A Concise Business Guide to Contract Law

Charles Boundy

Gower

Published by
Gower Publishing Limited
Gower House
Croft Road
Aldershot
Hampshire GU11 3HR
England

Gower
Old Post Road
Brookfield
Vermont 05036
USA

Charles Boundy has asserted his right under the Copyright, Designs and Patents Act 1988 to be identified as the author of this work

British Library Cataloguing in Publication Data

Boundy, Charles
    A concise business guide to contract law
    1. Contracts – England 2. Contracts – Wales 3. Business law –
    England 4. Business law – Wales
    I. Title
    346.4'2'02

ISBN 0 566 07921 0

Library of Congress Cataloging-in-Publication Data

Boundy, Charles, 1945–
    A concise business guide to contract law / Charles Boundy.
        p.   cm.
    Includes index.
    ISBN 0–566–07921–6
    1. Sales – United States.   2. Contracts – United States.
    3. Business law – United States.   I. Title.
    KF889.3.B589   1998
    346.7302—dc21

                                                                        98–6794
                                                                        CIP

Typeset in Palatino by Raven Typesetter, Chester and printed in Great Britain at the University Press, Cambridge.

Contents

List of figures   ix
Preface   xi
Acknowledgements   xiii

PART I – THE LEGAL PRINCIPLES   1

1   The elements   3
The framework of contract law – What is a contract? –
Contract requirements – Signature as a deed –
Incomplete contracts – Use of implied terms – When
contracts need to be in writing – A sample written
contract – Summary

2   Defect, mistake and misrepresentation   19
Past performance – You can't give what you don't
have – Gifts – Illegality / Provisions contrary to public
policy – Contracts with minors – Corporate incapacity
– Actual and apparent authority – Fraud –
Misrepresentation – Collateral contracts – Duress and
undue influence – Mistaken identity – Mistake as to
nature of the transaction – Mistake as to content or
commitment – Summary

3   Sale of goods and services   33
Legislation in the scheme of contract law – European
law – Terms implied by statute – Supply of goods and
services – Summary

4   Exclusion clauses and unfair terms   **47**
Commercial contracts – General principles relating to
exclusion clauses – Consumer contracts – Unfair Terms
in Consumer Contracts Regulations 1994 – The grey
list – Summary

5   Negligence and product safety   **57**
Claims against third parties – Negligence – Liability
in contract law and negligence – Consumer Protection
Act 1987 – Liability for unsafe consumer products –
Misleading pricing and advertising – Trade descriptions
– Consumer credit – Summary

6   Confidentiality and competition   **69**
Legal protection of confidential information –
Employment confidentiality and restrictions –
Confidentiality and competition in other business
relationships – Deleting unreasonable restrictions –
Remedies for breach – Restrictive Trade Practices Act
1976 – Other UK competition legislation – EU
competition law – Summary

7   Companies and contracts   **87**
Directors' duties – Directors' criminal liability –
Insolvency – Summary

8   Agency and distribution   **99**
Distinctions between agent and distributor – Protection
for the commercial agent – Contract terms – Termination
and its effects – Distributor or agent? – Summary

9   Consultancy and services   **115**
Consultancy distinguished from employment –
Corporate consultancies – Outsourcing, facilities
management and other agreements for services –
Summary

10   Employment contracts   **127**
Written contracts – Contract terms – Termination of
employment – Business transfers and employment
rights (TUPE) – Section 1 requirements – Summary

11 **Intellectual property** 141
Patents – Trade marks – Copyright – Computer
software – Know-how – Summary

12 **Franchising and licensing** 155
Features of a commercial licence agreement – Franchise
agreements – Franchising and pyramid selling –
Master franchise and area development licences –
Effect of competition law on intellectual property
licences – Summary

PART II – CONTRACTS IN PRACTICE 167

13 **Planning the contract** 169
Subject – Object – Effect – Cost – Benefit – Risk –
Tolerance factor – Making it work – Summary

14 **Standard form contracts** 183
Preparing standard conditions of business – Identifying
the goods or services – Delivery and inspection –
Price and payment terms – Risk and insurance – Title
and retention of title – Exclusion or limitation clauses –
Bringing the terms into the contract – Summary

15 **Boilerplate clauses** 195
Preliminary clauses or recitals – Term and notice to
terminate – Interpretation clauses – Confidentiality –
Notices – Force majeure – Entire agreement and no
variation clauses – Counterparts – Other typical
boilerplate clauses – Summary

16 **New technology and the international dimension** 205
Electronic contracts (fax, e-mail, worldwide web and
EDI) – Implications for businesses – Practical pointers –
Choice of law and jurisdiction clauses – Arbitration and
alternative dispute resolution – Checklist for the
international element

17 **Transferring contracts** 221
General principles of transfer and assignment –
Exceptions to the general principles – Change of
control – Novation – Summary

18   Dealing with problems   **229**
The contract review – Troublesome contracts –
Inducement to breach contracts – Anticipating
defence – Default notice procedure – Summary

19   Endings and breakdowns   **241**
Rescission – Restitution – Repudiation – Insolvency –
Death – Frustration – Termination by notice – Remedies
– Arbitration and alternative dispute resolution –
Summary

20   Working with contract law   **257**
Responsibility – Negotiation – Writing it down –
Into the future – Summary – Contract guidelines

A contract checklist   267
Glossary   271
Index   279

List of figures

1.1 Personal guarantee   14
2.1 Example: mistake as to content or commitment   31
3.1 Title to goods   39
3.2 Example: supply of goods and services   43
6.1 Alternative layout for summary   84
7.1 Example: secret profits   90
8.1 Agent or distributor?   100

Preface

This guide has been written for people in business. All businesses use – and need – the law. Contract law, in particular, underpins commercial life and provides the framework for business dealings, yet is often treated at best as a necessary evil and at worst as an obstacle.

It is easy to blame laws which may be seen as obscure or irrelevant, or indeed to blame lawyers who may be seen in the same way. England and Wales do not have an overall statutory commercial legal code and in many respects our law appears difficult to track down. At the same time, being less structured, it can be more flexible and adaptable to commercial requirements. Businesses may be reluctant to consult a lawyer, but to have no understanding of how the law affects business decisions only compounds the position. The average person in business is experienced in weighing up facts, making judgements and taking decisions. But without a working knowledge of how the law assists and impacts on transactions and agreements, those in business may find their objectives frustrated. Their decisions will be less informed and may be badly implemented as a result.

The business clients I have advised over the years have recognized that a better understanding of law brings immediate benefits in using contracts to their advantage. This book seeks to develop that principle. The particular challenge for me has been to produce a guide in an accessible style which will enable the business reader to gain a rapid understanding of the core issues. The main problem was what to leave out.

I have concentrated on the ground rules, the planning of contracts, an enquiry into some common forms of commercial contract and a glimpse of what can go wrong. The text contains examples, practical guidance and checklists throughout.

Commercial law is complex and continues to change at a bewildering rate. Whilst the book by its nature can give only general guidance, it should enable the reader to improve decision making with clearer knowledge of possible consequences and to decide when and how to seek further assistance. It can save management time and professional fees by identifying many of the key issues and showing where legal input is required. It is not a substitute for legal advice nor an alternative to checking current law and practice in any given case.

This book does not cover contracts relating to land or to company law, nor does it attempt to deal in any detail with financial instruments or other specialized contracts. Apart from reported cases, the examples are fictitious and not intended to have any connection with any person, living or dead, or any existing company or business. Although there are references to other laws and to the international context, this book covers only the law of England and Wales. The law of Scotland, for example, may be significantly different. To make the style more accessible, case and statutory references are not generally given. Those who wish may easily find more detailed reports in the many textbooks and casebooks on the subject. Within this framework the law stated is correct as at 1 April 1998.

Charles Boundy

Acknowledgements

My thanks to the clients with whom I have worked over the years for the chance to advise and work with them (and learn something in the process!); the Association of Women Solicitors who gave me the opportunity to enjoy giving refresher courses for those returning to the law; Landmark Education which taught me to start my future today; Roger Horton who made the contact; Malcolm Stern who encouraged creativity and gave shape to the book; Julia and Raymond Bellenger who spared their dining room for several days; Nicolas Greenstone who spared the time and sharpened the focus; Karen Warmoth and her team who tirelessly found information; David Robinson, Lisa Venables, Jessica Learmond-Criqui and other colleagues who gave feedback; Michelle Clark for being my secretary and right hand for longer than she likes to remember; and my family for accepting my domination of the family keyboard and screen and for their constant encouragement, love and support.

CB

PART I

The legal principles

1

The elements

Contracts are the building blocks of business. The legal relationships between a business and its suppliers, customers, employees and service providers are all based on the law of contract. It is according to the architecture of those relationships that a successful commercial enterprise is constructed. Knowledge of how those contracts work and what stops them working will help you to understand the legal side of business and the use of contract law for your advantage.

The framework of contract law

Unlike many other European legal systems, English law has no general statutory commercial code and relies on common (or judge-made) law and the principles of equity developed by our courts over centuries. To these have been added statutes, or law enacted by parliament, which have been supplemented by statutory instruments or regulations, setting out detailed procedures and obligations. There is also the law of the

European Union, much of which originates from directives of the European Commission. All this legislation may affect the way contracts are made and interpreted.

What is a contract?

There is a popular misconception that a contract is an agreement in writing. Sam Goldwyn's famous remark that 'a verbal contract isn't worth the paper it's written on' only adds to the confusion. The definition of 'contract' in the *Collins English Dictionary* (3rd edition) is 'an agreement with (a person, company, etc.) to deliver (goods or services) or to do (something) on agreed and binding terms, often in writing'. The *Concise Oxford Dictionary* (9th edition) refers to 'a written or spoken agreement between two or more parties, intended to be enforceable by law' and 'a document recording this'. For the purposes of this book a contract may be defined as 'an agreement which is legally enforceable'.

Consider a simple transaction such as buying a loaf of bread from a bakery. There is no written agreement when you go into the shop and request the loaf, but a contract is created between that moment and the time you walk out of the shop with the loaf in your hand. In law there is an offer to buy and an acceptance of that offer backed by payment of the purchase price. By the time the money is paid and the loaf handed over the contract has been made and completed. The only piece of paper that may have changed hands is a till receipt.

Let me return to the analogy of building blocks or, more particularly, concrete. The main elements of concrete are sand, cement and water. Other ingredients can be added and the relative proportions of the three basic elements can vary, but all those three are required. Equally there are factors which will destabilize concrete: it may be the proportions of the ingredients or the circumstances in which they are put together; or the addition of a new factor, such as the high alumina cement which was so disastrously used in the construction of buildings in the late 1950s or early 60s.

In construction terms these problems are known as 'inherent defects' and in technological (or even human) terms they would be known as 'viruses'. Similarly we can think of contracts as having certain ingredients or components which are necessary to their proper construction and other factors which can destabilize and destroy them. This chapter concentrates on the key ingredients required in the mix. The defects and viruses are considered in Chapter 2.

Contract requirements

A valid contract requires:

- offer and acceptance
- certainty
- consideration (something of value)
- an intention to enter into a legally binding relationship.

Offer and acceptance (Have we agreed?)

It takes two to tango and it takes two or more able and willing participants to make a contract. The dance is conducted through an offer and acceptance with the offer leading and the acceptance following. As will be seen, if the acceptance starts to lead, it will itself become an offer (known as a counter-offer). Leaving the dance floor and going back to the bakery, there are two possible interpretations of what happened. First, the shop was offering to sell the bread at a stated price and you accepted the offer by picking up the loaf and paying for it. Second, the shop was merely displaying the bread, you offered to buy it and the shop accepted the offer by selling it to you. English law is now clear that the display of goods or circulation of a catalogue is not, in itself, an offer but merely an invitation for an offer to be made. It is therefore the second analysis which is correct – you offer to buy the loaf and the bakery accepts by selling it. The question of who offers what first may seem academic in the case of a loaf of bread, but with a larger business transaction the issue can be highly significant.

To conclude the contract the acceptance has to be notified to the person making the offer. The acceptance is normally instantaneous, as in the case of an agreement made face to face or over the telephone.[1] But what if the acceptance is never received by the person making the offer? This is simple enough in a shop but more difficult when the contract is made by post. Under English law posting in an official postbox is regarded as due notification of acceptance, even if the postbox is destroyed minutes later. On the same principle, an offer can be withdrawn at any time before it has been accepted, but not afterwards since the contract will then have been established. The revocation of the offer must be received by the other party before acceptance. The mere posting of a revocation notice is not sufficient to withdraw the offer.

Certainty (What exactly is on offer?)

Agreements need certainty to be enforceable. Both buyer and seller must agree what exactly is being bought and sold. If you go into an office furniture showroom to buy a filing cabinet, you will be asked what type, size and finish and perhaps to select between other variations. There is no question of a contract being made at that stage, because the request is too vague. In a supermarket the situation is generally different; you select from the display and the transaction can be wordless. There is certainty because you select the product you want. The same is true of a catalogue with prices. The buyer will select from the range shown in a catalogue and submit an order on the basis of the details set out. The despatch of the goods is the acceptance of that offer.

Consideration (What will it cost?)

Consideration is the legal term for an obligation which has some real value. In most cases consideration is given by the payment or promise of payment of money. It may also be given by an agreement to provide other goods or services in return for those offered. Consideration is the main difference between a legally enforceable contract and an intention, hope

---

[1] And, in effect, by fax or telex, but not necessarily e-mail (see p. 206 et seq.).

or promise. There are two main exceptions to this requirement of consideration: cheques and other negotiable instruments and documentary credits, such as letters of credit, do not need consideration to be valid; likewise, a document signed as a deed is enforceable without consideration. The first exception is self-explanatory; the second is considered in the section 'Signature as a deed' later in this chapter.

Intention to be legally bound (Do I want to be committed?)

There will be no contract if all parties to an agreement do not intend to create a legally binding agreement. Most informal domestic commitments and arrangements with friends are not intended to be legal commitments. For example, you offer to prune your neighbour's roses in return for his lending you his rotavator. If your neighbour suggests, after you buy him a good meal, that he might invest in your planned mail-order rose bush business, would that be any different? The key question is whether there was a commitment which was intended to be legally binding. If not, as seen later, the arrangement will be, at best, a 'gentleman's agreement'.

Example offer and acceptance

Mary Morris runs a furniture manufacturing business, Morris Furniture Supplies Limited, specializing in office furniture. Walter Williams, a wholesaler and the owner of Williams Limited, is a regular customer. Morris offers to sell a filing cabinet to Williams for £50 and Williams accepts the offer by telling her that he agrees to pay that amount. A binding contract then exists. Alternatively Williams could offer Morris £50 for her filing cabinet, but there will be no deal unless and until Morris accepts Williams' offer.

The effect of acceptance on different terms

Any terms of the bargain, such as delivery of the goods and time for payment, must be included in the offer or added to the offer before it is accepted. Once the acceptance has been notified, the terms are fixed. On the other hand, if the person to whom the offer is made claims to accept but specifies different terms, the original offer is destroyed. The acceptance on different terms is then a counter-offer, open for the party making the original offer to accept or reject in turn.

So, if Williams said he would buy the filing cabinet, but only at £45, this would be a counter-offer which Morris could accept or refuse as she chose.

Mistake as to what is on offer

What if, outside their business dealings, Morris offers to sell Williams her car for £5,000? Williams knows only of her Porsche, not her five-year-old Ford. He is mistaken about the real subject-matter of the contract. It may seem simplistic, but in business such events occur all the time. A court may conclude that there never was agreement about what was to be bought and sold and may refuse to enforce the contract for either the Porsche or the Ford. It might, on the other hand, conclude from the evidence that Morris had misled Williams into believing he would acquire the Porsche and either enforce the contract for the Porsche or award damages against Morris for misrepresentation.

The message is that you must be clear from the outset what you are selling or buying, otherwise there might either not be a deal at all or not the deal you thought you had. These issues often go to the root of complex commercial negotiations and can create big problems. Leaving it to the accountants and the lawyers to decide what is to be included is no substitute for clarifying the issues at the outset – and before the price is agreed!

Adequacy of consideration

Although the consideration must have some value – known as money or money's worth – it does not have to be market value. The law does not, as a rule, like to judge whether people are getting a good deal (business might grind to a halt if it did), provided they deal fairly. Token consideration is sufficient, although the token pound has now replaced the token peppercorn (and may shortly make way for the token Euro).

The need for consideration can easily be overlooked. The fact that someone has for some time gratuitously permitted you to use their premises or their name or their copyright material, for instance, does not prevent them from withdrawing that permission at short notice. It may be worth making a payment or performing a service in return, even if the original consent is in writing. That original consent was merely an agreement not to sue for trespass, passing-off or breach of copyright for the past, not an agreement to continue the permission for the future.

Signature as a deed

Consideration is not required where an agreement is recorded in a document which is signed as a deed. In the not so distant past a document needed to be 'signed, sealed and delivered' in order to be effective as a deed. Now the law merely requires that it is expressed to be signed as a deed, witnessed (preferably by an independent person) and 'delivered', normally by being handed over. Whenever consideration is in doubt, because someone is asked to commit to something without receiving direct payment or anything in return, it is better to obtain that commitment in writing signed as a deed. Signature as a deed may also indicate the existence of a gift or trust or some other legal relationship which is not dependent on offer and acceptance. In such cases there is no intention to enter into a bargain and the rules of contract law will not apply.

Incomplete contracts

Unless the contract requirements are fully in place, a contract will not properly come into effect. Incomplete contracts can be distinguished from defective contracts as described in Chapter 2. The contract may be deemed:

- never to have come into existence in the first place (*null and void*), or

- to have come into existence but to be subject to a defect that can destroy it (*voidable*), or
- to be a valid contract but simply unenforceable in law (*unenforceable*)

and each of these situations can produce a different result in law.

Use of implied terms

There are some occasions where the law will imply additional terms into a written or oral contract, for example, terms implied by statute law in relation to the sale of goods and the supply of services (see Chapter 3). Terms may be implied from the circumstances. Typically such an implication arises when the term is so obvious that it did not need to be stated or where it is necessary to give the contract commercial effect. Terms may also be implied from a previous course of dealing (see p. 190) or by custom and usage, as is the case in many specialized trade markets.

'Gentleman's agreements'

An agreement will not be legally binding if there is no intention to enter into a legally binding relationship. Take, for example, the statement by one person to a friend: 'If you went into business, I'd be happy to put in £20,000'. What does this mean? Is it a statement that an investment of £20,000 will be made if the other person starts up a business, or is it a mere declaration of confidence or goodwill? Most courts would be reluctant to interpret the words as a legal commitment. Even if there is a genuine intention to enter into a legally binding agreement, are all relevant terms sufficiently clear between the parties so as to be enforceable?

Much new business is done on the basis of 'sounding out' other people. There is an apparently good meeting (particularly during a meal or drink) followed by an understanding and a handshake. Those present may go away having assumed certain facts, or with a different impression of what was agreed. A communication gap can arise because one party is simply too busy making their own point to listen to what the other party is actually saying – or not saying. We all tend to hear what we want to hear and disregard the rest. On other occasions, even if the attention was originally on the point, memory fails, especially if there is any benefit in overlooking something that might be inconvenient to remember.

Such cases create an expectation by one person which is not matched by the performance of the other. Often this prevents the certainty required to form a contract in the first place, or a contract is created which one of the parties is subsequently reluctant to honour. Either way, such situations are the foundation of disappointment, loss of business and possible litigation. Details must be agreed and clearly written down *at the outset* to avoid misunderstandings, upsets and disputes, any of which might be fatal to the new business.[2]

Subject to contract

Where there is correspondence setting out the terms of a proposal in some detail and you do not want to be legally bound, use the words 'subject to contract', preferably at the head of your letter or proposal. These words will prevent a contract coming into existence, but they cannot undo that contract if it has already been created. The phrase 'subject to contract' should not be confused with the words 'without prejudice'. The latter is appropriate only where there is a genuine negotiation to try to settle a dispute or a difference of opinion. Its effect is to prevent the evidence being produced in court as an admission or as a sign of weakness. Putting 'without prejudice' in an abusive letter, for example, will not prevent it being defamatory because there is no genuine attempt to settle a dispute.

Unlike 'subject to contract', the words 'without prejudice' will not stop something becoming a binding commitment; a 'without prejudice' offer can be accepted in the same way as any other offer and can become binding if all the terms and

[2] The issue of contract planning is explored further in Chapter 13.

conditions in the offer are accepted. If you are negotiating a settlement and do not want your offer to be accepted without further thought, then you should head correspondence 'Without prejudice and subject to contract' to cover both aspects.

Agreement to agree

In some ways the agreement to agree is a variant of the previous type of incomplete contract, but it deserves special mention because it is so common. Consider the statement that 'Morris will supply Williams with such products at such prices as they may both agree', or even 'You will supply me with filing cabinets against purchase orders with payment to be made within 30 days'.

On their own these statements would be unenforceable because the key elements relating to the number and type of products and the price are omitted. In some cases it is possible to decide the terms by reference to other factors, such as a known distributors' list price, a quoted commodity price or even a reference to a fair market price to be fixed by an arbitrator. In the absence of such provisions and anything to identify the products, the 'agreement' is merely a statement of intention.

The same principles can apply in the middle of a complex document, such as a supply agreement. Sometimes the problem is simply that the parties have not checked or agreed a vital piece of information. If the missing part is key to the whole deal, the whole contract could fail. If the omission is less important, the clause itself may be unenforceable although the rest of the contract could stand. All too often the result is an expensive dispute as to whether there is a contract and, if so, what the terms of that contract are.[3]

When contracts need to be in writing

The general rule is that contracts do not need to be in writing,

[3] See, for example, the 1997 case of *VHE Construction plc* v *Alfred McAlpine Construction Ltd* on p. 231.

although there are several exceptions. The principal ones are now briefly reviewed.

Contracts relating to land

Contracts relating to freehold or leasehold property are likely to be unenforceable (and may be void or voidable) if not in writing in a single document. This specialist area is not covered further in this book, but you should check that no part of your contract relates to land or buildings. If it does, this aspect may need to be covered separately.

Guarantees

A guarantee can be enforced only if it is evidenced in writing, which does not mean that the actual guarantee must be written, but that there must be written evidence of the guarantee having been given. It is one of the longest standing legal rules designed to stop spurious claims against individuals based simply on oral evidence. Consideration – or signature as a deed – is still required to make the guarantee enforceable.

Example

If Morris is asked to supply 500 filing cabinets at £50 each to Williams Limited on 30 day payment terms and Morris has doubts about the creditworthiness of Williams Limited, Mary Morris may ask Walter Williams for a personal guarantee of the purchase price. Since Williams Limited is buying the goods, Walter Williams will not be receiving any direct personal benefit from the contract. Morris should ensure that the personal guarantee is in writing and, to avoid arguments over consideration, she should have the guarantee signed as a deed by Walter Williams personally (see Figure 1.1). For example:

'To Morris Furniture Supplies Limited

You have, at my request, agreed terms with Williams Limited for you to sell and Williams Limited to buy 500

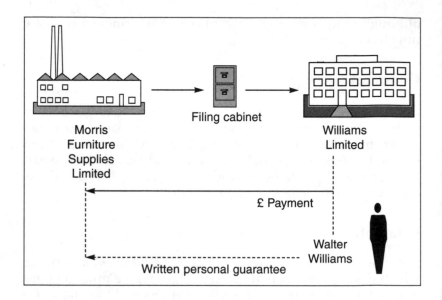

FIGURE 1.1   PERSONAL GUARANTEE

filing cabinets in accordance with and on the terms of your quotation [or their order] number 657/9. I, Walter Williams, guarantee to you that Williams Limited will pay the price and fully and promptly comply with all its obligations in relation to such sale and purchase.

Signed and delivered as a deed
by Walter Williams   [signed Walter
                                                                    Williams]

in the presence of
[witness signature]
[witness full name and address]'

If guarantees can be this simple, why are most guarantees so complex? The reason is that the law is at pains to ensure that guarantors should be responsible only for the deal they first agreed to guarantee and then only if the party to whom the guarantee is given acts promptly against the principal debtor, in this case Williams Limited. Otherwise, particularly if the obligations increase, the law will not simply limit the guarantee to the original terms but release the guarantor completely. To avoid this result (although it is possible – and often advisable – to write much lengthier clauses) Morris should add:

'This guarantee will remain in force despite any delay in your enforcing the obligations of Williams Limited or any variation of the terms of the order or contract.'

Guarantees should be distinguished from indemnities and representations, which do not need to be in writing to give legal redress. For example if Walter Williams said to Mary Morris 'I give you my word that I'll pay you for any loss if anything goes wrong', this could be enforceable against Williams personally as an indemnity if anything did go wrong. If Williams said 'I guarantee that I have a customer lined up who will give you another order for the same amount on the same terms', this might be a misrepresentation on which Morris Furniture Supplies Limited could sue if they would not have done the deal at that price otherwise. In neither case would written confirmation be required if other evidence were clear enough.[4]

Consumer contracts

The law increasingly regards private consumers as needing special protection when buying goods or services from businesses, especially when it comes to consumer finance. Where we select products or services from a brochure we are used to looking at printed details and making a decision in reliance on the information given. This is the reason why there is now so much legislation to protect the public (or 'consumers' as we are known in our private lives). If we are used to making decisions based on brochures, those brochures need to be clear, accurate and not misleading. Moreover, suppliers offering those goods or services are not now allowed to put in terms and conditions, in large or small print, which act to the unfair detriment of consumers. In other words, when selling to the

[4]Indemnities are dealt with further on p. 62 and misrepresentations on p. 23.

public suppliers cannot give with one hand and take away with the other.

Consumer credit transactions must also be in writing and comply with formalities to ensure the bargain is accurately and fairly recorded and the customer not misled.

Many laws now allow the consumer a 'cooling-off' period in which to cancel the contract. They may also give the right to claim compensation if the information given was inaccurate and, in some cases, can make the supplier criminally liable for false representations or unlawful exclusions.

Employment contracts

An employment contract is created by job offer and acceptance. Even starting work can be acceptance. The law does not require the contract to be in writing, but it does state that certain minimum particulars of the terms of employment are given by the employer to the employee when the latter starts work. The subject is considered in more detail in Chapter 10.

A sample written contract

Creating a written record of a contract can be straightforward. Whilst it is sensible to record contracts in writing, no great formality is required. A letter can be quite sufficient. The following example assumes that Williams, the wholesaler, writes on Williams Limited letterhead to Mary Morris at Morris Furniture Supplies Ltd.

'It was good to meet you again on Monday and to discuss future developments. I am impressed by the new Morrisey wood-finish range of cabinets which you have developed and write to confirm what we discussed as the first stage.

You will supply 500 of the Morrisey range, finished in teak, as inspected by us and as described in your Spring 1998 brochure, being 300 3-drawer units and 200 2-drawer units. Based on these quantities, we agreed a price of £86.50 each for the larger units and £74.80 each for the smaller units. Prices are exclusive of VAT and delivery. You will deliver between 1 and 31 August this year, giving us at least five days' prior notice of delivery. You will invoice us for the cabinets on delivery and we will pay in full by the end of the month following. We will see how they sell before making further plans!

I believe that covers everything. I would be grateful if you would sign and return the duplicate of this letter to confirm your agreement.

Regards

Walter Williams
For and on behalf of Williams Limited'

If Morris signs and returns the duplicate without further comment, a clear contract will have been created on the terms set out in the Williams letter. If Morris Furniture Supplies Ltd as manufacturer make the offer formally first, they will doubtless include their standard terms of business. The advantage in Williams writing to Morris first is that Morris may overlook the normal procedures, which is why a well-organized Morris would reply with an official order form on Morris' conditions of sale. We can see the effect of this counter-offer and dealings with standard terms of business in more detail in Chapter 14.

Summary

Certain fundamental ingredients need to be present for a contract to have legal effect. The sequence of the negotiations may be relevant to decide which terms were actually incorporated into the contract. Although some contracts must be in writing, in most cases they can be created by the spoken word, but it will still be necessary to prove the agreed terms. Make sure that the terms are fully thought through and recorded in writing and that there is 'consideration', unless the contract is signed as a deed.

Consider a contract you have just made or are about to make:

● Are there two or more parties who are each clearly identified?

- Is the agreement intended to be legally binding?
- Is each party agreeing to do something of value for the other or others?
- Were all the relevant terms agreed before the deal was done?
- Are the assets, products or services to be sold clearly identified?
- Does the contract include everything you want the other person to do?
- Is the price clearly established? If not, is there some mechanism for establishing the price?
- Are there any assumptions which have not been checked?
- If you told an intelligent stranger all the details, what further questions would they ask?
- If payment is involved, when and how is it due?
- What do you need to do to make it work and are you able and committed to do it?
- If so, are all these points in writing and signed?
- Does the agreement need to be signed as a deed?

■ 2

Defect, mistake and misrepresentation

Chapter 1 described what makes a contract. This chapter looks at the inherent defects or viruses which were referred to, and their effects, and some of the other forms of legal relationship which might be created during the negotiations.

English law has developed empirically over the years, recognizing situations where new rules are required and others where the existing rules have ceased to operate fairly. This latter principle, known as 'equity', gives its name to 'equitable remedies', where the court has a discretion based on fairness as between the parties. Equity itself then developed its own rules, which became so complex that common (judge-made) law had to re-interpret them to try to restore the original fairness. Many of the principles or legal remedies which follow are derived from those rules of equity for reasons which will become apparent. An example of the operation of some of these rules is set out at the end of the chapter.

Part performance

The law does not like to permit one person to take advantage of another where the first has encouraged or permitted the second to believe that a binding agreement exists. If, as a result, the second person acts to their own detriment and cannot easily go back to where they were, there may be a legal remedy. The principle is known as 'part performance' because the second person will have partly performed the contract which the first (wrongly) led them to believe existed. This applies even if there has been no express promise or consideration provided by the second person. The part performance doctrine is generally available only by way of defence and is therefore something of a 'last ditch' attempt which is not to be relied on as a legal right.

You can't give what you don't have

In law you cannot sell or transfer a better right of ownership of something than you have yourself. This is known by lawyers as the 'nemo dat' rule (*nemo dat quod non habet* – no one can give what they do not have). Even buying the goods in daylight in one of the long-established London markets will not now rectify bad title. If the goods are stolen, they must be handed back to the rightful owner. One of the few practical exceptions to this rule is that someone will be prevented (or in legal terms 'estopped') from denying something that they previously represented as true. For example, if the rightful owner tells the buyer that the thief does own the goods, and the buyer buys in reliance on that statement, the owner will be precluded from suing the buyer later for the return of the goods. Again the principle is something of a 'last ditch' defence.

Gifts

By their nature gifts are not intended to be in return for anything of monetary value. They are, at least in theory, given freely. However, it is sometimes difficult after the event to tell what was the original intention and it is all too easy to mistake a loan for a gift. Always check and confirm assumptions in good time. Even if it is embarrassing to request, a written confirmation of the intent to make a gift might save much heartache later.

Illegality/Provisions contrary to public policy

The courts will not generally enforce a contract which contains terms that are illegal or contrary to public policy, because the civil law does not wish to support activities which are either contrary to the criminal law or to that most difficult of standards to judge – public morals. Thus a contract to pay fines for criminal offences would be unenforceable, although the actual payment might be legal. Remember this point if you are dealing with governmental regulations which contain criminal sanctions for breach and contracts which, for example, attempt to evade tax or VAT laws or which might contain transactions which are illegal under company law.

Contracts with minors

Apart from so-called 'necessaries' (on which most cases date from Victorian times) contracts entered into by individuals under the age of 18 are not enforceable against them unless the minor adopts the contract after reaching the age of 18. Adoption requires some clear approval or course of action consistent with acceptance of the obligations of the contract.

Corporate incapacity

A validly incorporated company is, for many purposes, deemed to be able to enter into any lawful transaction, even if it is beyond the powers laid down in its memorandum of association. Check that the company is validly incorporated, that it has not changed its name and that the contract would not be an abuse of the powers of the company nor an offence under any other legislation. There may be particular risks in dealing with a company which is potentially insolvent. This subject is considered in more detail in Chapter 7.

Actual and apparent authority

Is the person you are dealing with authorized to commit their company? There is no problem with a sole trader because he or she has full personal responsibility. If you are dealing with a partner in relation to the business of a firm, the same position applies and the partner will bind or commit all the other part-ners on a joint and several basis (but it is as well to check that they are indeed a partner).

You can generally assume that a company director can commit the company to anything within its normal course of business, but what about other employees? Some employees are authorized to deal with third parties on behalf of their company, either because the law says so (as with directors) or because the board of the company has expressly authorized them to that effect. Others are put in a position by their com-pany where they have apparent – or ostensible – authority to make commitments on behalf of their company. This will generally include managers and senior executives whose titles indicate their authority when acting in the course of their normal work, but not, for example, a junior office assistant. If the person who agrees the deal has neither the actual nor the ostensible authority to do so, the agreement will not bind their company, although it may bind the individual, unless the company actually adopts or approves it.

Fraud

Fraud potentially invalidates any contract. It can arise where there has been an intention to deceive or a deliberate conceal-ment of relevant facts which misleads the other party. Fraud is, however, extremely hard to prove since it requires evidence of intention on the part of the fraudster. To revert to the example of the car in Chapter 1, it is possible that Mary Morris inten-tionally duped Walter Williams into believing that she would sell him the Porsche for £5,000, for example by pointing to the car or giving him a ride in it. She might go further and switch the number-plates with the Ford, having agreed to sell him a car referred to only by its number-plate. But to establish fraudulent intention might be difficult in all but the last of these cases and claims for pure fraud are limited to the most exceptional cases. For this reason specific remedies were brought in by legislation for misrepresentation where fraud could not be established.

Misrepresentation

If a seller, to encourage a sale, misrepresents something to a potential buyer, the buyer may be able to claim compensation and, in extreme cases, to cancel the contract. The leading legal cases under the old common law deal typically with the lies that are told when selling cars. There are cases about a Bugatti being sold as a general touring car, a car being represented as 'a good little bus – I'd stake my life on it' and a car that would not even start, prompting one eminent judge, who had obviously not attended car mechanics night classes, to state that 'a car that will not go is not a car at all' (although this statement should no longer be regarded as good law!).

These cases all involved a clear misrepresentation about the car, whether about its suitability for the intended purpose, its condition or the fact that it simply did not work. The Misrepresentation Act of 1967 makes it clear that a misrepresentation can give rise to legal action even if made innocently. It applies both in the course of business and outside it, although it may be more difficult to establish a sufficient level of misrepresentation outside business dealings.

So what would be the position if Mary Morris did misrepresent to Walter Williams the car she was selling? If Williams could prove this, he could insist that the Porsche be sold to him for the £5,000 or claim damages for the difference between the £5,000 and the value of the Porsche, which could prove an expensive lesson for Mrs Morris. She would be advised to distinguish between:

1   General statements extolling the virtues of the goods or services, but which are not intended to be relied on by the buyer (ironically known by judges over the years as 'mere puffs') – *unenforceable*.

2   Representations as to quality, performance or some other factor specifically designed to encourage or comfort the buyer in the choice of product or in its suitability, although not included in the contract – *likely to be enforceable* as if they were terms of the contract, unless actually and fairly excluded by the contract itself.

3   Actual terms of the contract – *fully enforceable* as terms of the contract except to the extent that the contract fairly excludes liability of the seller in relation to them.

Misrepresentations of the second and third kinds may entitle the buyer to rescind the contract (i.e. to treat it as void from the outset) and/or to a claim for damages. The court may limit the claim to damages rather than rescission where the representation was not made fraudulently and damages would be a sufficient remedy. Sellers and their sales representatives need to be cautious about the statements they make and their ability to live up to them if things go wrong, even where there is a great deal of evidence of what actually happened. The courts will also usually refuse to look behind the terms of a written contract to bring into account terms agreed orally, as oral terms are deemed to have been absorbed into the written terms (the 'parol evidence rule'). The main exception to this is where the written terms are themselves unclear and evidence of earlier dealings is necessary to explain them.

Collateral contracts

In their struggles to find acceptable legal solutions for unfair situations the courts also discovered the collateral contract. This is a side agreement running alongside the main terms, which may be useful where the terms in question were not part of the main contract but were part of the basis upon which the parties agreed to do a deal. There is sometimes a fine distinction between a representation and a collateral contract; the point to note is that a collateral contract which appears unenforceable for lack of consideration may in fact be binding simply because it is itself consideration for another contract.

Duress and undue influence

It is not surprising that the law will not enforce a contract made under duress. The more difficult question is the extent of duress which would need to be proved. Fear of imminent physical danger is likely to be accepted by the courts. Mere timidity or general fear of circumstances on the other hand is unlikely to suffice. In the middle are a range of responses which might arise. In general the courts will require a fairly high level of proof that the obligation is one that would not have been undertaken were it not for the pressure that had been exerted. This in turn will depend on the nature and vulnerability of the person alleging duress. By the very nature of the subject there are few cases of duress that ever come to court.

There are, nevertheless, certain situations where people are in a position of particular trust or responsibility, such that the law recognizes that those relying on that trust must be protected. Thus if someone has what is known as undue influence over another, they must not abuse that influence so as to benefit themselves or unfairly disadvantage the person relying on them – for example, in family situations where one relative, especially if elderly, relies on another for business advice; or solicitors and doctors who have acted for many years for clients who rely on them for making decisions or taking action. Accountants may be in a similar position and also directors of family companies in relation to their shareholders. In these areas independent advice should always be taken as soon as a potential conflict of interest or uncertainty arises.

Mistaken identity

Legal textbooks are full of fascinating examples of how one person can enter into a contract with another thinking that the other is really someone else. If this happens, the apparent contract will almost certainly be void and ineffective, but in business this is rare. It is more likely that the mistake relates to what the other person is selling or spending, what their authority is or what they can deliver. Where there are cases of mistaken identity the dispute is often between two innocent parties because 'the rogue' has generally already disappeared or become insolvent. If the rogue has simply given an alias, this is unlikely to be grounds for avoiding the contract. It will normally need to be shown that the rogue is impersonating another party with whom the innocent person would have done business.

The real question is often whether or not the identity of the person is a key element of the bargain between the parties. If I advertise to sell my car and a buyer responds to the advertisement, I am probably not concerned about his identity so long as he pays for the car. If the buyer gives me a false name, it does not invalidate the transaction. Certainly the buyer would have no grounds to escape from the deal and I would have no grounds to do so unless the buyer's identity was essential for clear and stated reasons. On the other hand identity may be relevant in different circumstances and deliberate deception goes back to Jacob and Esau. As fraud becomes more prevalent and the lies of fraudsters more outrageous, a check on identity is increasingly recommended.

Finding the right people with the right names to be parties to the contract sometimes causes remarkable difficulty. An agreement with an impostor or company which does not exist may be of little benefit. Where there is any doubt, and a person's identity is important, look at the passport and make a credit check as to their financial standing. The passport should also confirm that the person with whom you are dealing is the same as the person checked out. Having the same name might be mere coincidence, or may be part of a deliberate fraud, as one bank found out to its cost. A bankruptcy search against the individual is also cheap and useful protection.

Companies can be more of a problem as they can change their names very easily, provided there is not another alphabetically or phonetically identical name on the register already – which also means that companies can switch names. Jacob Limited and Esau Limited, fellow subsidiaries of Isaac Limited, might actually have been Esau Limited and Jacob Limited respectively a few months ago. You thought you were dealing with the smooth company but find you are dealing with the hairy one instead. How can you tell the difference? There is one certain way. The company number does not change, even if the name does. For safety, check the company number and put it in the contract and carry out a company search just before you sign to check that all is well and there have been no sudden name or other last-minute changes. Remember that a new company name must be used immediately and exclusively from the day the change of name certificate is issued, but not before.

Mistake as to nature of the transaction

If someone hands you a document to sign, how can you be sure that it is what you are told and not something entirely different? Many cases relate to the elderly. For example, a trusted personal assistant might pass the company boss a document that looks like a normal order form or a property lease but which is in fact a transfer of the company's freehold property to the assistant's nominee company. What the boss believes is being signed and what is actually being signed are entirely different documents. In such cases the legal principle of *non est factum* (not my deed) might save the day if all else fails. The transaction would be void at the request of the person duped, even if there were no actual misrepresentation.

Mistake as to content or commitment

The law will not assist a business person to escape from a bad bargain unless there is fraud, misrepresentation, mutual mistake or similar circumstances as outlined. The law expects people in business to take care with the commitments they are undertaking and the documents they are signing and will not permit them to escape from an obligation simply because it turns out to be onerous. Thus the fact that you did not read a contract before signing, and did not realize its obligations, will be no defence to an action by the other party to enforce those obligations.

Example – a cautionary tale
See Figure 2.1 on page 31

Walter Williams, the wholesaler, deals regularly with Ronald

Richards, a retailer with a number of office equipment stores. One day they are discussing a good deal for some filing cabinets which Williams is able to negotiate. The deal is only open to the end of the month. Richards tells Williams that one of Richards' customers needs the same type of cabinet and that the customer could be very interested. Williams and Richards provisionally agree a price but Richards says that the customer needs credit and Richards' own cashflow would not enable him to pay for the cabinets on normal terms. In exchange for the cabinets, therefore, Richards agrees that, if the deal goes ahead, Williams can sell some purpose-made desks which Richards has bought and paid for but which Williams is continuing to store.

Williams is to deliver the new cabinets direct to the customer and Richards is to confirm the order with the customer. The customer is keen and Richards tells Williams that it looks as if the order can be delivered by the end of the month provided that Richards can confirm the final terms with the customer. In fact, Richards never finalizes terms to sell on to the customer. His deal with Williams was provisional and there is therefore no contract between Williams and Richards or between Richards and the customer. However, Williams tells Richards that he is planning to deliver that Friday to the customer, in the belief that the deal has been done. Because Richards is still hoping to finalize a deal with the customer he does not tell Williams the true situation. Williams believes that he has an agreement with Richards on the terms originally discussed. Williams delivers as planned and then sells the desks which he was holding for Richards.

Meanwhile the customer, who has been in financial difficulty, sells the cabinets on to a third party, Threlfalls Limited, and goes into liquidation. Richards claims that as there was no contract between Williams and Richards, Williams should return the desks or pay compensation.

On the face of it there is no final contract between Williams and Richards. Richards appears to have a valid claim against Williams, leaving Williams to try to recover his losses from the customer. There are, however, a number of areas to consider:

1   A claim by Williams that his action in delivering the filing cabinets to the customer and selling the desks was part performance of the contract which Richards had led Williams to believe existed. Williams may therefore have the same defence as if there had been a duly agreed contract.

2   A claim by Williams against the customer who received the cabinets and re-sold them. There was no direct agreement between Williams and the customer, but was Williams delivering on behalf of Richards or possibly Richards negotiating on behalf of Williams? Here there was either a complete contract, in which case payment is due for the cabinets, or there was no contract, in which case the customer did not own the cabinets and therefore had no right to sell them to Threlfalls.

3   A claim by Williams against Threlfalls, the third party who bought the goods from the customer. If the cabinets never belonged to the customer, the customer had no right to sell them to anyone else. Unless Threlfalls can prove that one of the limited exceptions to the *nemo dat* rule applies, they must hand the goods back, even if they were buyers in good faith and paid a fair price.

4   The law of agency (dealt with in more detail in Chapter 8), may be relevant. Was Williams entitled to sell the desks which were the property of Richards? Richards might argue that the sale of the desks was conditional upon the sale of the filing cabinets and no agreement was ever finalized. He in turn might seek to recover the desks from Williams' customer, but in this case there are significant differences. Richards had stood by and left Williams to believe that a deal had been done, causing Williams to act to his detriment by delivering the filing cabinets to Richards' customer and by selling the desks.

There are other issues that could be examined here, but you can see that there is enough in this relatively simple situation to keep a team of lawyers busy for weeks. That prospect alone should be enough to concentrate the minds of those involved to find a practical solution. Even then it would be difficult to predict the outcome of a court case on the subject because, quite apart from the complex legal issues, much would depend on how the evidence was presented and received by the judge. There are one or two practical pointers in such a situation.

First, Williams and/or Richards should write to the liquidators and Threlfalls and say what has happened. The priority is to let Threlfalls know that they should not part with the cabinets and that if they dispose of them, they will be liable for their full value. There are a number of complications. Richards, the retailer, is really responsible for the situation but has ultimately derived no benefit from it. His customer has had the benefit but is now insolvent and the chances of recovering from the liquidator are probably remote. Threlfalls, the third party sub-buyer, has paid for the cabinets in all innocence and will be full of indignation at the prospect of losing out. Threlfalls would have a claim against the customer but, like Williams or Richards, is faced with a potentially worthless claim against the customer's liquidator.

Who is to be the loser? In law there is no question of loss being shared out proportionately among those involved. There are competing claims and so far as the law is concerned Threlfalls, despite acting in good faith throughout, must hand the cabinets back. Worse still, Threlfalls must be clear about handing the cabinets back to their rightful owner. If they do this wrong they might lose the cabinets and still have a claim against them for their value from the rightful owner. The practicalities of the situation may be less clear. Threlfalls may consider that possession is nine-tenths of the law and refuse to hand back the cabinets, leaving Williams to pursue Richards and the customer first. Much will depend on the business relationship between Williams and Richards and whether Richards (or Williams) wants to preserve goodwill by agreeing some form of deal under which the loss is indeed shared in agreed proportions. Whether legal action is ultimately taken will depend on all the circumstances, including the amount of the claim and the good sense of the parties.

This example is illustrated in Figure 2.1.

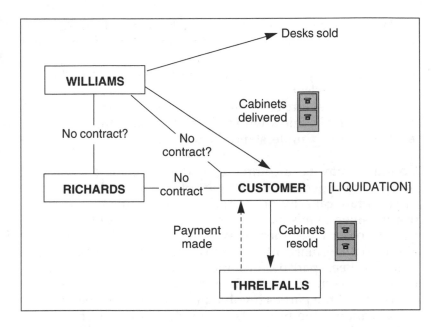

FIGURE 2.1 EXAMPLE: MISTAKE AS TO CONTENT OR
COMMITMENT

Summary

- Are the terms of all relevant contracts fully clear?
- Is there anything which has been left outstanding?
- If the terms are not finalized, has anyone partly performed the intended contract?
- Does each party have the ownership or other rights to do what it is proposing?
- Is there any element of gift and, if so, how is this evidenced?
- Is the contract connected with anything which is illegal or against public morality?
- Are all the parties over 18?
- Are the companies' names and numbers correct and up to date?
- Does the person signing have authority to do so?

- What scope for fraud exists and what would be the effect?
- Have any representations been made on which reliance is being placed?
- Are there any side agreements or collateral contracts – are their terms clear?
- Has any pressure been put on anyone to sign?
- Do you really know who you are dealing with?
- Do you really understand the transaction?

Contracts may be incomplete or defective for a variety of reasons: defective title on the part of a seller; lack of personal or corporate capacity or authority; fraud; duress or pressure, or fundamental mistake as to person or nature of the transaction. In other cases there may be legal remedies despite the absence of a formal contract, or in addition to a contract, where there has been part performance, misrepresentation or a collateral contract. Whilst the law provides remedies in several areas, one of the parties involved may have to be the loser. By understanding the principles at work you should be able to put your business in the strongest position to achieve your objectives and to reduce foreseeable risks.

See also: Chapters 1, 3, 8 and 13.

■ 3

Sale of goods and services

Certain terms will be implied into your business dealings if you, or the other parties to them, take no further action, and this chapter explains how these terms might operate in practice. The issues are taken further in Chapter 4, in relation to exclusion and limitation clauses, and in Chapter 14 in terms of working with standard form contracts and conditions of business. Relevant statutes and regulations will be discussed. For ease of reading they will be repeated occasionally, but the following abbreviations will also be used:

SGA   Sale of Goods Act 1979 (as amended by the Sale and Supply of Goods Act 1994 and the Sale of Goods (Amendment) Acts 1994 and 1995)

SGSA Supply of Goods and Services Act 1982 (as amended).

Legislation in the scheme of contract law

Since there is no commercial code in English law, our judges, in theory, do not make new law. Rather they interpret and clarify what the law is, even if in the process it appears that the law changes. At times this process is not adequate for the purposes of the community and parliament enacts legislation which seeks to cure the problem or fill the gap. The legislation may be prompted by a particular decided case, or by the Law Commission, or by political considerations. The pace of legislative change can itself vary, especially where social and technological change generates new areas requiring protection or regulation. These new rules are in turn tested by the practical demands of business and decisions of the courts until amendments are brought into force to correct any irregularities or clarify uncertainties in the earlier statute. This legislation in turn may be consolidated in a new Act or statute and so the process continues.

European law

Our laws are increasingly being driven by the requirements of the European Union (EU). European law is often treated as being remote and mysterious, but in fact it is an integral part of our law. It could even be said that the Treaty of Rome, the bedrock of the European Community which is now the EU, is our written constitution. Certainly the treaty is the basis of European law and the source of the authority of the European Commission.

The Commission, in consultation with the other bodies of the EU, develops European law primarily through regulations and directives. Regulations have direct effect in member states from the date that they come into force. Directives, on the other hand, require member states to introduce the necessary legislation in their own countries within a given time. In the UK that legislation usually takes the form of statutory instruments, which have the same effect as a formal statute but do not go through the same debating process in parliament. At the same time the increasingly international nature of trade is giving additional impetus to the harmonization of cross-border terms and practices of trading even outside the strict framework of legislation.

Terms implied by statute

Suppliers must comply with certain obligations which statute law implies into their contracts with buyers. To counteract this, suppliers may endeavour to limit their liability by an express term in the contract, even in a standard form contract. They will be successful only if the limitations do not change the basis of the bargain and are fair and reasonable for the type of contract in question. Particular formalities may also be required where consumers buy supplies in a personal, non-business capacity.

What are goods?

Goods are things or products which have a physical character, apart from money which is governed by a separate set of laws. The definition specifically excludes intangible items such as copyrights and trade marks. The distinction can be significant.

In 1996 the Court of Appeal dealt with a dispute arising from the supply by ICL of a new computer system to the City of St Albans. The system was required to 'cope with all statutory requirements' for the old community charge, with software which was to be 100 per cent error-free. Early versions of the software contained an error which produced an overstatement of the number of residents available to pay the community charge. As a result, the council fixed a lower charge than it would have done or needed to do and consequently suffered a shortfall in income.

Sales of computer systems frequently involve a combination of hardware in the form of drive unit, screen and keyboard and software in the form of a disk. Custom-made software is notoriously liable to imperfections or 'bugs' which impair its working but which generally do not prevent it working altogether. The sale of goods legislation requires that goods must be of satisfactory quality and fit for their intended purpose. Software is not goods since it consists of copyright material (although there may be other rights also). Is the disk on which the software is loaded goods or not, such that the implied terms of quality and fitness apply to it?

In the ICL case the court decided that the sale of a disk incorporating software was a sale of goods and approved an Australian decision that the sale of an entire system including hardware and software was a sale of goods. As a result, the terms as to quality and fitness for purpose implied by statute applied to the sale of the whole system including the software. Implied terms as to quality and fitness for purpose can only be excluded in sales to business to the extent that the exclusion would be reasonable and cannot be excluded at all in sales to consumers. This highlights the distinction not merely between goods and other items but also between business and consumer transactions.

Price and payment

Where the price is not specified the courts may sometimes imply a reasonable price by reference to trade custom, clearly known market price or even previous dealings between the same parties. This implied price should not be relied on since, as already seen, the failure to agree a price, or at least a mechanism to establish the price, may invalidate the contract altogether. So far as payment is concerned, the SGA implies that payment is due on delivery. Let buyers beware: as there is no implication of any credit period – it should be specifically stipulated in each case.

Delivery and acceptance

Detailed provisions are contained in the SGA covering delivery and acceptance, subject to different intentions expressed by the parties in the sale contract. Suffice it to say that if the intention is that the goods be delivered by the seller or that the place of delivery is other than the buyer's normal place of business, those intentions should be clearly agreed and recorded. Subject to some rare exceptions, there is no implication as to delivery date other than that it should be within a 'reasonable time', which is inevitably a question of fact in each case. If time is made of the essence in this respect (see p. 186) and the seller is a day late, the buyer can refuse delivery and terminate the contract. Again, unless otherwise agreed, the buyer is not obliged to accept partial delivery, but may accept some parts and reject others which are defective or delayed. The SGA does set out detailed rules as to acceptance which will apply and should be consulted if the parties have not expressly agreed on the issue.

Title to goods (SGA, ss. 12 and 18)

SGA implies a term in the contract that the seller has title to the goods (also known as ownership of or property in them) and a warranty that the seller can pass good title to the buyer free from any third-party claims. The Unfair Contract Terms Act (see Chapter 4) reinforces this by making void any attempt to exclude the implied warranty. Indeed, an attempt to exclude the warranty in a consumer transaction is also a criminal offence.

It is often difficult to establish the precise point when the title or property in the goods passes to the buyer. Title may be critical to the question of who bears the loss if anything adverse happens to the goods. Here the SGA starts to use words like 'specific, ascertained and unascertained goods'. The following example is pertinent. If I go to my local off-licence or supermarket and select a bottle of wine, the goods will be specific. If, on the other hand, I join a wine club which selects the wine within a pre-agreed price bracket, the wine will be unascertained (at least by me) until I am notified what it is or it is actually delivered. Under the SGA the title to unascertained goods cannot pass until they have become ascertained. The rest of the equation is not so straightforward, as the SGA rules only apply if the intention of the parties is not clear. In other words the parties to the contract can agree when title passes and in this case they can override the implied terms of the SGA. The rules in SGA, s. 18, are summarized as follows:

1   In a case where all preconditions have been met, the goods are specific and are ready to be delivered, the title passes

when the contract is made – even if the price has not been paid and the delivery not yet made. If I order a case of specific wine from the off-licence and they agree to deliver it, the wine is technically mine already. If payment is expressed to be a precondition of handing over, however, such as cash on delivery, the wine does not become mine until the condition is satisfied by payment being made.

2   If the goods are not in a state to be delivered, the title does not pass until they are ready and the buyer has been informed.

3   Where the seller has to carry out a step such as weighing the goods in order to fix the price, title does not pass until the weighing has been done and the buyer informed.

4   Where the buyer needs to approve the goods or there is sale or return, title only passes when the buyer accepts the goods or retains them for an unreasonable length of time. Consumption of the wine (without complaint), for example, might be safely regarded as acceptance, as would giving it away to friends.

5   With unascertained goods title passes when they are 'appropriated' to the contract, i.e. effectively selected for the purpose, provided they are ready to be delivered and there are no preconditions. The point here is that once the goods become ascertained they are specific and the other rules apply.

So if I order my mystery case of wine, it becomes specific when the bottles are selected and the case is picked up by the carrier for delivery to the waiting tipplers. What if I am out and the case is left in my front porch from which it is removed by a thief? (See Figure 3.1.) It depends on whether the title to the wine has passed to me. In the circumstances mentioned, assuming that I had already paid the bill or that I was a trusted customer who paid later on receipt of the wine company's account, the SGA rules would say that the property in the goods had passed to me. The loss would therefore be mine.

If the parties do not agree other terms, s. 20 of SGA states that risk passes when title to the goods passes, irrespective of possession of the goods. The exception is where there is late delivery and the late delivery causes the loss, when the party

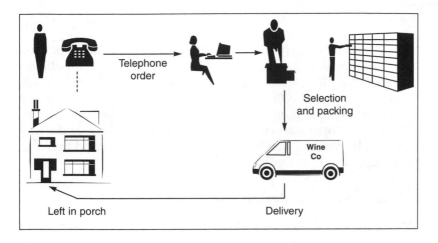

FIGURE 3.1   TITLE TO GOODS

at fault will be liable. Sale of goods cases therefore often depend on whether, and to what extent, the parties are insured and may then be fought by the insurance companies. In the wine example, the suppliers' terms might have stated that risk passed to me on delivery, although title is retained until payment is made. The loss would then be mine, whether or not there were preconditions.

Retention of title

The main risk to a seller is that, if he is giving the buyer credit, title to the goods will pass before the seller is paid. Even if the buyer becomes insolvent, therefore, title will have passed and the seller will have lost his goods and, very likely, his money too. It is to prevent this situation that retention of title clauses have developed. They are expressly permitted by the SGA and operate so as to defer the passing of title until either the goods have been paid for, or all payments due from the buyer to the seller have been made.[1]

---

[1] Retention of title is dealt with further in Chapter 14, p. 188.

Bailment

A bailment arises where one of the parties has to store or look after the goods in some way and there may be special obligations on that party (the bailee). Whilst not covered by the SGA, in general the law will imply a duty of reasonable care on the bailee where payment is made for the storage services or where they form part of the overall contract. The standard of care will be much less where no payment is made and the storage is provided on a voluntary basis.

Compliance with description (SGA, s. 13)

Where the sale is negotiated by reference to the description of goods, they must comply with that description. This will be the case where the buyer has relied on the description and has not seen the goods and may also be the case where the goods have been seen but there is still reliance on the description and the non-compliance was not readily apparent. On the other hand, experts, for example in fine arts, would be expected to rely on their own expertise and could not therefore rely on the implied term. Reference to description includes the quantity or weight of goods, their measurements and their overall presentation and packaging. Minor discrepancies may be overlooked.

Quality and fitness for purpose (SGA, s. 14)

The goods must be both of 'satisfactory quality' (which replaced the former concept of 'merchantable quality') and fit for their purpose. Satisfactory quality is a broad concept, judged by whether the goods are of the standard which a reasonable person would regard as satisfactory in all the circumstances, including the price charged for them. Appearance, finish, safety, durability and freedom from minor defects may all be relevant. The question of fitness for purpose is associated with the question of quality, but the question may arise as to whether the seller knew of the purpose for which the buyer intended to use the goods. Usually, but not always, this will be fairly obvious. It is in the interests of the buyer to make the intended purpose of the goods clear to the seller. The implied term will not apply to cases where the buyer is an expert, or where the seller declares he has no expertise in relation to them, or the buyer expressly agrees to take the goods as they are. 'Sold as seen' is not necessarily a reliable disclaimer if the seller has not specifically drawn the attention of the buyer to any defects, or the buyer has not expressly taken time to examine the goods or agreed to accept them with any inadequacies they may have.

Sale by sample (SGA, s. 15)

Where a buyer sees a sample of the goods and agrees to buy by reference to that sample, he is entitled to expect the remainder of the goods to conform to the sample. Section 15 confirms this and gives a reasonable opportunity for inspection before the goods are deemed to have been accepted by the buyer.

Supply of goods and services

The Sale of Goods Act applies to goods which are actually to be sold. The Act does not deal with the supply of services or with hiring and leasing agreements and agreements for the supply of goods short of outright sale. The statutory protection was accordingly extended by the Supply of Goods and Services Act 1982 (SGSA). Hire purchase and credit sale are not covered by this Act and are regulated separately.

Part I of the SGSA covers a set of implied terms which are largely parallel to the implied terms in the SGA for circumstances where there is a supply, but less than a full or outright sale, of goods. These terms also apply where there is a mixed supply of goods and services, such as under a building contract where the builder supplies the materials as well as the labour. The materials must comply with implied terms as to quality and fitness for purpose equivalent to those set out in the SGA.

Part II of the SGSA deals with services supplied in the course of a business. The supplier of those services has an implied obligation to provide them with reasonable care and skill. The standard is based on the level of care and skill that an ordinary competent supplier of those services would be expected to possess. That level in turn relates to the standards that the supplier of the services actually professes to possess (either expressly or by implication) in relation to the nature of their calling. So if you ask an electrician to carry out wiring work, you are entitled to have the work carried out to the standard that a competent electrician would be expected to achieve. But if you asked a carpenter to carry out electrical work, you could not expect the same standard unless the carpenter represented that he was indeed a competent electrician. With services also, there is no obligation on the supplier to achieve a specific result unless the contract included such a term. A similar situation would arise with a lawyer acting on a piece of litigation. All reasonable skill and care should be used but a successful result cannot, of course, be guaranteed!

In contracts covered by the SGSA there is also (s. 15) an implied term that the buyer will pay a reasonable charge for what is supplied if the parties have not agreed a price. If, therefore, you ask a builder to carry out some work for you, and you do not fix clear terms of reference with him, the law will imply terms as to the quality of the work and materials and the price of the deal. That still leaves open the question of how much work the builder was asked to do in the first place and how far that original agreement was changed subsequently. This is an area where disputes can be as frequent as disputes on price and quality and far more difficult to resolve. As there will be no implied term that the work will achieve any given result, the statutory implied terms are no substitute for sensible contract planning.

Example

This example is illustrated in Figure 3.2. Cruncher & Co., chartered accountants, are refurbishing their offices and planning a new file storage system. They engage Stargazers Design, space planners, to design and install the new layout. Stargazers Design, after measuring up the site and discussing the requirements of Crunchers with their facilities manager,

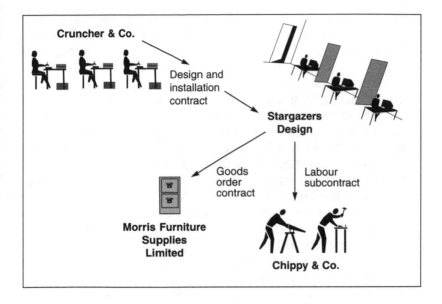

FIGURE 3.2   EXAMPLE: SUPPLY OF GOODS
                          AND SERVICES

design a system which consists of a number of standard
units linked to purpose-made cabinets and shelving.

Terms are agreed and client approval is given. Stargazers
order the standard cabinets from Morris Furniture Supplies
Limited and engage Chippy & Co. to carry out the carpentry
work. Everything is installed and Crunchers move back into
the space. To their dismay they find that several of the cabinets have been put in different places from the agreed plan
(limiting their office layout). Because they did not fit in the
space originally proposed, some cabinets are of the wrong
size for their files. Some of the shelves are loose and unable
to support heavy files and overall the space is substantially
short of the firm's new filing requirements.

The main contract is between Crunchers, the accountants,
and Stargazers, the space planners. Stargazers have entered
into a separate contract with Morris for the purchase of cabinets and with Chippy & Co. for the carpentry work. There is
therefore a sale of goods contract between Morris and

Stargazers which would be governed by the SGA, and supply of goods and services contracts governed by the SGSA between Stargazers and Chippy (assuming that Chippy had supplied additional materials) and between Stargazers and Crunchers.

Stargazers, as space planning specialists, have an implied duty to exercise reasonable skill and care at a level which would be expected of competent space planners, i.e. a greater duty on the planning side than would be expected of a general builder or carpenter. Crunchers would be entitled to assume that Stargazers would correctly measure the space and the cabinets and would have relied on their expertise in this respect. Moreover, Stargazers were the contractual suppliers of all the materials to Crunchers. The shelves, for example, should have been expected to bear the weight of papers and were therefore unfit for their purpose as well as probably being of unsatisfactory quality. The poor fitting is also Stargazers' responsibility to Crunchers under the SGSA, as is the fact that the cabinets were put in the wrong positions. Stargazers may have their own claims against Chippy & Co. for the work, but their claims will depend on how far Stargazers could show that they had relayed to Chippy exactly what was required.

The question of the lack of adequate filing space may be more difficult. There will be no term implied by the SGSA that Stargazers, as suppliers, guaranteed to produce any specific minimum amount of filing space, but there may well be an express or implied term in the contract arising from discussions between Crunchers and Stargazers. Stargazers may accept liability for the defective work but resist a claim for the 'lost' filing space and the misplaced cabinets. It will then be a question of going through the papers and taking statements from the parties to decide whether those issues were agreed as terms of the contract.

In planning the contract, Stargazers, like ICL in the St Albans case, might have considered how far they could exclude or limit their liability by incorporating suitable terms of business in their contract with Crunchers, assuming of course that Crunchers would have agreed to this.

Summary

- Are you dealing with goods (as defined for this purpose) or services?
- When does title pass (for specific and/or ascertained goods or otherwise)?
- Do the goods need to comply with description and/or sample?
- Are the goods free from all defects or has the buyer expressly agreed to accept specific faults?
- Has the intended purpose of the goods been made known and are they fit for that purpose?
- Are services being supplied in addition to goods and, if so, is a particular result required?
- Are all these points clearly agreed in writing?

Certain terms will be automatically implied into the sale or purchase of your goods unless you exclude or modify them. These terms are mainly concerned with ownership of, or title to, the goods, when title passes to the buyer, whether the goods are satisfactory, comply with description or sample and whether they are fit for their intended purpose. Different terms are implied to services and there is no implication of a specific result. You must understand the terms that are implied in order to enforce them against other parties if necessary, or to modify your obligations in the sale contract as far the law permits. (See also Chapters 4, 5, 13 and 14.)

■ 4

Exclusion clauses and unfair terms

It is often possible to exclude or limit terms which are implied in contracts (see Chapter 3) or liability for breach of contract generally. This chapter sets out the rules relating to contracts between businesses and also those relating to consumer contracts. Statutory references are as follows:

UCTA   Unfair Contract Terms Act 1977
UTCCR   Unfair Terms in Consumer Contracts
            Regulations 1994.

Commercial contracts

The reference in this chapter to commercial contracts is to those between two or more businesses. Such contracts should be distinguished from those between a business and a customer acting in a private capacity, but note that the legal definition of consumer contracts does vary among the different statutes and regulations.

In relation to unfair contract terms in commercial contracts there are two main areas to consider: first, the extent to which the courts have found exclusion clauses valid under the common law; second, the statutory rules under the UCTA. In effect the UCTA tests have been grafted onto and are additional to the common-law tests, although both make considerable use of the traditional British question of 'reasonableness'. The UTCCR tests do not apply to commercial contracts as defined above, but are considered later in the chapter in relation to sales to consumers. To avoid repetition, references to 'limitation' clauses include 'exclusion' clauses and vice versa, unless otherwise indicated. It is also assumed that the seller is the party seeking to rely on the exclusion clause, although in some cases it is large buyers who 'call the shots' and trade on their own terms of business. The provisions relating to unfair contract terms can equally well apply to them.

General principles relating to exclusion clauses

- A well-drafted contract will set out exactly what it covers and, expressly or by implication, what it does not cover. It is better to state clearly at the outset what you are going to do (or even what you will try to do but are not committed to do) and what you are not going to do, rather than to rely on broadly-worded obligations and an exclusion clause.
- A contract term will only apply if it is properly incorporated in the contract in the first place. You cannot limit liability after the contract has been entered into.
- An exclusion clause (one which excludes liability altogether) or a limitation clause (one which limits liability to a specific amount or in some other way) will be interpreted by the courts very strictly. An exclusion of liability regarding, for example, defective design, would not be regarded as covering defective workmanship.
- If there is a wide exclusion clause the courts will not rewrite it, but will regard it all as void if it is too wide. It is therefore usually better to break the clause into more specific parts so that, if any part is void, the court may delete just that part (the so-called 'blue-pencil test') and leave the rest standing.

- The courts will also interpret exclusion clauses against the party seeking to invoke them. This will generally be the party drafting the contract or that part of the contract in question (a principle known by the Latin maxim *contra proferentem*).

- National laws will vary as to what is and what is not permitted. There will, however, be a similar position on consumer contracts among member states of the European Union since the law is derived from European directives.

- Any attempt to exclude or limit liability for death or personal injury resulting from negligence will be void and may well be a criminal offence.

- Any exclusion of the implied warranty of title will be ineffective in either a business or a consumer sale (see Chapter 3).

- The exclusion of the implied terms as to description, quality, fitness and sample, and/or any other attempt to exclude or limit liability for breach of contract or negligence, will only be valid so far as it is regarded as reasonable within the tests set out in the UCTA.

- What is reasonable is judged with regard to the circumstances which were known or ought to have been known or considered by the parties when they made the contract. Each situation will depend on its own facts.

- Special rules apply where one party trades under standard written terms of business which are incorporated into the contract. The UCTA states that, except so far as the contract satisfies the standard of reasonableness, such terms may not exclude or limit any liability for that party's own breach or permit a major departure from the obligations under the contract. The UTCCR also deal with standard form contracts in relation to consumer sales.

- The Unfair Contract Terms Act is really a misnomer since it is not limited to contract terms, but also covers negligence and is more concerned with the reasonableness of a term than its fairness. When considering the reasonableness of a clause under the UCTA, the courts will have regard to:

  - the alternatives open to the other party
  - the relative bargaining strength of the parties

- whether the buyer received an 'inducement' to enter into the contract (such as a special price for a lower standard of liability), and
- the availability of insurance for one party or the other.

• As limitation clauses in contracts will not limit liability to third parties, indemnity clauses are increasingly used to require a party to a contract, who may be responsible for actions causing loss, to indemnify the other party in respect of any such claims. These clauses are not limitation clauses as such, and are not therefore directly covered by the unfair contract terms laws, even though they may operate unfairly between the parties.

Notices on premises which seek to exclude liability for any form of loss however caused are almost certain to be void, because they include an attempted disclaimer of liability for death and personal injury. Such a disclaimer is itself void and since it is not possible to 'sever' the offending parts, the whole exclusion would fail. If the clause were limited to loss or damage to vehicles or their contents, then the test of reasonableness would apply. What should you reasonably expect from a car park? Is it reasonable to expect that cars will be protected from thieves or vandals, or merely that the staff of the car park themselves do not break in?

Blanket limitation clauses are dangerous, even in commercial contracts, but may still be upheld in surprising circumstances. In a celebrated case in 1980 (*Photo Production Ltd* v *Securicor Transport Ltd*) Securicor were hired to provide security for a warehouse building. The night was cold and the security guard lit a fire to keep himself warm. His heating system was too effective and the warehouse burned down. The House of Lords' decision finally resolved many legal disputes on the issue of wide-ranging exclusion clauses. They held that Securicor were able to rely on an exclusion clause in their contract with the warehouse owner, even in respect of the gross negligence of one of their own staff. Whilst the destruction of the warehouse was not the result expected from a contract designed to protect it, the court decided that an exclusion clause in a commercial contract could not be struck down merely because it was unreasonable or because the effects of the breach were serious. It was up to the warehouse owners, as experienced business people, to have understood and accepted the exclusion clause. The case is a reminder that it is always necessary to take careful note of contract terms, including standard terms, analyse the risks against the benefits and be prepared to renegotiate if necessary. Despite this, the Securicor case remains anomalous, and how the principles of that judgment can be fully reconciled with the UCTA tests is still an open question.

Summary

Attempts to contract out of or restrict liability are strictly construed and controlled by the courts, but should be considered by most sellers in commercial dealings as a relevant way in which risks may be validly reduced. The question of risk and cost is dealt with in more detail in relation to planning the contract in Chapter 13. Sellers must ensure that their clauses are precise and relevant; buyers, for their part, should take such clauses seriously and consider the possible risks and whether they should negotiate, or even pay for, additional protection.

Consumer contracts

Businesses who deal with individuals in their private capacity must be aware of the outlines of their responsibility to them.

Who is a consumer?

Consumers are given special protection. In the UCTA the reference to a party to a contract 'dealing as a consumer' covers the following situations, assuming that the consumer will be the buyer (although the regulations are not limited to this role):

● The buyer neither makes the contract in the course of a business nor pretends to be doing so (so that the private buyer masquerading as a trade buyer cannot invoke the consumer protection).

- The seller makes the contract in the course of a business (which excludes the private seller to private buyer deal being a consumer contract).
- The goods supplied are of a type ordinarily supplied for private use or consumption (an increasingly fine distinction in the case of office furniture, but perhaps more obvious with industrial machinery).

The UTCCR definition is slightly different and covers individuals acting for purposes outside their business. Both definitions of consumer will therefore include a business person buying or selling outside the scope of their normal business, but the UCTA definition can also include a partnership or company acting in this way.

What additional rules apply to consumer transactions?

Broadly all the rules relating to commercial contracts, as referred to earlier, apply (so far as they are relevant) to consumer transactions. A number of others are set out below. In addition the UTCCR tests set out in the next section may also apply.

- Provisions excluding liability for the seller's own breach or permitting a great variation in the subject-matter of the contract are subject to the test of reasonableness under the UCTA, whether or not they are part of the seller's standard terms of business.
- Provisions limiting the statutory implied terms of description, quality, fitness for purpose and compliance with sample are completely void. Furthermore, the display or publication of such terms is a criminal offence.
- Any guarantee or statement of the consumer's rights must contain a statement that the customer's statutory rights are unaffected by the guarantee or statement. (This relates to the sale and supply of goods, but not of services.)
- Where there is a defect in a product, there can be no exclusion or limitation of liability by contract or notice on the part of the manufacturer or supplier to the customer in

respect of loss caused to any person as a result of that defect (Consumer Protection Act 1987, s. 7).

Unfair Terms in Consumer Contracts Regulations 1994 (UTCCR)

The 1994 regulations stemmed from a 1993 EC directive which aimed to harmonize member states' laws in relation to the health, safety and economic interests of the consumer, a principle which goes back to the Treaty of Rome. The purpose of this harmonization, or standardization of approach between the member states, is not only to ensure a similar approach in each member country but also to break down trade barriers arising from the existence of different consumer laws in different countries, which might tend to isolate national markets and be a barrier to free international trade.

The UTCCR are part of a range of directives and regulations relating to consumer services, consumer credit, misleading advertising, defective product liability and the negotiation of contracts away from business premises, many of which are specialist areas outside the scope of this book. Because the UTCCR are additional to existing regulations there are separate definitions in the UTCCR and indeed different concepts. The main differences are:

- the UTCCR are much wider than the UCTA in relation to consumer contracts,
- they are based on a continental European concept of good faith and fairness rather than the classic Anglo-Saxon test of reasonableness (the fairness, or rather unfairness, test concentrates more on the effect and the reasonableness test more on the cause or justification,
- the UTCCR apply only to consumers and only to standard form contracts – those which have not been individually negotiated.

The UTCCR cover all contracts except those relating to employment (which is separately regulated), inheritance (where there are great national differences), family law rights and the rules relating to the formation and constitution of companies and partnerships (which are already heavily regulated). This leaves within the new rules the relevant provisions of financial services contracts and insurance policies, other than the risk and liability definitions which relate directly to premium levels. The transfer of property rights in land is outside the regulations, but provisions relating to the supply of services in a building may well be within their ambit. In these areas the UTCCR again go further than the UCTA, but clearly only in relation to consumer transactions.

There are three key UTCCR tests:

1   Taking into account the relative bargaining strengths of the parties and the existence of any inducements, do any of the contract terms create a significant imbalance in the relationship between business and consumer contrary to the requirement of good faith?
2   Are the written terms in plain, intelligible language? If not, the consumer is to have the benefit of the doubt.
3   In particular, do the terms fall within the 'grey' list of 17 terms which will be unfair if they have certain objects or effects?

Complex terms in small print are unlikely to pass muster. Indeed, those dealing with consumers should make their terms of business clearly phrased in plain, intelligible language and clearly printed, and give the consumer time to read them. Consumers should also be given the chance to amend the terms so that they are individually negotiated, although perhaps an understanding of the basics of contract law by the sales assistant would be advisable!

The grey list

The 17 terms mentioned in the directive and the regulations are given as an indication that they may operate unfairly rather than by way of an automatic ban. They are quite carefully worded but the main provisions, summarised here, are those which:

- limit liability in respect of the death or personal injury of a customer resulting from an act or omission of the seller or supplier (potentially wider than the UCTA provision)
- 'inappropriately' limit the rights of the consumer where the supplier has not fully performed
- permit the supplier to retain the customer's deposit if the customer decides not to go ahead with the deal, unless the customer is given a similar right against the supplier
- require a 'disproportionately' high payment by way of compensation for non-fulfilment of the contract
- permit the supplier, but not the customer, to opt out of the contract or to retain amounts paid by the customer where the supplier has terminated the contract
- entitle the supplier, but not the customer, to terminate the contract on short or no notice (except where there are serious grounds for doing so)
- entitle the supplier to extend a fixed-term contract without notice to the customer
- bind the customer to contract terms which he or she has had no proper opportunity of studying
- enable the supplier to vary the terms of the contract unilaterally without good reason
- give the supplier the sole right to decide if there has been a breach of contract
- permit the seller to raise the price without giving the customer the right to cancel
- restrict the buyer's right to take immediate legal action for breach.

You may still see such clauses, but they are now unlikely to be upheld. Although the UTCCR do not go as far as the UCTA in actually banning some terms, the potential of the UTCCR in consumer contracts is far wider and deeper than the UCTA. To reinforce this, the European Commission is pressing member states to attack suppliers who persist with unreasonable terms and the 1993 directive places an obligation on member states to prevent such terms being used. The mobile phone industry was one of those singled out by the Office of Fair Trading (OFT) in the early stages to mend its ways and improve the fairness of its contracts. The OFT does have considerable enforcement powers if due note is not taken. The consumer may now make a complaint direct to the Director General of Fair Trading who will, if appropriate, enforce the new laws, by securing undertakings from any offending suppliers or a court injunction if persuasion does not succeed.

UTCCR summary

The provisions of the UTCCR apply to you if: (a) you supply goods or services to a consumer and (b) you use standard terms of business. If so, use the following checklist:

● Are all your contract terms clear in print and language?
● Are the price and basic terms clearly (and perhaps separately) stated?
● Do the terms include any on the 'grey' list (unless there is good reason for these)?
● Do the terms cause a significant imbalance in the relationship, which is unfair to the customer;
● Has the customer's attention been drawn to the terms before the contract is signed?
● Has the customer been given a fair opportunity to consider the terms, including, if appropriate, a reasonable cooling-off period for any longer-term commitment?
● Have any problematic terms been re-negotiated?
● Do your sales assistants and agents only make claims for the goods or services that they are authorized to make and can substantiate?

(See also: Chapters 3, 5, 13 and 14.)

■ 5

Negligence and product safety

Because it is not possible to enter into a contract with everyone whose activities might impinge on our own, we must understand how other areas of legal liability cross-relate to obligations created by contract and how they may need to be dealt with in the contractual process. Whilst this chapter indicates laws and distinctions which businesses should be aware of in relation to contracts, it is not a definitive guide to all other areas of potential liability. The only safe prediction in this respect is that, as life becomes more complex and the impact of one person's activities on others becomes more widespread and more immediate, the law will become more, rather than less, complex.

Claims against third parties

We can immediately identify with claims against third parties which arise from incidents on the road. Drivers, cyclists and pedestrians all use the road and the activities of any of them can directly affect all road users and other third parties. The effect may range from fear at a narrow miss, through damage to vehicles, to personal injury and death. There may be further consequential losses in all these cases. The car may be out of action when it is needed and the loss of earnings following injury or death could undermine the financial well-being of a family. How far does the law compensate people in these circumstances and how do those rules relate to the law of contract? Further, what happens when the general duties that we owe to others in everyday life interact with more specific contractual duties?

One of the first questions that anyone asks after the shock of an accident is 'How did it happen?' closely followed by 'Who is to blame?' The question of blame may have enormous legal repercussions because of the cost of repairs, the loss of business which may result and the individual losses caused to those affected by the situation. The decision that the police officers on duty at Hillsborough after the football ground disaster could claim compensation for stress and emotional suffering reminds us that the categories of person affected by an incident may go well beyond those who were first involved. Innocent bystanders suffering nervous shock as a result of an accident, and relatives away from the scene but suffering from the shock arising from the news of death or injury to their family, have all been regarded as people likely to be affected by a negligent act.

Negligence is not necessarily a crime. It may be a crime where it amounts to a specific criminal offence, such as driving without due care and attention or even dangerous driving. It may also be criminal if it is reckless, particularly where life is put at risk, such as a grossly negligent failure to supervise children on an activity holiday where there were predictable risks and dangers which should have been foreseen by those responsible. The law has accordingly developed rules in circumstances where a right of redress for such 'wrongs' should be given by the civil law. These cases are known as 'torts', a reminder that some of our law dates from Norman times. The most common tort is negligence.

Negligence

The main features of negligence are very straightforward:

1 There is a duty of care which one person owes to another.
2 There is a breach of that duty of care.
3 Loss or injury results from that breach.

Anyone who has ever studied law will probably remember the case of the snail in the bottle of ginger beer. Whether it was the part of the snail which the lady drank, or the effect of the discovery of the part still left in the bottle afterwards which caused the illness, the manufacturer was liable for the injury despite the absence of any contract between manufacturer and consumer. Our law of negligence is still largely based on the words of Lord Atkin in the 1932 House of Lords decision in *Donoghue* v *Stevenson* when he said:

> You must take reasonable care to avoid acts or omissions which you can reasonably foresee would be likely to injure your neighbour. Who then, in law, is my neighbour? The answer seems to be persons who are so closely and directly affected by my act that I ought reasonably to have them in contemplation as being so affected when I am directing my mind to the acts or omissions which are called in question.

In the case of a traffic accident, therefore, there is a clear case that road users have a duty of care to other road users who can be expected to be affected by their mistakes. If a mistake then occurs which is classified as negligence and which causes personal injury or death, or simply physical damage to a vehicle or other property, the negligent road user will be liable for the loss which results directly from the breach to the extent that the loss could have been reasonably foreseen at the time of the negligent act.

Negligence may be no more or less than a single error of judgement, as is the case with many traffic accidents. It may also be the result of a number of errors which need untangling in order to find out the real cause of the accident. The law fully recognizes the concept of contributory negligence, where for example one of the parties to an accident is travelling too fast or is poorly positioned on the road or fails to react quickly enough. Where that fact did not cause the accident but contributed to the result, the award of damages will be reduced by a factor to reflect the contribution.

Interrelation of breach of contract and negligence

Consider how the laws of negligence and contract would apply to a construction project such as, for example, the laying of a pipeline as part of a larger commercial development. Let us assume that there is a site owner client (perhaps represented by a project manager), the head or main contractor responsible for the whole project, the specialist pipeline contractor and a number of other subcontractors. The main contract will be an extensive document with detailed specifications attached, setting out the works and construction methods in detail and incorporating standard terms with agreed variations. The various subcontracts will include reference to the relevant parts of the main contract and impose similar terms and conditions on specific parts of the project. Any of those involved could be liable for defective workmanship by reason of all or any of the following:

- breach of the contract with the client (in the case of the head contractor) or the head contractor (in the case of the subcontractors)
- breach of any collateral contract which a subcontractor may have entered into in favour of the client and/or any party (such as a lender) associated with the client
- negligence.

There may also be liability for breach of a statutory duty, i.e. a duty laid down by legislation or regulation, typically relating to construction methods or health and safety issues (which can give rise to a claim by those suffering loss as a result in a way similar to the law of negligence).

Liability in contract law and negligence

The same default can, therefore, incur liability for the party responsible across a range of legal areas, but there may be different sanctions and different levels of liability in damages in respect of those areas. The measure of loss in contract claims is the amount that would be necessary to put the innocent party in the same financial position as if the contract had been properly performed. In a construction contract this means the position in which the client or head contractor would have been if the work had been carried out in accordance with the specification and on time. A claim in contract in these circumstances might cover the cost of repair or rebuilding, the loss of materials which have been wasted, the cost of rectifying any other part of the construction damaged as a result and loss of the direct financial benefits of the contract. These financial benefits must be carefully considered and can only include items which arise as a direct result of the breach of contract, and not from a separate cause. They can also only include matters which were, or could reasonably have been, contemplated by the parties when the contract was first entered into.

Because it may be difficult to identify the true loss, and to avoid later arguments, a clause may be inserted into the contract specifying an agreed amount of damages in respect of each day or week during which completion is delayed. This is often referred to as 'liquidated' (i.e. a known figure) damages or, in construction and other contracts, liquidated ascertained damages (LADs). The parties will therefore know at the outset what they will be liable for if there is a delay, if indeed it can be shown to have been the fault of the contractor. The figure must be a realistic pre-estimate since a penalty figure will be unenforceable in the courts.

The contractor, for its part, may wish to limit its liability. Obviously this is not a consumer transaction and exclusion or limitation of liability is permissible subject to the rules of common law and the UCTA (see Chapter 4). The position in relation to negligence is different because it may not be practicable to limit liability for negligence to third parties. There are cases where notices may be issued to third parties, such as the notice in a car park disclaiming liability for loss or damage.

These notices have their place in warning people of the dangers of going onto building sites. In general, however, whilst an exclusion clause may limit liability to other contracting parties, it will not assist against third parties.

Indemnity clauses

The head contractor will have overall responsibility for the site and the construction works and will be first in line for any claim. If it is sued for something which is really the responsibility of a subcontractor, it will want to be able to pass the claim on to the offending subcontractor. If there is a clear breach of the specification or other contract terms, there will be a straightforward claim for breach of contract, but in addition the head contractor will probably require the subcontractor to provide an indemnity in respect of third party claims arising out of the subcontractor's negligence. The head contractor will seek an indemnity which will provide cover, not merely against proven liability to third parties but also against the cost of dealing with any claims brought by them. The subcontractor giving the indemnity will in turn wish to ensure that it is given early notice of any claim, the opportunity to deal with any allegations, the chance to repair any defective work (if practicable) and the ability properly to defend any legal proceedings brought against it.

How far, then, can the claim in negligence proceed, as opposed to a claim in contract? In cases of negligence, the measure of damages is the amount necessary to compensate those affected for loss or injury which could have been foreseen by a reasonable person. In some cases it is enough that loss of that type could have been foreseen, even though the extent of loss was greater than expected. In the law of negligence, the concept is that 'you take your victim as you find him' under the graphically named 'thin-skull rule'. If your victim has a thin skull and, in an accident, is struck a glancing blow over the head which would not have seriously injured many people but kills the victim, you are liable for the death because it follows from the act and it could be foreseen that the victim might have a thin skull. Once the negligent act has been committed, you, as the perpetrator, run the risk of the extent of loss to that victim. On the other hand you cannot be expected to be able to foresee and be responsible for what is called 'pure economic loss', i.e. that which goes beyond the immediate effects of the case and includes matters such as loss of profits and goodwill from contracts or business which have not yet been made or concluded and which may or may not happen.

Consumer Protection Act 1987 (CPA)

Under the law of negligence a person complaining about a product must show that the product was defective when it left the factory. Because this may be difficult or impossible for a buyer to prove, additional protection has been given to the consumer by the CPA. This Act should be interpreted in accordance with the intentions behind the European Product Liability Directive of 1985. It gives additional rights to consumers beyond those under contract law or negligence and shifts the burden of proof from consumer to producer. Awareness of the obligations under the Act (and the other statutory liabilities referred to in this chapter) is important for businesses who deal, at any stage in the chain, with consumer goods. The potential liabilities may be relevant to any sale, purchase, agency or distribution contract made between any of those parties. The main points are now considered in turn.

The CPA gives the right to a victim of a defective product to claim compensation against any producer of the product for any damage which the victim can show that the product has caused. For this purpose:

- Damage covers personal injury, death and damage to private property, loss of or damage to the goods themselves or pure financial loss.
- Defective means that the safety of something is not at the level that people are entitled to expect. There is an objective test according to all the circumstances, which covers how the product is marketed, what is expected to be done with it and any instructions or warnings given with it.

- Producer can include the manufacturer and any others in the production chain who produced the raw materials or processed, packaged, imported or branded any part of the product.
- Product is widely defined and includes ingredients in another product. It may also include labelling and product information which might make the product unsafe.
- Suppliers who are not producers are generally not liable unless they fail to identify the producer when requested to do so by an affected customer. All suppliers should therefore keep adequate records of the businesses from whom they obtain particular products or batches of products, which may be a complex procedure when several sources are used.

If the victim can show that a product has caused damage which could not reasonably have been expected, then the producer will be on the defensive. To escape liability the producer will have to establish one of a number of defences. These defences require the producer to *disprove* his involvement in the chain or the cause of the defect, or prove that the defect resulted from compliance with relevant legislation or regulations, or that the defect was not known as a risk in the light of scientific and technical knowledge at the time of supply. The producer may not disclaim or contract out of liability under the CPA, but the victim must bring the claim to court within three years of discovering the damage or the link with the product or the identity of the producer. There is a ten-year long-stop cut-off date.

Liability for unsafe consumer products

Part II of the CPA (supplemented by the General Product Safety Regulations 1994) sets up a régime for unsafe consumer products. Breach of this part of the Act is a criminal offence. Again there are defences including compliance with relevant regulations or approved safety standards. Retailers may also bring a defence that they did not know, and had no reasonable grounds for believing, that the products did not comply with general safety requirements or that all reasonable steps were taken or the offence was due to the default of another.

There is power under the Act for the government to make safety regulations including safety standards and information and warning requirements. Local trading standards officers are responsible for enforcement and have wide-ranging powers. The fact that something has been sold without complaint for some time is no protection against the view of a trading standards officer that the product is unsafe. Kitchen equipment, children's toys – and products which might be mistaken for children's toys – are particular examples where great care needs to be taken. The enforcement authorities' powers include ordering suspension of the production or sale of products which they consider unsafe, even without a court judgment, coupled with power to apply for offending products to be forfeited and destroyed.

Retailers would do well to seek, as a written term of the contract with their suppliers, a clause that if any products are alleged to be defective the supplier will take them back at a full credit. Retailers should also request an indemnity from the suppliers against any claims made in relation to those products. All producers, suppliers and retailers down the chain should in any event ensure that their product liability insurance is in good order. All involved should take even greater care in relation to goods for export, especially to the US. Laws there may impose strict liability for any defects, regardless of where the manufacturer or distributor is based, with damages awards far in excess of UK levels.

Misleading pricing and advertising

Part III of the CPA covers misleading pricing in advertisements, tickets, notices, catalogues or various other forms. The price will be misleading if it indicates a lower price than is actually the case, or that it is dependent on other conditions. If the price is not fully inclusive, e.g. of VAT, that fact must be clearly stated. A voluntary code advises that all prices to consumers should include VAT. There are limited defences available.

The Control of Misleading Advertisements Regulations 1988 are wide-ranging, although they do not cover advertisements relating to shares and other investments with their own statutory régime. These regulations catch advertisements, firstly, if they deceive or are likely to deceive and, secondly, if they influence or are likely to influence the 'economic behaviour' of those reading the advertisement. There may also be an offence if they are likely to deceive or injure a competitor of the advertiser. The sanction is a complaint to the Office of Fair Trading which acts as public watchdog and which can also step in of its own volition. It does not obtain compensation orders for individual complainants, nor deal with complaints about commercial radio, TV, private advertisements or party political advertisements.

Trade descriptions

The Trade Descriptions Act 1968, combined with the various regulations made under it, is the main statutory weapon for protecting consumers against inaccurate or misleading descriptions given to goods by someone in the course of a business. The goods must actually be supplied or offered for supply. Those at risk are retailers, suppliers, wholesalers, manufacturers and company officers of those companies. The following conditions apply:

- The Act and regulations refer to 'supply' which includes hire and exchange agreements where ownership either does or does not pass.
- An offer to supply covers not only goods on display, but also goods in the possession of a supplier (such as those under wraps downstairs.)
- There is strict liability in relation to goods, so that it is irrelevant whether the person committing the offence knew or should have known that they were doing so.
- A trade description can cover almost anything said about the product, from size, through method of manufacture or composition of the product, to statements about its performance.

- Any approvals or recommendations must be true and capable of being supported.
- The description can be written, oral or implied, as in the case of car mileometers which imply the correct mileage.
- There is a defence that the supplier exercised all due diligence and the commission of the offence was due to mistake or the fault of some other party. Due diligence requires a wide-ranging and generally effective system to be set up and not merely reliance on the statements of others.
- In relation to the supply of services the statement made must be known by the supplier to be false or the supplier must be reckless as to whether it is false or not. Prime candidates are travel and holiday companies where the blandishments offered to customers have, since the Act, been matched by the readiness of customers to complain. There may also be a civil breach of contract claim.

Consumer credit

The common law and legislation relating to the sale and supply of goods proved insufficient to deal with the legal demands of the ever-growing consumer credit business. Accordingly the Consumer Credit Act 1974 introduced a system of licensing, regulation of individual agreements and control of credit advertisements. Its main aim is to ensure that consumers have a clear statement of the terms of any deal in a way that can be compared with other deals and that they are suitably protected from entering into arrangements that they would not, on more careful consideration, have agreed to. The Act applies wherever payment is deferred, even if no interest is apparently being charged. The law relating to consumer credit has been further extended and developed by a series of Consumer Credit Regulations – where detailed working knowledge is required, or where specialist advice should be taken. Non-compliance is a criminal offence and the agreement will be unenforceable against the consumer, potentially leaving the supplier without goods or money.

Summary

Many other areas of law impinge on the law of contracts. They range from the common laws on negligence to detailed consumer protection regulations regarding product quality, pricing, advertising, description and credit. Some practical suggestions are set out below.

- Consider where performance of the contract may impinge on the rights or well-being of third parties and the rights of those third parties against one or more of the parties to the contract.
- Consider where you may be at risk from any claim resulting from breaches of contract or other defaults of other parties to the contract.
- Does the contract set out clearly who is responsible for safety, quality, pricing, packaging, labelling and advertising?
- Does the contract provide an effective claims handling procedure so that you are fully indemnified for loss caused as a result of any breach by the other parties?
- Where you are required to indemnify, does the contract give you the right to be notified immediately any possible claim comes to light and an early opportunity to deal with it and to repair or replace as appropriate? Do you have the right to deal with legal proceedings direct, provided that the claim will not commercially embarrass the party being indemnified?
- Have you checked your insurance cover – and full disclosure to the underwriters – especially in relation to goods which may be used in the US?

(See also Chapters 3, 4, 13 and 14.)

■ 6

Confidentiality and competition

Laws relating to confidentiality and unfair competition seek:

● to preserve a fair market
● to prevent unfair advantage being taken of one business by another, and
● to avoid distortion of competition by unreasonable restrictions or removal of a material competitor from the marketplace.

At one extreme there may be a restriction on a middle manager in a private company and at the other the law is concerned with regulating a merger between multi-billion pound conglomerates. This chapter examines the legal principles involved and how these affect contracts. Failure to appreciate these principles and plan for maximum business advantage could expose a business to serious and unanticipated threats.

Legal protection of confidential information

The competition law of the European Union (EU) is designed to create a free and open marketplace with equal economic opportunities. English law, on the other hand, has historically taken the approach that the law should interfere as little as possible in an open market, provided the public interest is not seriously affected. The protection of confidential information has underpinned the development of the law relating to restrictions against employees wishing to compete with their former employers. Restrictions on individuals and business sales are still largely regulated by historic English legal principles, whereas ongoing restrictions on business dealings are more likely to fall within the ambit of EU law.

The principles of EU competition law are set out in articles 85 and 86 of the Treaty of Rome; subsequent delegated legislation and court decisions follow clearly from the principles set down in those articles. Because of its historical development, however, there is no single piece of English competition law legislation which sets out our laws relating to confidentiality and competition although the new competition laws and proposed law making it illegal to use or disclose a trade secret without authority will change the balance. In the meantime it is necessary to look to case law for the concepts, reconciling decisions which often seem to conflict with one another, and to statutes and regulations for the more recent provisions. This chapter sets out the ground rules on the basis that, as so much with legal life, each case has to be judged on its own facts and merits.

Protecting confidential ideas

Whilst the law will not protect ideas as such, two notable cases illustrate how the law of confidence can, in appropriate circumstances, be used to protect anything from sensitive financial or marketing information to a business concept. *Seager v Copydex* 1967 concerned an inventor who developed a revolutionary form of carpet grip. When seeking backing, the inventor discussed the concept and details of the scheme with a company which then decided to develop the idea itself without further credit or payment to the original inventor. In *Fraser v Evans* 1983 an all-female rock band approached a television company with the idea that their story would make a good television series. The underlying concept was that, if the idea was taken up, they would have the opportunity to star in the show themselves. The television company, having apparently ignored the proposal, then went ahead to produce the show with different band members who rose to fame because of it. In both these cases the courts held that an original business idea had been communicated in confidence, that there had been a breach of the duty of confidence on the part of the companies to which the information had been disclosed and that substantial compensation should be paid to those who had lost out on the exploitation of the idea.

To be protected, the information must have the necessary quality of confidence about it and have been treated as confidential. It is no good making information freely available to all and sundry and then claiming it is confidential. It should be clearly so marked and its circulation and reproduction strictly controlled. Potentially it may be protected indefinitely. Equally, the ideas must be sufficiently detailed and original. By contrast, in a 1997 case, an idea for a style of night club discussed at a dinner party was held to be neither original nor confidential.

Confidentiality undertakings

Communication of confidential information should therefore be protected by a suitable undertaking from the party receiving it (the user) in favour of the party supplying it (the provider), including:

● reference to the nature of the information and the purpose for which it is supplied
● a prohibition against the user disclosing the information to anyone else or using it for their own purposes
● permission for the user to involve certain senior employees and advisers – subject to the user taking all reasonable care in providing the information and perhaps also holding the

user responsible for any breach of undertaking by those third parties or requiring the third parties to give direct undertakings to the provider

- requiring that all copies of the information be returned to the provider or destroyed if the negotiations are unsuccessful
- providing that the restrictions will cease to apply if the information becomes public ('in the public domain') unless it has become so as a result of breach of the undertaking by the user or their employees or agents.

Some confidentiality undertakings also prohibit the user from offering employment to the provider's own staff, which might otherwise be a cheaper way for the user to take advantage of the employee's knowledge of the business as an alternative to buying the goodwill. These clauses must be sufficiently limited in extent and in time to be enforceable by the provider, but they could easily catch out an unwary user who innocently takes on the provider's staff shortly after negotiations prove abortive. Confidentiality undertakings therefore require careful drafting by those seeking to protect information with regard to the circumstances in hand and careful review by the receivers of information before they are signed. Experience shows that documents called confidentiality agreements or undertakings may go well beyond the protection that might be expected. Again there is no such thing as a standard form and both provider and receiver of the information should take the time to negotiate the agreement that is appropriate to the circumstances and the particular parties.

Employment confidentiality and restrictions

Employees may be prevented from taking unfair advantage of their employers or ex-employers. During employment employees have a duty of fidelity to their employers and may be accountable for disclosure of confidential information or any breach of their duty which damages their employer's business. After employment they are, in the absence of express restrictions, able to use in the open marketplace the general skill and knowledge which they have built up in relation to their industry, but they may not unfairly exploit information which can be shown to be confidential and unique to their former employer. The employer must, however, have a legitimate interest in the information or business which it is seeking to protect and the protection should go no further than is reasonably necessary to protect that interest. Many employers assume that there is no point in including restrictive covenants in an employment contract since they will be unenforceable. That is certainly not the case. Neither is it the case that blanket restrictions can be imposed, which was established many years ago in the case of a celebrated opera singer. The courts refused to uphold a clause preventing her from singing opera anywhere else for a lengthy period when the contract ended. Since opera was what she was known for and had trained in, the restriction both acted against the public interest and prevented her from earning a living in her chosen profession. The following guidelines further illustrate these principles.

Restrictions during employment

- There is an implied duty on an employee to act honestly and in good faith towards an employer, including the duty to pass on relevant information and not to indulge in harmful competition, nor to use or disclose information which is confidential to the employer.
- An employee in a senior managerial or executive position is expected to exercise a greater duty in these areas.
- Senior employees can be validly restricted from working in other businesses during the course of their employment.

Restrictions after employment

- Employees cannot be prevented from using the general skill and knowledge of the industry which they have built up as part of their general industry, product or service experience.
- Ex-employees may be restricted from using or disclosing trade secrets which are specific and unique to the employer's business and have been treated as highly

confidential by the employer. A stricter test applies after employment than during employment.

- An employee will be released from restrictive covenants applying after the end of employment if the employer terminates the employment in breach of contract. Particular care must be taken with payments in lieu of notice.
- The restrictions should go no further than is strictly necessary properly to protect the legitimate interests of the employer.

Express restrictions

The most difficult aspect of restricting employees relates to clauses which seek to limit their choice of work in the future – after the current employment has ended. It is best to discuss such restrictions openly at the outset with the employees concerned to secure a clear understanding and commitment at that stage. A restrictive covenant is an important provision which should not be left hidden in the small print but rather identified in discussions as part of the responsibility equation, perhaps as a counterpart to promotion and remuneration. Restrictions against canvassing the customers of a former employer are normally uncontentious but difficult to prove and enforce. In many industries highly paid sales people are taken on precisely because of their customer contacts and their ability to bring customers from one business to another. Although brought in for the purpose, such individuals can make or mar the fortunes of a company and their contracts deserve careful consideration. The following points are relevant:

- the area of operation of the employer's business and the extent of the employee's influence
- the area to be covered by the restrictions
- the definition of the type of business to be restricted
- whether there is any commercial justification in seeking a blanket restriction against the employee being involved in that particular aspect of the business within a given area

- alternatively, whether it will be sufficient to restrict the ex-employee only in respect of existing customers of the business (a much easier restriction to enforce)
- the identification of the customers to be protected
- how much time the employer needs to establish customer connections after the departure of the employee
- the length of time each of those restrictions should apply
- the interrelation between notice periods / garden leave and restrictions post termination. (See also p. 134.)

There are no standard approaches with restrictive covenants and the courts have constantly emphasized that each case must be considered on its own merits. Employees should, however, note that a restrictive covenant in the hands of an ex-employer can be a powerful weapon since there are relatively few ex-employees who have the financial means to defend a legal action by their former employers, particularly given the uncertainty of court decisions and the debilitating effects of an injunction.

Confidentiality and competition in other business relationships

Judges are likely to consider partnership agreement restrictions as matters between parties of equal status and to have less regard for the concepts of the legitimate business interests of the partnership and the reasonableness of the restrictions on a departing partner. As such, pure non-competition obligations in partnership agreements would probably be upheld. The courts are also more likely to enforce restrictions underpinning the value of a capital asset, such as the goodwill of a business, to prevent the seller from reducing the value of what has been transferred.

Similar principles apply to most commercial agreements. In a joint venture agreement, for example, any substantial financial investments by the parties may require protection when the parties go their separate ways. Much depends upon whether the joint venture business is to continue and what type of protection would be reasonable. At the other end of the scale is the individual agent or distributor who, when ceasing to work for one principal or supplier, goes to work for another in relation to the same type of products or services. A balance must be found between preventing the agent or distributor from earning a living at all and permitting them simply to relocate the customers to a new supplier.

Deleting unreasonable restrictions

The courts have power to delete (or, in legal language, sever) from a restrictive covenant words or provisions which make it unreasonable, but no power to re-write the bargain between the parties. If the removal of the offending words leaves something incomplete or incoherent, then the whole clause or restriction will fail. In the case of a series of restrictions, for example, the courts might delete a restriction against pure competition whilst leaving intact restrictions protecting existing customers and staff. It is therefore better to set out restrictions separately and to fix a reasonable time period. If there was only one clause against competition, then deleting that would remove all restrictions. For the same reason buyers, employers, principals and suppliers should avoid pressing their lawyers to include greater or lengthier restrictions than are reasonably necessary to protect the interest in question.

Remedies for breach

It is advisable not to enter into a fight in the first place. If you are caught by a restriction and liable to be in breach of it, consider whether you can agree some modified form of undertaking with the other party which might give them the protection they need and still leave you sufficient flexibility. Such an approach might also persuade a court, in a borderline case, to refuse an injunction if it considers that the undertaking you have offered would be adequate protection. Whilst any party subject to a restriction can seek a court declaration as to its validity, most cases that come to court do so because the party which fears being damaged seeks an injunction or court order against the other party from breaching the restriction. If you are at risk of being the victim of another party's breach of a restrictive covenant, you should act immediately the breach or imminent breach of contract becomes known to you so that you do not lose your rights through delay. Employees considering breaching restrictive covenants, on the other hand, should remember that if the employers have some indication of the intended competition and seek a formal undertaking from them not to breach their existing covenants, a failure or refusal to give that undertaking may, coupled with the other evidence, be a sufficient basis for the employer to seek an injunction before any breach actually takes place.

Restrictive Trade Practices Act 1976 (RTPA)

Until 1998 English law treated agreements restricting competition as matters of public record: only in extreme cases should they be unlawful. The RTPA and the regulations under it therefore require certain agreements, under which two or more parties accept restrictions on their freedom to compete, to be submitted to the Office of Fair Trading (OFT). Failure to do so within three months from the date of the agreement makes the restrictions potentially unenforceable. Most agreements are generally exempt or capable of registration by the OFT without the need for reference to the Restrictive Practices Court. Although the RTPA is a trap for the unwary, a 1997 regulation exempts many agreements from registration and provides for an aggregate turnover exemption below £50 million for the participating businesses.

New UK Competition Act

The RTPA will be replaced by a new Competition Act, probably as from 1999. This is based broadly on Articles 85 and 86 of the Treaty of Rome (see p. 78 onwards), but with reference to matters affecting trade within the UK rather than within the EU. At the time of writing the detailed final text and regulations are awaited, but some of the outlines are clear.

The Competition Act will provide for the granting of both individual exemptions and block exemptions. The overall process is administered by the Director General of Fair Trading (DGFT). Block exemptions may provide for individual exemptions where the block exemption does not apply generally but where specific criteria are met. This should give some greater flexibility in UK block exemptions than exists in those in the EU.

Where the agreement falls within Article 85, but is exempt by virtue of an individual exemption or block exemption, a 'parallel exemption' applies under the UK regime. The DGFT can disapply this exemption in certain cases. Care should be taken with comfort letters. As these are not exemptions as such, applications may still be required to the DGFT even if a comfort letter has been obtained from the European Commission. It appears that similar regimes are being established in several other EU member states. Unfortunately this could mean that a business seeking a comfort letter from the European Commission, in circumstances where the restrictions are not *de minimis* and where a block exemption is not available, may also have to apply to the competition authorities in each of the countries which may be affected by the trade in question.

In relation to dominance, the monopoly provisions of the Fair Trading Act remain. Only sections 2–10 of the Competition Act are repealed. The new provisions are similar to Article 86 and refer to abuse of a dominant position if it occurs in the UK and may affect trade within the UK.

There are major new powers of investigation for the DGFT, more similar to those available for the EC Commission. These include powers of entry into premises, although generally one day's working notice must be given except where a dawn raid is justified (where someone is 'reasonably believed to be breaching' the prohibition).

There is a right for third parties to recover damages, but only following non-compliance with a decision made by the DGFT. This may be more restrictive than the position under Articles 85 and 86.

This will be a *de minimis* exception, but the extent of it is not known at the time of writing. If it is lower than EU levels, many agreements which are not subject to the Article 85 regime will nevertheless require application to the DGFT if they affect trade in the UK.

Other UK competition legislation

The Competition Act 1980 gives rights to the director general of the OFT to investigate potentially anti-competitive behaviour. It can refer the matter to the Monopolies and Mergers Commission to consider whether the conduct operates against the public interest. Undertakings from the business in question may be sought and ultimately a prohibition order can be made, but competition references are rare and generally only made in the case of substantial businesses where there would be a clear public interest issue. Here again, changes in the new Competition Act will harmonize the English approach with prevailing EU law.

The Fair Trading Act 1973 may also be invoked in the case of monopolies and mergers if there is a business or group of businesses which represents at least 25 per cent of the buying or supply power in a particular product or service market within the UK. The Act also applies if a group of businesses act together to the same effect. It is up to the OFT to monitor the activities of potential monopolies and there is no obligation on the businesses themselves to notify the OFT if they cross the 25 per cent limit.

EU competition law

The separate régimes of articles 85 and 86 of the Treaty of Rome are now well developed. Although the Treaty of Amsterdam, signed in October 1997, significantly amends the Treaty of Rome and changes many of the article numbers (see Glossary), it is convenient here to retain the original numbering. Article 85 is general in application and article 86 deals with situations where there is abuse by a business of a dominant market position. The provisions of the legislation and the various regulations and block exemptions relating to it are complex and specialist professional advice is essential, but it is important for businesses to recognize that these laws may affect what otherwise appear to be ordinary commercial transactions. Similar provisions apply in the European Economic Area states. The following outline guidance indicates where you are likely to need further advice.

Article 85: anti-competitive behaviour

- There must be two or more independent businesses involved. Arrangements made between parent and subsidiary do not qualify and article 85 likewise does not generally apply to an agreement between principal and agent. It will, however, apply to the relationship between a supplier and distributor, even if the distributor is mistakenly called an agent.
- The practices involved must actually or potentially restrict or distort competition within the EU. Trade within the EU may be affected even if the arrangements apparently involve only one member state, since the result in practice may be to prevent other businesses trading in the EU from entering that market. Trade within the EU may also be affected as a result of the activities of companies based outside the EU and article 85 could then apply.
- The effect on trade must be perceptible. Are any of the participants prevented from competing in the market as fully as they might otherwise have done? Are third parties restricted from competing as effectively in that market? If the agreement or practice in question makes no difference to the way that other businesses behave or will behave, it is unlikely to have a perceptible effect on trade.
- The European Commission has issued an updated notice on agreements which it deems as of 'minor importance'. Effectively this is an exemption from article 85 and applies if the parties together have no more than 10 per cent of the relevant market – in the case of 'vertical' agreements – or 5 per cent in the case of 'horizontal' or hybrid agreements. For this purpose 'vertical agreements' are those between manufacturer/supplier and distributor/dealer, and 'horizontal agreements' are those, for example, between two or more manufacturers where there is greater likelihood of anti-competitive behaviour. There is a further exemption, regardless of market share, for businesses with fewer than 250 employees *and* a turnover of less than 40 million ECU (close to £30 million).

- The Commission has also issued a notice seeking to clarify how the 'relevant market' is defined. This will usually involve considering how far one product can be substituted for another without materially depriving the customer of choice. The lack of substitutes indicates a narrow market and vice versa. This is also a relevant issue for article 86 and the question of whether there is a dominant position, as considered later in this chapter.

- The fact that the agreement fails the minor importance test does not mean that it will necessarily have a perceptible effect on trade within the EU. Nevertheless, the parties must keep the position under review since, if a venture becomes highly successful, it may create an effect on trade which did not exist at the outset and thus cause the agreement to fall outside the exemption at a critical time.

- If article 85 appears to apply, and the agreement is not within the *de minimis* thresholds, those involved should consider whether there is a relevant block exemption. Block exemptions are designed to avoid an excessive number of applications to the European Commission and to set down permitted, non-permitted and possibly permitted provisions (the so called 'white', 'black' and 'grey' clauses) relevant to the particular types of agreement covered by the block exemption. These exemptions deal with contracts such as exclusive distribution, exclusive purchasing, franchising, technology transfer, research and development and specialization and also cover specific industry sectors such as insurance, car distribution and transport.

- If the contract falls within the relevant block exemption, then all is fine so long as it continues fully to do so. Many commercial contracts for major trading relationships are now drafted from the outset wherever practicable, so that they fall within a block exemption. However, this may not always be possible, as in the case of an area development licence in relation to trade marks and know-how (see Chapter 11), which currently falls outside both the franchising and the technology transfer block exemptions. Again, the effect of changes and future growth over the 10- or 20-year life of an agreement should be considered at the outset. Is it possible that the circumstances during the intended life of the agreement will change so that the arrangements will come to have a perceptible effect on trade or the *de minimis* thresholds will be exceeded? If so, should the agreement be drafted from the outset to fit within the block exemption?

- Where the agreement may have a perceptible effect, but falls neither within a block exemption nor within the minor importance tests, an individual exemption should be sought. Notify the European Commission in Brussels on the prescribed form A/B with full details of the agreement, the activities of the parties and the markets affected. The Commission may give an individual exemption or a negative clearance, which amounts to confirmation that the agreement does not appear to be caught by article 85. Frequently the Commission will issue a comfort letter which is an indication that it intends to take no further action unless circumstances change. Either way, these procedures can be lengthy.

- Non-compliance has serious effects. If an agreement infringes the rules, the restrictions may be unenforceable and the Commission has power to levy very substantial fines on the parties involved. In addition, since the infringing provisions are unlawful, third parties affected by the restrictions may have the right to seek injunctions, and possibly damages against the companies involved in the agreement.

Article 86: abuse of a dominant position

Dominance in a market is for the most part determined by whether or not the relevant business has the power to behave, to an appreciable extent, independently of its competitors or customers. In short, does it have the power to dominate those around it? Dominance is also considered by reference to market share. In general a share of 40–45 per cent indicates dominance, but there may still be dominance with a market share of 25 per cent if most of the other players in that market have only very small shares.

In defining the relevant market the Commission has various tests. One is the extent to which there are acceptable substitutes for the products supplied. Businesses whose products are unique, where there is no real alternative to them, are more likely to fall foul of article 86. Examples of the abuse of a dominant position are unfair prices, price discrimination, refusal to supply and fidelity rebates. In such cases block exemptions are irrelevant and individual exemptions are not available. Breach of article 86 and the dominant position rules have the same sanctions as breach of article 85. A similar régime will now also be an integral part of English law.

World trade

Although issues of world trade are really beyond the scope of this book, it is worth noting that international co-operation on trade issues is gathering momentum. The World Trade Organisation (WTO) based in Geneva now provides a set of binding rules relating to trade and investment in world markets and has a direct affect on how WTO member states are able to legislate nationally. A machinery exists to bring defaulting states into line.

WTO has developed from GATT (General Agreement on Tariffs & Trade) and taken on the role as a principal international trade forum. Nearly all the main trading nations are members and China, Taiwan and Russia are negotiating terms for joining. The EU states have individual membership but speak and work through the European Commission. It seems likely that WTO will be exercising a growing influence in future in the development of cross-border trading issues.

Summary

The law will imply only limited duties of confidentiality in circumstances where fair dealing requires it, otherwise express clauses must be included within the contract. Like exclusion clauses they should go no further than is necessary to protect the business in question, and they must satisfy certain tests if the restrictions are liable to distort the market. Distortion in this case is on a wider scale, but the effects of breach of the

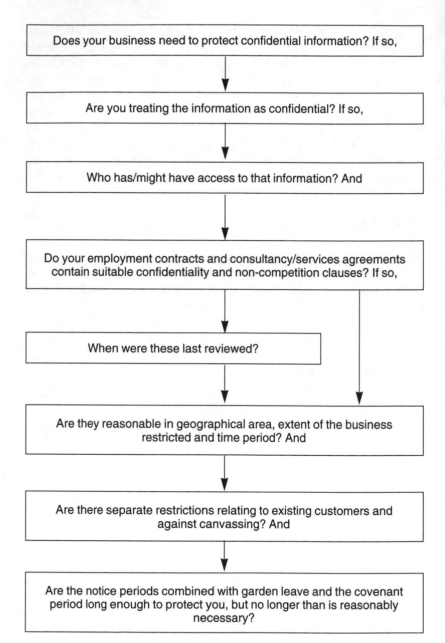

FIGURE 6.1   ALTERNATIVE LAYOUT FOR SUMMARY –
CONTINUED

A Concise Business Guide to Contract Law

Charles Boundy

ISBN 0 566 07921 6

ERRATUM

This is a corrected version of the flowchart that appears on pages 84 and 85.

Please accept our apologies for any inconvenience.

Gower Publishing Limited

(a) Employment confidentiality and competition

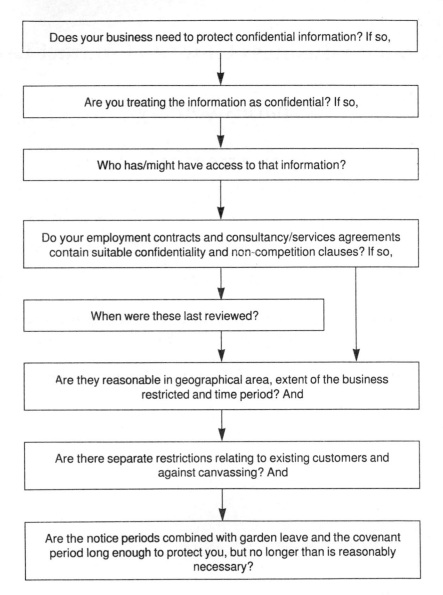

FIGURE 6.1   ISSUES RELATING TO

(b) Business competition

Do you have any restrictive agreements with other businesses, including exclusivity arrangements of any type? If so,

Do they involve another UK business accepting restrictions (RTPA) or might they cause a perceptible affect on trade within the EU? if so,

Do they fit within any relevant block exemptions? Or if not,

Can they be amended to do so? Or

Are you within the minor importance/*de minimis* thresholds? If not,

Are you a potential monopoly, or do you have a potentially dominant position?

Do you have disgruntled competitors who might be seeking to report you to the European Commission if they can?

Should you apply to the European Commission for negative clearance or a comfort letter?

CONFIDENTIALITY AND COMPETITION

Gower

Gower House, Croft Road,
Aldershot, Hampshire
GU11 3HR   UK

(a) Confidentiality

> Do you have any restrictive agreements with other businesses, including exclusivity arrangements of any type? If so,

> Do they involve another UK business accepting restrictions (RTPA) or might they cause a perceptible effect on trade within the EU? If so,

> Do they fit within any relevant block exemptions? Or if not,

> Can they be amended to do so? Or

(b) Competition

> Are you within the minor importance/*de minimis* thresholds? If so,

> Are you a potential monopoly, or do you have a potentially dominant position? If so,

> Do you have disgruntled competitors who might be seeking to report you to the European Commission if they can? If so,

> Should you apply to the European Commission for a negative clearance or a comfort letter?

FIGURE 6.1   ALTERNATIVE LAYOUT FOR SUMMARY – CONCLUDED

competition laws can themselves be far more wide-reaching than the loss of the contract itself. This is expanded in Fig. 6.1.

(See also Chapters 8, 10, 11 and 12.)

■ 7

Companies and contracts

Directors generally have authority to make contracts on behalf of their companies. The concept is simple enough, but below the surface there are a number of factors which can undermine the authority of a director or prevent the other parties to the contract from relying on it. A broad understanding of the responsibilities of directors is therefore an important part of contract planning. The subject is a large one and this chapter concentrates on day-to-day business contracts, rather than issues which are more related to pure company or securities law. The statutory duties of directors and their companies, and their potential liability under the laws of negligence, insolvency and the criminal law, may all in their turn have an impact on the validity or enforceability of a contract.

Directors' duties

The primary responsibility of a director is to the company he or she serves and through the company to its shareholders.

Even if a director is appointed to represent a particular section of shareholders, such as a financial investor or joint venture partner, the responsibility is owed first and foremost to the company itself. A company director should always recognize and deal with this inherent conflict. Similar considerations apply if a director puts a personal interest ahead of the interest of the company.

- Directors have a 'fiduciary' duty to act honestly and in good faith in relation to their company. This duty requires a director to avoid, or deal fairly and openly with, any conflict which might arise between the interests of the director and those of the company or its shareholders and to deal fairly as between shareholders.
- Before entering into any contract, the directors of the company must satisfy themselves that the transaction is within the powers and in the best interests of the company which they represent.
- Directors may not make secret profits out of their role with the company.
- Directors must perform their duties with reasonable skill and care, including the skill and care reasonably to be expected from a person with that particular director's knowledge and experience. The specialist knowledge and experience of a director can therefore require a higher standard from that person either generally or in relation to that subject.
- Where matters are outside the scope of their day-to-day authority, the directors should obtain full board consent. Company law also requires the consent of the shareholders to certain transactions, such as 'substantial' property transactions between the company and the director, and payment for loss of office to a former director in excess of the company's strict legal obligations.
- Although a third party dealing in good faith with the company may presume that the directors are duly authorized to commit the company to the contract in question, breach of the obligations mentioned above may cause the transaction to be set aside. The defaulting director may also be required to indemnify the company against any loss or to

repay the amount of benefit obtained by the director.

- In general, references to a director will include each executive and non-executive director and any person known as a 'shadow director' who is used to having a major influence on the activities and direction of the company. In technical terms, this is a person 'in accordance with whose directions or instructions the directors of the company are accustomed to act', even if such a person has not been formally appointed to the board. A substantial, but unseen, backer or even a holding company might be held to be a shadow director and be as liable as those duly appointed to the board.
- Further problems may arise where the company or any of the other parties to a transaction are actually or potentially insolvent at the time of the transaction or become insolvent shortly afterwards.

The following examples illustrate these principles.

Secret profits – a cautionary tale

Peter Perks, full-time development director of a property company, Devland Ltd, in the course of his usual work for Devland, becomes aware of a possible redevelopment site which is not on the market but which has enormous profit potential. He decides that he could finance the venture himself and sets up a new company, Pekinese Projects Ltd (Pekinese), in nominee names to negotiate the site purchase, funding, development and pre-lets. The project is not reported to the Devland board. Pekinese, directed behind the scenes by Perks, buys the site, develops it and sells it at a handsome profit. This is illustrated in Figure 7.1.

Although the purchase contract is beneficial to Pekinese, assuming it is 'at arm's length' (i.e. between independent businesses) and there are no further unusual circumstances, it will be valid and binding. The law will not rescue the seller of the land from a bad bargain unless there is evidence that the seller was misled by the buyer. The finance, development, pre-lets to the occupying tenants and the final sale on would all have been on open market terms and (again assuming no other

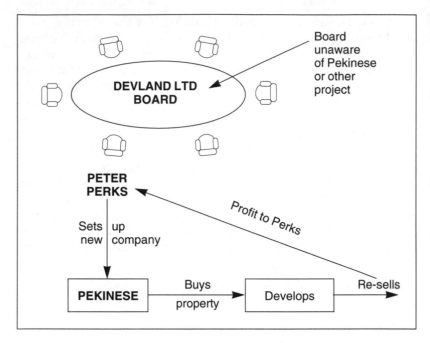

FIGURE 7.1   EXAMPLE: SECRET PROFITS

features) will be valid. The mischief here is that Perks has used for his own benefit an opportunity which became available to him in his capacity as a director of Devland. The result would be that Devland, when it finds out, could sue Perks, not simply for damages but for the full amount of the 'secret' profit which Pekinese made from the transaction. It would also have good grounds for dismissing him for gross misconduct. There are three other considerations.

1   In this case Perks was a full-time working director of Devland, and had a service contract which prevented his undertaking any similar work without the consent of the Devland board. The position might be different if he had still been a director but only an occasional consultant to Devland for specific projects. His consultancy contract (see Chapter 9) may not have obliged him to report all opportunities to the Devland board.

2   If Perks had been a full-time employee but not a director, he would still have been in breach of his obligation of good faith towards Devland, but it might be more difficult for the company to recover all the profits of the enterprise. The principles are clearly important for those considering starting their own ventures. The timing of events will be critical. Even if Perks had left Devland by the time the development was under way, the fact that he had set it up whilst being a full-time director of the company would make him still accountable for the entire profits.

3   The duty not to make secret profits exists even where there is no bad faith. It can be breached inadvertently by a director failing to seek board guidance and approval. Perks could have been liable simply for forgetting to bring the opportunity to the Devland board, even though he had no dishonest intention.

Directors as parties to a transaction with the company

Alternatively, Devland may hold a property which has been on its books for some time and for which planning consent has been refused. Through his contacts, Perks discovers that planning consent can be obtained if certain adjustments are made to the scheme. He does not pass on the information to Devland but offers to buy the property at a knock-down price to 'get it off the company's books'. The board agrees and sells it to him. He then makes the adjustments to the scheme and re-sells at considerable profit.

Here again there is a secret profit. There is also an actual sale of a property between the company and one of its directors. This transaction may require approval by the shareholders of Devland if it is of the 'requisite value' within s. 320 of the Companies Act 1985; in broad terms, where the value of the asset is more than £100,000 or 10 per cent of the company's asset value (as defined in the section). If the transaction is one for which shareholders' approval should have been, but was not, obtained, the company may have the transaction set aside, unless either (a) restitution is no longer possible (or the company has already been separately indemnified, e.g. by Perks himself); or (b) rights acquired by third parties in good faith, for value and without notice of the contravention would be affected; or (c) the shareholders themselves affirm the transaction within a reasonable period.

Third parties dealing with a company director therefore need to fit within category (b). So long as they are acquiring something for value and in good faith and without notice of any contravention of the section, they should be safe in relation to any subsequent action they take. If there is any connivance or awareness of the mischief on the part of a buyer, the transaction may be set aside. On the other hand, the defaulting director and any person connected with the director ('connected' having a broad meaning), will be liable both to account to the company for the benefit arising and to indemnify the company against any loss resulting from the transaction. Indeed, persons connected with a director may be treated in the same way and as accountable as the director. The message in this context is therefore clear. If you acquire something of value from a company without paying a fair price, or are aware of any bad faith or failure to obtain shareholders' approval on the transfer of an asset, the arrangement may be set aside and you may have to pay up for any loss caused to the company.

Transaction outside the powers or not in the interests of the company

If the directors enter into a transaction which is not for the benefit of the company, they may be acting outside their powers and the transaction may be liable to be set aside; for example, where the assets or financial strength of one company are being used to support another company, or a person connected with the company, in a way which gives no material benefit to the first company. This was the situation in one of the myriad cases following the Maxwell affair in the early 1990s, when it was held that, before signing documents transferring assets out of a company, the directors must satisfy themselves that the action is in the company's interests. Failure to do so may result in personal liability on the directors for breach of fiduciary duty and, in extreme cases, to the transaction being set aside as an abuse of the powers of the company. Generally third parties are protected, unless they knew or ought to have known that the transaction was beyond the powers of the company.

Transaction not duly authorized

On rare occasions courts have set aside transactions as being unauthorized actions of the company. One such case involved Thomas Ward, a former director of Guinness, who was ordered to repay a £5.2 million fee paid to him by the company in connection with its takeover of Distillers. Ward argued that the payment was authorized since it had been approved by the remuneration committee of the board. The court reaffirmed that there was no general authority for the full board to delegate its powers and held that the authority given to the remuneration committee was only to fix directors' remuneration for work carried out in the ordinary course of business and not exceptional fees for special circumstances. This fee was of such an unusual nature and magnitude that it was outside the scope of the delegated powers and required approval by the full board.

Incorrect company name

Directors must not be careless with the company name. If the name is not added to a contract, or is materially incorrect, the director who signed is at risk of being personally liable on the contract. A director who signs a cheque on behalf of a company where the company name is missing from the cheque will be obliged to honour it. This stems from the long-held concept that limited liability status is a privilege and is not to be implied.

Directors' personal negligence

Directors may incur personal liability if they exceed proper legal bounds in their actions or act negligently, for example by recommending a defective product, even on company letter-head, or commissioning on behalf of their company an act which was itself wrongful.

In a 1996 case, *Williams and Another* v *Natural Life Health Food Ltd and Another*, Mr Mislin was the managing director of a company offering franchises for health food shops. He put together a brochure and details about the advantages of the franchises which the company was offering, including financial projections of the potential turnover and profits of a typical operation. The court found that these projections were based largely on a personal venture which Mr Mislin had run in a different area some years before and amounted to a negligent misrepresentation of the likely levels of performance of a franchised outlet of the new business. Mr Williams and Ms Reed relied on the figures and statements and made a disastrous investment in the franchise. There was a clear duty of care and obligation on the part of the company (which had since been dissolved) not to mislead Mr Williams and Ms Reed, but should Mr Mislin, who had not taken active part in the negotiations, also have been liable? The Court of Appeal held that, whilst the circumstances must be exceptional for a director to be liable, Mr Mislin, even though he did not personally deal with the franchisees, played an important role behind the scenes and must be assumed to have taken personal responsibility for the negligent misstatements made on behalf of the company. He was therefore liable to Mr Williams and Ms Reed for their losses. The lesson is that where directors of companies provide information on which those dealing with the company are likely to rely, the directors must be able to verify that information and establish that it is not being used in a misleading way. Note that the franchise closed after eighteen months' operation in 1989 and the case came to the High Court after six years, in December 1995, being upheld on appeal just a year later.

Using a company as a cloak

The law will sometimes step in to save an innocent party from exploitation where a wrongdoer deliberately uses a company with no assets to carry out a wrongful act, leaving the innocent party with a claim against a worthless company. In these rare cases the courts have the power – rather fancifully named 'lifting the corporate veil' – to look at the person behind the scenes who is really creating the problems. This will generally apply only if there is evidence of fraudulent intent or subterfuge from the outset or, perhaps, recklessness.

Directors' criminal liability

Directors, and those dealing with them, should be aware of their potential criminal liability in relation to contracts in two main respects. First, there are an increasing number of areas where directors are made personally liable for breaches of the criminal law by their companies. Examples include health and safety at work, weights and measures, data protection, consumer protection, trade description, financial services and environmental health. The level of involvement may vary and in some cases there will be absolute liability irrespective of awareness of the circumstances. In these cases there will be a breach of statutory duty on the part of the director, and those affected by the breach may also have a personal claim against the delinquent director as a result. Second, some circumstances might amount to criminal negligence by the directors. The issue was left open in the Zeebrugge ferry case, but the prosecutions in the later Lyme Bay canoeing disaster left no doubt that directors and managers will be expected to face the full barrage of the criminal and civil laws in cases of failure to have proper regard for personal safety. These liabilities will override all contractual limitations or exclusions which will, in any case, be ineffective in relation to claims for death or personal injury.

Insolvency

All too often the defaulting company stops trading and goes into insolvent liquidation, whether preceded by receivership or not. The liabilities and preferential debts of the company make it pointless for trade and ordinary creditors to sue and they turn their attention to possible claims against the former directors. In the cases mentioned above, those affected can take specific action at law against the directors concerned. In insolvency the situation is different. Most of the claims that may be brought under insolvency legislation are only available to a liquidator. Whilst the claim is strictly for the benefit of the company, any proceeds will probably be swallowed up by other creditors with equal or preferential claims. The most likely areas of claim are summarized below.

- Wrongful trading – trading and incurring or continuing liabilities past the point where the company had no reasonable prospect of recovery and the directors then failed to take every step possible to protect creditors.
- Fraudulent trading – deliberately trading with an intent to defraud creditors.
- Preferences – making payment or giving an advantage to one creditor at the expense of others and without clear commercial need.
- Sale of assets at an undervalue – enabling the transaction to be set aside where the sale was on terms materially below market value, especially if the transaction was with another company or a person closely associated with the insolvent company or any of its directors.

Summary

In general it is safe to deal with a company by acting through one of its directors, but you should take care if there are any unusual circumstances, or if you know that there has been a contract entered into between the company and the director regarding the same subject matter. For their part directors should take care that they are acting lawfully, in accordance with their company's memorandum and articles (and any shareholders' agreement), within their authority and in good faith.

- Take sensible steps to check that the company you are dealing with really exists, by making a company search, and that there are no insolvency notices registered.

- Check that the company name is correct.
- Use the company number if the contract is of any substance. Company names can be changed easily but the company number remains constant.
- Check that the person who purports to be a director has been appointed to the board or is clearly held out as such. Again, if there is any doubt, a company search will reveal the names of current directors.
- If you are a director of a company, check that you are authorized to negotiate and sign the deal in question. Be sure that the board and, if necessary, the shareholders know exactly what is proposed, approve it and, if appropriate, that it is duly minuted, signed by the chairman and you have a copy.
- If you are the director negotiating a transaction in which you or a member of your family or a close business associate have, or may be likely to have, a personal interest or stand to gain, go to the board and disclose your position fully. If necessary ask the shareholders to approve it too.
- Where the transaction is at all unusual, not in the company's ordinary way of business or long-term, ask for evidence of its approval by the company's full board of directors. A minute, or an extract from a minute containing the relevant section, of the board meeting signed by the chairman should suffice.
- Take extra care if there is anything unusual or suspicious about the transaction. It is better to risk an upset in diplomatic relations than to act unlawfully or lose both asset and price. Look out for cases where a director has a personal involvement or there is an obvious underpayment or a suggestion of hoodwinking or bypassing the board of directors.
- Double care is required if the company is having trouble paying its debts – you don't want to be forced to hand back property and be left with a worthless claim.
- Take professional advice if you are in any doubt.
- If you are the other party and all seems fine, leave well alone. As the law stands it may be better not to investigate further if there is nothing suspicious.

Postscript

If, as a director, you remain unscathed after walking through this minefield, remember that there is still the Company Directors Disqualification Act to catch out those who have been indolent, injudicious, improper or just plain incompetent in their stewardship of a company's affairs. If you are a director, take your responsibilities seriously and minimize the risk of problems later on.

(See also Chapters 2 and 9.)

■ 8

Agency and distribution

When a company decides to use outside help in selling its products or services, it may first consider appointing either an agent or a distributor, or occasionally both. The similarities and significant differences between the two are considered in this chapter. They are also illustrated in Figure 8.1.

Distinctions between agent and distributor

It is convenient to refer to a business which appoints an agent as the principal and a business which appoints a distributor as a supplier. These are the most commonly found terms in commercial agency and distribution agreements. This chapter also focuses on the sale of goods rather than services.

In an agency, the principal (typically, but not always, a manufacturer) appoints the agent to sell the goods of the principal. The goods remain in the ownership of the principal until they are sold to a customer. The agent never takes title to them but is paid a fee by the principal, normally by way of

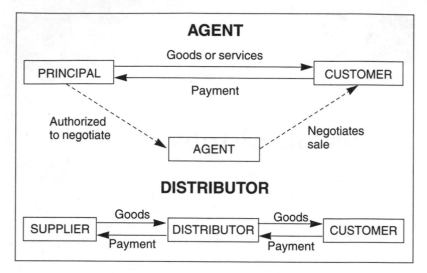

FIGURE 8.1   AGENT OR DISTRIBUTOR?

commission. By contrast, in a distribution arrangement, the supplier sells the goods to the distributor who then resells them to the customer. In the process the distributor takes title to the goods and is paid by reference to the difference between the price at which he buys from the supplier and sells to the customer.

The term distributorship is also used frequently to describe the appointment of a distributor, to distinguish the type of distribution agreements referred to in this chapter from what might be called logistical distribution arrangements, i.e. those mainly concerned with transporting or distributing goods from one place to another. Clearly there are many arrangements under which transport and other companies store and distribute products for others without title in the products ever passing.

There are significant differences in terms of control and risk between agency and distribution. An agent can be given precise terms on which the goods can be sold, including price. Legislation[1] effectively prevents suppliers from insisting on

---

[1] The UK resale price legislation. There would also be issues under competition law.

minimum resale prices by distributors. As a result, a supplier will have much closer control over customer sales through an agent than through a distributor. The position is similar with risk. With agency the goods belong to the principal until sold to the customer and accordingly the principal is not directly at risk if the agent defaults, provided the customer can pay. It follows that the principal will be directly affected by the creditworthiness of the customer and will want to know that the agent carries out adequate credit reference and other checks.

The supplier to a distributor will be concerned only indirectly with the creditworthiness of the ultimate customer, since the distributor may rely on being paid by its customer in order to pay its supplier. If the customer does not pay, the supplier may be faced with the difficult decision of cutting off supplies to its own distributor or hoping the distributor can trade out of the problem. The distributor in this situation, for its part, risks giving the principal the opportunity to terminate the distributorship for breach.

Different kinds of agent

The term 'agency' covers a multitude of arrangements including, for example, estate agents, insurance agents, agents on commodity markets and implied agency situations where one party is given authority by another to act on that other's behalf. There are also more specific legal designations. The term 'special agent' applies not only to the James Bonds of this world but also to those appointed to act for a specific transaction outside their ordinary course of business. As such they are distinguished from a general agent. There are brokers who are normally expected to deal as agents and not as principals; there are factors who may deal as both, although the term is now more commonly used in relation to debt finance. A specific type of agent, known as a *del credere* agent, is unusual in that the appointment is a guarantee to the principal that the third-party customer will perform the contract, leaving the *del credere* agent at risk if the customer does not pay. This chapter concentrates on the commercial agent who acts generally in seeking product sales for one or more principals.

Authority and obligations of agent

To what extent can the agent bind the principal? If an agent is given actual authority to enter into contracts on behalf of the principal, those contracts will be binding upon the principal if made in the name of the principal or if made in the name of the agent expressly on behalf of the principal. By contracting or signing on behalf of a principal, the agent warrants an entitlement to act in that way and will be liable to a third party who relies on that warranty and who suffers loss because the principal fails to confirm or honour the order.

Frequently the third party does not check the position and relies on the apparent authority of the agent. Mostly the agent will have 'usual authority', that which is expected of a person holding the position in the ordinary course of their work. In cases of doubt some form of actual or implied representation must be shown that the principal did authorize or 'hold out' the agent to carry out the transaction. When dealing with an agent, therefore, even if the act appears within the agent's authority, it is much safer if the principal expressly signs the contract.

The obligations of the agent are to perform the agency duties with reasonable care and skill and to observe and act within the lawful and reasonable instructions and authority given by the principal. The agent also has an overriding duty of good faith to act in a financially responsible manner and to account properly to the principal. It is advisable to spell out these obligations in the contract and to clarify any conflict of interest issues.

Over the years the English common law has protected the agent's basic right to earn commission, but little more. If the principal terminates the agency agreement, the only remedy given to the agent by the common law is to be paid what was properly due during the contract period, including a proper period of notice. The fact that the agent may have spent years building up the business interests of the principal, only to be deprived of all further benefit from the connections, was not something which the law recognized. In some continental European jurisdictions, on the other hand, the potential unfairness of this result has long been recognized and was ultimately codified in an EEC Council Directive of December 1986 on the protection of commercial agents.

Protection for the commercial agent

New regulations were finally introduced in Britain by the Commercial Agents (Council Directive) Regulations 1993 as from 1 January 1994, which were designed to establish a form of commercial code between principals and commercial agents. Known as the Commercial Agents Regulations (or sometimes simply as the Agency Regulations), they aim to harmonize treatment of agents in the UK with those in other member states.

Commercial Agents Regulations

- The regulations relate to both individuals and company agents, provided they are independent from the principal.
- They relate only to agents who sell (or buy) goods, not services. 'Goods' for this purpose do not include land.
- There should be some form of continuity in the agent's authority. A single agency commission will not suffice, but the agency does not need to be in writing.
- The regulations do not relate to agents who are mere representatives with no authority either to negotiate or to negotiate and conclude sales on behalf of the principal.
- The regulations do not cover agents whose agency activities are secondary to another main activity, such as a distributor with only occasional agency transactions.
- A formal duty of good faith is established both ways between principal and agent.
- The agent is entitled to an account from the principal at least quarterly and to be paid within one month after the end of the quarter. The obligation to pay strictly arises, in the absence of any provision in the contract to the contrary, when the goods are delivered and invoiced, not when they are paid for.
- The principal may terminate the agency only by written notice of between one and three months, dependent upon

how long the agency has lasted. Notice must expire at the end of a month unless the contract states otherwise.

- The agent is entitled to receive commission, not only on orders secured before the agency terminated and delivered afterwards, but also on orders secured afterwards which were 'derived from the agent's efforts' before termination.
- The contract may include provision for commission to be shared between old and new agents where it is equitable to do so. Principals should take care to avoid double commission payments.
- Unless the agent terminated voluntarily, with no fault on the part of the principal, or the principal terminated on the grounds of such a serious breach by the agent as would justify summary termination, the principal must pay the agent compensation or an indemnity. This will broadly represent payment for the goodwill which the agent has built up for the principal (see below). In some respects the commercial agent's statutory right to compensation is similar to that of an employee who has been unfairly dismissed, although there are no minimum qualifying periods.
- There are limitations on the extent of restrictive covenants which may be enforced by the principal against the agent.
- Most of the regulations cannot be excluded from the contract.

Goodwill or termination payments

The regulations specify two methods of goodwill or termination payments, compensation or an indemnity. Although there is a different basis of calculation for each of them, the intention is to value the benefit which the principal will be receiving from taking over the customers and business generated by the agent and/or the loss to the agent from termination of the agency. If the agency agreement does not specify otherwise, compensation will be payable, rather than an indemnity; compensation is potentially unlimited. By contrast, a written agency agreement may specify an indemnity payment, rather than compensation, which can be limited to an amount equivalent to one year's commission averaged over the last few years of the agency. Moreover, if the contract specifies an indemnity and the principal can establish that the agent has not generated any new customers or increased business with existing customers, no indemnity payment will be justified.

The goodwill payment concept is relatively new to the UK and, in assessing compensation or an indemnity payment, the courts have tended to look to continental Europe, and in particular Germany and France, which have had many years' experience in this area. The courts have to consider how far the agent has built up the business of the principal, any additional costs which the principal has encouraged the agent to incur, and how far the business will remain with the principal and be lost to the agent. Judgments will often be for the equivalent of three or six months' commission, but in some exceptional cases, such as that of an individual agent approaching retirement, awards of several years' commission have been made.

A goodwill payment is due even on the retirement, illness, infirmity or death of the agent, to reflect the value 'inherited' by the principal. In these circumstances shorter fixed-term periods may be helpful, with careful monitoring of the agent's performance and, where appropriate for the principal, termination at the optimum time. For principals granting or renewing agency agreements of any lengthy period, an express indemnity clause may be preferable which will limit the maximum amount payable. Agents, on the other hand, should guard their new rights but keep funds in hand for a potential battle with principals who are less well informed!

Agency Regulations – the international aspect

The Agency Regulations apply to the activities of commercial agents which are carried out in Great Britain and there are equivalent regulations for those operating in Northern Ireland. It is the place where the agent operates, not where the principal is located, which decides the issue. It is possible to make agency agreements subject to the law of another EU member state, where equivalent protection should be available, although there may be some differences. For example, whilst Germany has adopted the indemnity system, France has generally applied compensation which may give rise to payments of two years' commission, double the English law indemnity maximum.

Contract terms

Although the legal structure of agency and distribution agreements is significantly different the contractual framework involves many of the same issues. The following terms apply:

- *Territory*   It is usual for the appointment to apply and be limited to a particular territory, ranging from an entire country to a small, clearly defined geographical area. Parallel arrangements are then set up with other agents or distributors for other territories with the concept that each will concentrate on his/her own area.
- *Exclusivity*   The reference to appointment as 'sole' agent or distributor means that the principal/supplier will not appoint another agent/distributor in the same territory for the same purpose. It does not mean that the principal/supplier will not itself sell the same products direct into the same area. The word 'exclusive', however, operates to exclude the principal also. It is unnecessary to refer to 'sole and exclusive' as the latter automatically includes the former, but not vice versa. (Exclusivity also has competition law implications – see Chapter 6.)
- *Principal's freedom to sell direct*   An associated point with exclusivity. Both types of agreement may see principals or suppliers reserving the right to sell direct into the territory. The right may be limited to international accounts – for example, where there is a customer with headquarters or at least a base in another territory – or national or large accounts, particularly where there may be suppliers for a number of depots – or house accounts, customers who are traditionally serviced direct. These exclusions should be very clearly defined to avoid abuse or disputes.
- *Restrictions on agent/distributor during the agreement*   The counterpart of the exclusivity given by principal/supplier. The agent/distributor may be required neither to deal

in competing products produced by third parties, nor to sell outside the exclusive territory of the agreement. Competition law implications should be considered.

- *Term of the agreement*   Whereas an agent will be entitled to compensation on the agency coming to an end, there is no such entitlement for a distributor who may find that his business is suddenly lost without compensation. A distributor will often therefore wish to negotiate a longer period for his agreement, potentially with renewal rights if the contract has been complied with. The supplier may resist, unless confident that the distributor will continue to exploit the territory to maximum advantage. A longer term or a renewal right may be given by the supplier in return for the supplier's right to terminate if minimum purchase or sales targets are not met. (This is an example of setting clear objectives as referred to in Chapter 13.)

- *Minimum sales targets*   Some clauses require careful thought and drafting. They will be examined in great detail when expectations are not fulfilled and they can result in litigation. Distributors should beware of absolute commitment to targets which may cost them substantial damages if not met. For a supplier, a clear minimum obligation on the part of the distributor is to be preferred to reliance on clauses requiring 'reasonable endeavours' to sell. Here again you should consider competition law implications; a minimum level of purchases by the distributor from the supplier is expressly permitted under the exclusive distribution block exemption (see later in this chapter), but there is some question as to whether a minimum sales target will cause the exemption to be disapplied. Termination is a last-ditch remedy because it may cause the distributor to rush into the arms of a competitor of the supplier. Suppliers should therefore consider including suitable post-termination restrictions (see Chapter 6); distributors should be equally wary of losing the distributorship and being out of the market for a period.

- *Commission or margin*   Commission rates for agents are normally agreed, but if not can be fixed by the courts in accordance with market rates. With distributors, profit depends on buying and selling prices. The customer price is very much dictated by the market but suppliers will rarely wish to tie themselves long term to sell at fixed prices to their distributors. There will probably be an export or similar list price, with or without discounts, which will be the basis used between the parties. Distributors will, at the very least, wish to ensure that they are given adequate notice of price rises and are protected against price rises on existing orders unless these can be passed on to their customers. Occasionally suppliers will be prepared to limit price rises to increases in their base costs. List prices or discount terms which differentiate between territories should suggest potential competition law problems.

- *Exchange rates and payment terms* Payment terms for commission or, with distributors, payment for the products should be set out clearly. These terms will include proper accounting arrangements.
- *International aspects to the sale* The contract should stipulate the currency and place of payment. Distributors should be cautious about currency fluctuations when buying from a supplier based overseas and when buying and selling in different currencies. Many of these considerations are avoided if using an agency.
- *Allocation of responsibilities* Careful arrangements should be made about packaging, labelling, delivery, risk/insurance, title in the goods and delivery notes to ensure that both parties are kept fully up to date with the position. The pricing structure should reflect the delivery costs at each stage.

Termination and its effects

Like death and taxes, termination is inevitable. Think about it and plan for it from the outset, both as to how and when it is likely to happen and what the effects will be. So far as the agent is concerned, the break will be reasonably clean, with continuing commission in some cases and the possibility of a compensation or indemnity payment. With a distribution agreement the supplier will not want the distributor to unload the remaining stock onto the market at a low price when the agreement expires. Accordingly many distribution agreements will include a provision which enables the supplier to repurchase stock from the distributor at cost (or similar) on termination. There is a view that such a clause may take the agreement outside the exclusive distribution block exemption. If the agreement is otherwise likely to fall foul of article 85 and the *de minimis* thresholds do not apply, it may be best that the agreement merely gives the distributor the right to require the supplier to buy back the stock.

Employee transfer regulations

The implication for employees of termination of either an agency or distribution agreement should not be overlooked. Termination of the agreement may result in a technical transfer of the agency or distributorship business back to the principal/supplier and possibly on again to another agent or distributor. This subject is covered in more detail in Chapter 10 and may not apply to so-called 'second-generation outsourcing', but you should consider whether the Transfer Regulations apply to those employees who are assigned to the business in question. The principal/supplier should consider the question at the outset. If the regulations apply, the affected employees will automatically transfer to the supplier and possibly then on to any new distributor (or franchisee in the case, for example, of motor vehicle distributors) who will inherit any problems that exist. Where there is this prospect, it may be appropriate for the principal/supplier to include in the agreement specific clauses about dealings with employees before termination of the agreement and an indemnity claim in respect of any employee claims resulting from operation of the Transfer Regulations.

Exclusive distribution block exemption

Competition law generally was considered in Chapter 6 but specific reference should be made here to the exclusive distribution block exemption which dates from 1983. The exemption expired at the end of 1997, but has been extended until 1999, pending consultation and decision as to the terms of a new exemption. The supplier, and possibly also the distributor, may wish to bring the agreement within the block exemption where it is practicable to do so. The following points should be noted:

- The exemption applies only to exclusive agreements – on the basis that the supplier is then interested in promoting sales within the contract territory so as to justify exemption. The only permitted restriction on the supplier is not to supply others in the territory, although there are limited rights to supply certain reserved accounts direct.
- The exemption will not apply if the products are processed or altered by the distributor, other than by way of repackaging.
- The agreement must involve no more than two companies (bilateral only).
- Special rules apply to the sale of alcohol on licensed premises, fuels in service stations or the sale of motor cars.
- The distributor must not be a competing manufacturer – since this restricts competition – unless the arrangement is one-way only and the competing manufacturer has an annual turnover of less than ECU 100 million.
- The agreement may prevent the distributor from producing or distributing competing goods or actively seeking customers or operating a branch or depot outside the agreed territory.
- On the other hand the distributor may not be prevented from accepting *unsolicited* orders from customers outside the territory, nor restricted on the resale price for the goods or from supplying certain categories of customers but not others. This would prevent exemption for agreements for distributing goods in a stated territory only to different markets within that territory.
- The agreement may validly include obligations on the distributor to purchase minimum quantities, to sell the goods under the supplier's trade marks or design and to comply with certain promotional and training requirements.
- The agreement may require the distributor to buy the goods only from the supplier, but may not prevent users or

customers from obtaining an alternative supply of the goods from a source outside the agreed territory. Nor may the agreement require the supplier to prevent or limit unsolicited parallel imports by third parties into the agreed territory.

All provisions of the block exemption must be complied with. Breach of any of its provisions means that the block exemption fails to apply as a whole, not only the offending provision. The block exemption is irrelevant to agency contracts unless they are distributorships or the agent's activities are not closely integrated with those of the principal. If the agent can act largely independently of the principal, the normal principles of articles 85 and 86 will apply.

Distributor or agent?

So should you appoint or be appointed as a distributor or an agent? An agent is more under the control of the principal than a distributor and, if resale prices are important, the agent may be the natural choice. The principal will have to accept higher risk, not only regarding the creditworthiness of the customer but also any product liability and contractual problems which will come direct to the principal. The distributor, on the other hand, is likely to concentrate not only on sales and delivery but also on marketing and after-sales service of the type which many agents cannot supply. The distributor will deal direct with any customer problems in the first instance and will often resolve installation and service issues and supply spare parts from stock, relieving the supplier of the problems of small orders and individual customer attention. Indeed the distributor should be very experienced and knowledgeable in the market in question, a valuable asset when dealing across international borders.

Perhaps the main issue is that of the customers and customer details. The principal of an agent will contract and deal directly with the customers and can take active steps to retain them when the agreement ends, whereas the supplier may not know the end destination of the distributors' sales and, even so, is unlikely to have a significant relationship with the customers in many cases. Perhaps that is why the commercial agent is entitled to a goodwill payment, whereas the distributor is not. The ultimate decision may depend on how the parties see their relationships with the customers during and after the agreement period.

Summary

Agency and distributorships are two of the most common ways for a company to extend its sales and marketing reach without increasing its own headcount. Agency tends to be, but is not always, a lesser risk, shorter-term option, which in most cases will now be subject to the Agency Regulations thus adding a termination cost. Distributorships pose other questions. They will remain the primary link with the customer and distributors may be as ready as agents to supply competitor's products unless precluded from doing so. Distributorship terms are more likely to be caught by competition law. Questions to consider are:

- Do you wish to control resale prices?
- Can you fix a certain (non-discriminatory) price list for distributorship sales?
- Who is to bear the packaging, delivery and insurance costs?
- Do you wish to appoint an agent who can negotiate and / or take orders on your behalf, or a representative who can merely seek orders which you will process?
- Do you wish to accept prime responsibility for dealing direct with customers?
- Are you able and prepared to supply after-sales service?
- Do you wish to be concerned with the creditworthiness of all customers?
- Are you prepared to make your agent a goodwill payment on termination?
- Are you prepared to rely on one business to supply all of your products (or all products of a certain type) in one territory?
- Do you want, and are you able, to prevent your agent or distributor from dealing with your competitors?

- Do you wish to reserve the right to supply certain accounts direct?
- How long do you want to commit yourself to the agency or distributorship?
- Are there to be minimum sales targets? What will be the effect of failing to meet those targets?
- What currency is payment to be made in?
- Who is to bear the risk of exchange rate fluctuations?
- Who is responsible for labelling, packaging and delivery?
- What will be the practical effect of termination and how should your position be protected?
- Are there likely to be any employees who are subject to the Transfer Regulations and does the agreement cover this position?
- With distributorships, have you considered the possibility of offending competition law and, if so, whether you come within the terms of the block exemption?

(See also: Chapters 6, 9, 10, 11, 12 and 13.)

■ 9

Consultancy and services

An employee works for, under the direction of, and on behalf of, an employer. A consultant or a service provider is an independent contractor who provides agreed services to a client in much the same way as a producer of goods might provide those goods to a customer. Although many of the hallmarks of employment and even agency apply to consultancy, the legal independence of the consultant is one of the main features of the relationship. Within this broad framework there are a full range of possibilities which are considered in this chapter.

Consultancy distinguished from employment

Consultants are paid fees rather than salary and benefits. Those fees should take into account that the consultant is not working full time for the client and should include the cost of benefits which an employer might otherwise provide, such as car expenses, pension contributions and insurances. To this should be added an allowance for the lack of employment protection and cover for holidays and sickness. Thus an hourly rate of remuneration for a consultant may be substantially higher than the hourly rate of an equivalent employee.

The different tax treatment of consultants and employees is also significant. An employee is taxed under Schedule E, subject to PAYE and national insurance, the latter payable by both employer and employee. An independent consultant is taxed under Schedule D as a self-employed person and pays a reduced level of national insurance (albeit with lesser benefits). It has long been a temptation for parties to a contract to treat what is in essence an employment relationship as a consultancy in order to mitigate tax, but the Inland Revenue net has been tightening steadily over the years. If the relationship is, on Revenue tests, one of employment, the Revenue can claim direct from the effective employer the tax and national insurance which has not been deducted together with interest and penalties. Those tests may be summarized in three questions:

1   Does the 'consultant' come to the relationship complete with all skills and, if appropriate, all tools to do the job and accept the risk of providing the services with reasonable skill and care and of being accountable for failure to do so?
2   Does the 'consultant' have a large measure of discretion as to how and when, within an agreed timescale, the services are performed?
3   Can the consultant be said to be working on his or her own account?

The following factors tend to indicate employment:

● control of the way the work is done, of disciplinary issues, of precise working hours and of holiday approval
● right of the 'employer' to dismiss the 'employee'
● payment of a regular and consistent wage or salary
● provision of a company car and/or other equipment
● paid holidays, sick pay and other 'employee' benefits
● eligibility to join a company pension scheme
● obligation on the 'employer' to provide regular work.

The following factors tend to indicate self-employment although their absence does not necessarily indicate employment:

- ability to turn down work
- a fixed sum for the work, rather than an hourly rate
- right to work for others during the contract period
- right to subcontract some or all of the work.

The decision between consultancy and employment may have significant consequences, not only in relation to tax, but also as regards employment protection and liability for accidents and injuries. In some cases, the wrong choice may even be adjudged to be a fraud on the Inland Revenue.

Consultant and company director

In most cases an executive director will carry out a managerial role and be a company employee. A non-executive director, on the other hand, is more likely to be self-employed as someone whose role in the company is limited to matters of overall direction. A non-executive director may also have a consultancy with the company in a specific professional or advisory area.

Corporate consultancies

Individuals may run their own consultancy companies for commercial reasons. An engineer, for example, who is designing a project where a flaw could have serious repercussions, may feel better protected by operating through a limited company. The contract would be between the client and the limited company with the client's redress in contract limited to the assets of the company. The engineer would still be personally liable in negligence, which may not help the individual engineer who has been negligent but could protect the owner of the business from the worst effects of an employee's mistake.

The client, on the other hand, may take little comfort from this. Clients entering into contracts with consultancy companies should always consider joining the individual consultant as a party to the agreement. Apart from the question of personal liability of the consultant, the client will wish to ensure that the contract provides for the work to be carried out, or at least directly supervised, by the individual whom the client knows and has entrusted with the work. An obligation on the corporate consultant to provide the services of a named individual is thus consistent with the principle that a contract for personal services is to be performed by the individual in question and is non-assignable (see the comments on personal contracts on p. 223).

Example

Let us assume that Williams the wholesaler decides to engage the business advisory services of consultant Cheryl Chambers. This is a two-part engagement, the second part being dependent on the Williams' directors accepting the initial Chambers' report and recommendations. Chambers may write with a statement of her general terms and conditions, but this example assumes that Williams wants something more specific and writes to Chambers accordingly.

'Dear Cheryl,

Further to our meetings I am pleased to write to confirm the terms we have agreed for you to provide consultancy services ("the services") to Williams Limited.

1   The first stage of the services will be to investigate and report on the current markets in which this company carries on business, to consider other suitable markets into which it might extend its operations, to advise on the advantages and disadvantages and potential returns from each of those markets and to provide detailed and reasoned recommendations, together with cost and profit implications, of a revised marketing strategy ("the project"). In the second stage you will then advise and assist us further in implementing the chosen strategy.

We will be relying on your experience, skill and knowledge in considering your report and, in all probability, acting on it.

2   The first stage project report is to be completed and in final form for presentation to my board no later than 31 January next. In view of the need for the new plan to be in place before the international trade fair on 20 February, time for completion of the project will be of the essence. The second stage will probably continue six months after that, but must be completed by no later than 30 November in any event. The second stage is conditional upon the board approving your report and recommendations, in which case we require you to be available throughout that second stage period, as set out below. If the board does not agree, neither we nor you have any obligation to take matters further.

3   You will be carrying out the work from your own office and you will be responsible for all the research and collation work. You will decide and let us have preferably two days' prior notice (by fax to me or my secretary) of the days when you would like to attend or use our offices and of any facilities you wish to use or documents to which you require access. We will do our best to assist you without disrupting our normal activities. (As you know, our space is already somewhat cramped!). It is up to you how many hours you and your team put into the first stage. During the second stage it will be up to us to let you know when we need you, but each month we will require up to ten hours of your own time and potentially up to ten hours of the time of one of your assistants.

4   Your fee for the services will be according to the two stages. For the first stage it will be the fixed sum of £7,500 plus VAT for the project, this to be invoiced on presentation of your completed, final project report with payment 30 days after invoice. For the second stage it will be at the rate of £750 per day for yourself and between £300 and £400 per day plus VAT for an assistant. These second stage fees are to be invoiced each month for work carried out at our request in the

previous month with payment again to be 30 days after invoice. In addition we will reimburse you for invoiced travel and other direct third party costs for the second-stage work (but not the first stage which is covered in your overall first stage fee) reasonably incurred by you in accordance with our requests.

5   This agreement may be terminated by either of us on written notice to the other if the other breaches the agreement and the breach, if capable of remedy, is not remedied within 21 days of written notice identifying the breach and requiring its remedy. As indicated, a failure on your part to deliver the project report by the due date will be incapable of remedy. Either of us may also terminate this agreement on written notice to the other if the other becomes insolvent, including liquidation, receivership, administration, voluntary arrangement or bankruptcy.

6   You will treat, and take all practicable steps to ensure that all your staff treat, as confidential all information you or they receive in providing the services regarding our company, its business, finances, suppliers, customers and actual and potential marketing plans. You and they must not make use of any such information for any purpose or disclose it to any third party without our prior written agreement. This restriction will not apply to information which becomes public knowledge without breach of this agreement on your or their part. You will promptly return to us on completion of the services all property belonging to us, including all documents and copy documents in your possession or under your control.

7   You have confirmed that you are self-employed and are to be treated as an independent contractor and that you will be responsible for all taxation and similar liabilities arising in relation to the fees payable to you. You accordingly undertake to indemnify us in full against all claims or liabilities in relation to income tax, national insurance contributions, costs, penalties or other charges against us which arise from, or relate to, the services.

8   This agreement is personal to you and is to be performed by you personally except where stated otherwise. It may not be subcontracted or assigned except that you may assign it to your company, Chambers Consultants Limited, subject to our prior written consent which we will not unreasonably withhold provided that the company is and remains under your control and you continue personally to remain a party to this agreement.

I trust this letter is a fair reflection of our discussions. If so, please sign and return the duplicate to me to confirm your agreement. If not, please telephone me as soon as possible so that we may seek to resolve matters. The board is very excited about this project and we look forward to working with you and seeing your report.

With kind regards
Yours sincerely

Walter Williams
for and on behalf of
Williams Limited'

Comment

This letter, in fact, covers a great deal of ground and gives Walter Williams the chance to set out clearly his own expectations. It might be sensible to have an interim approval stage to highlight any early misunderstanding. Williams might also like to consider some form of restriction prohibiting Chambers from doing similar work for a competitor for a period. Whether or not this is feasible will depend on the nature of the work which Chambers normally does. Legal assistance should be sought to draft an appropriate restriction.

There are more points for Cheryl Chambers to consider, for example:

● any limitations on the work, e.g. specifically excluding certain types of specialist subjects and/or setting a maximum level of liability and specifically excluding claims for economic loss and the like

- seeking to negotiate out of the time of the essence clause in view of the severe implications of missing the deadline; providing that the right information must be available on time from Williams to enable deadlines to be met
- provision for non-availability due to holidays or incapacity not exceeding stated periods
- Chambers' own terms of business if she has them, which might cover some of these other points and might be incorporated into a contract by agreement
- specifying a minimum time involvement under stage two in case she and her team have to be available but are never called upon
- provision for interest on late payment of invoices
- ability to subcontract by delegating more work to other consultants.

Restrictions after termination

Remember that a consultancy team may be in very close contact with the clients or customers of the business which engages them. Take the case of a specialist IT team sent in by an external consultancy to perform a three year project which is an important part of a client's development plan. If the project finishes before the end of the three years, the parties may move on to something else. On the other hand, the relationship between the team and the client may have developed to such an extent that the client wishes to take on the team – or its members – as direct consultants or even as employees, thus bypassing the original consultancy. Does the contract cover this possibility? It may seem unreasonable to prevent the client from offering employment at the end of the contract term, but the consultancy may have invested heavily in the recruitment, training and development of the team members. An introductory commission would be appropriate in these circumstances. Similar considerations could apply if the team was encouraged to become autonomous and pitch for the new contract itself, probably undercutting the consultancy in the process. Here the consultancy should consider suitable non-competition provisions included in the team members' contracts before the venture starts. This is merely an example and each case must be carefully considered on its own facts.

Outsourcing, facilities management and other agreements for services

Businesses often contract out functions to third parties. These may be either new facilities management functions resulting from growth, technical innovation or reconstruction, or they may be outsourcing of functions such as catering which were previously carried on by their own staff. Most outsourcing to date has been in the field of services rather than production and there are now many specialist forms of contract applicable to specific functions or industries. The framework of such agreements is much the same as that of consultancy agreements, except that there is likely to be a longer contract period and greater certainty as to the level of work and fees. There may also be much more stringent quality control provisions, especially where the contract is for a longer period.

Where the outsourcing work is carried on by former employees you must show that there has been a genuine change in status to a self-employed basis, recognized by both employment law and the Inland Revenue. Otherwise the responsibilities under employment, tax and other laws will remain with the old employer. Because of the effect of the Transfer Regulations, you should take care if the outsourced part of the business is capable of being an independent economic unit retaining its identity, i.e. it is the nucleus of a self-contained business in its own right. For more detail, refer to page 109. Although it is now very doubtful how far, if at all, the Transfer Regulations apply to second generation outsourcing (i.e. when an operation is outsourced and comes up for termination or re-tendering), possible implications would include that:

- the employees engaged in the section which is outsourced may automatically transfer to the new operation on their existing terms of employment when the change takes place, even if there is no actual transfer of business

- any dismissal of employees for redundancy (other than for an economic, technical or organizational reason entailing changes in the workforce) or any detrimental change of their terms of employment which is in any way connected with the transfer may give rise to a claim for unfair dismissal
- each time the services contract comes to an end and the same business is put out for tender or the work finally comes back in-house the same principles may apply (depending upon the precise facts and the most recent court decisions at the time).

For these reasons the client is advised to include clear provisions as to service and quality control issues and the right to object and require the contractor to take disciplinary action against any of its staff who fail to come up to required standards. There may also be provisions against changes of staff, especially in the last few months of the contract, unless it is with the consent of the client, and the client may also require, both for itself and any new contractor, an express indemnity claim against the contractor if the client inherits undisclosed liabilities or substandard staff when the contract terminates. All these issues should be considered at the original contract or tender stage. Remember, under current rules, it will be the transferee or new owner who will inherit the employees and the liability for any past defaults.

Summary

Consultancy and services agreements will be relevant where a business wishes to use the skills of people without employing them. Agreements may apply to individuals or teams and may range from information technology skills to cleaning or catering services. There should be flexibility for all parties, but the price of flexibility may be additional uncertainty. Consider the following questions:

- Is it appropriate to appoint a consultant/service provider rather than an employee?

- Are you certain that the arrangement is not one of employment?
- If you are appointing a company, is the controlling director to be an additional party?
- Is the project or task clearly defined?
- Are there any specific milestones or standards to be achieved?
- Is the fee structure clear?
- Where is the work to be done?
- What is the term of the agreement and the arrangements for termination?
- Have you considered confidentiality and assignability?
- Should there be restrictions on either party during or after the agreement?
- Are the Transfer Regulations likely to apply?

(See also Chapters 8, 10, 11, 12, 13 and 16.)

■ 10

Employment contracts

The employment relationship exists first and foremost as a matter of contract law. Until the 1970s there was relatively little in the way of statute law relating to the creation and termination of individual jobs. Only in the last thirty years have our employment laws developed. This chapter will first consider the contractual position, then the terms implied into the contract by law and then those statutes and regulations which supplement and may override the contractual position.

First, a word of warning. Employment law is a minefield where specialist knowledge and up-to-date advice is an asset. This book concentrates on the contractual aspects, which will help businesses to formulate and think through the main terms of the relationship, but there may be many other aspects which you should consider. Employers should remember that legislation is most likely to apply where the contract terms fall below minimum legal standards, where there is any form of discrimination or unfair treatment and when the contract is terminated.

Written contracts

Statute law requires a written statement of principal terms and conditions, rather than a formal contract, to be given to employees within eight weeks of starting work. Although it is customary to give detailed written service agreements to senior management and directors, it is advised that terms and conditions for all employees be written down and agreed before the contract is created.

Example

Williams Limited, the wholesaler, takes on a new sales representative, Sam Roberts. The sales director writes to him:

'Dear Sam
    Further to your interview here on Friday 12, I am pleased to offer you the position of sales representative with this company commencing on 1 September at a salary of £12,000 a year plus commission. Please let me know if you would like to accept the offer, in which case I look forward to seeing you here at 8.30 am on 1 September.

Yours sincerely

Simon Williams
Sales Director'

In the sequence of offer and acceptance the position is clear. The job advertisement was not an offer but an invitation to apply. The offer may be made at or immediately following the interview or, as in this case, by letter afterwards. All Sam Roberts has to do is to communicate an acceptance either in person, by telephone or by letter. The letter specifies the nature of the job, the salary and starting date, but there is a great deal that is not covered. In addition to matters such as holidays, there is the question of the level of commission. The letter suggests that Williams has not fully worked out its policy on commission and it may be that Sam Roberts, pleased to accept the job, does not wish to create difficulties by asking for clarification. There is fertile ground for dispute here and in the interests of both good employment relations and employment law the terms of the commission scheme should be sorted out at an early stage. If the employer fails to do so, the employee can apply to a court or tribunal for a declaration as to what the terms should be with no certainty that the decision would not favour the employee more than the employer expected.

Although there can be valid oral offer and acceptance at interview, many employees now await written offers before accepting a position, so as to check the precise terms before handing in notice to their current employer and/or deciding between competing offers. Wise employers should likewise not make an offer at interview, but rather state their intention to make an offer and follow this up by letter. In this way, any uncertainties or misunderstandings can be resolved by clear written terms.

Conditional employment offers

The offer should specify any preconditions, which should be acceptable to the employer and should not leave open the question of what, objectively, is 'acceptable'. At the same time, it must not discriminate against an actual or prospective employee on grounds which might be regarded as relating to sex, race, religion or 'disability' within the meaning of the Disability Discrimination Act 1995.[1] In the case of work permits the time-scale may also be relevant and it is wise to limit the time within which a permit will be obtained. UK businesses need to remember that there are now criminal penalties for employing non-EU nationals without first making sufficient checks on their right to work in the UK. Similarly, with senior executives and sales managers – check that there are no restrictions in their previous contract which would limit their activities in the future.

---

[1] The definition of disability is wide-ranging and the obligation extends to availability of jobs and interview conditions. Further advice should be taken.

Agreeing the contract terms

In the example offer letter from Williams to Sam Roberts note that only a limited number of terms were agreed at first. The statutory terms and conditions would be notified after the contract was created. It is not uncommon to find that they include provisions with which the employee does not agree.

To avoid this an employer should clearly set down the terms in writing, from the outset, which are then countersigned by the employee. It is less clear as to how this is best done. At one end of the spectrum there is the short offer letter, such as that sent by Simon Williams to Sam Roberts; at the other end an employer might send a complete set of offer letter, terms and conditions of employment and staff handbook to a prospective employee as part of a composite offer letter. By doing so the employer ensures that the prospective employee is aware of and accepts all the relevant terms from the outset. However, it is expensive to produce a handbook, particularly for an individual who may not accept the job, and it will take the employee some time to read and absorb the information before deciding whether to accept or reject the offer. Some individuals will be impressed by the composite approach and others will be oppressed by the volume of paper. What might be suitable for a senior executive may be intimidating to a production worker.

For this reason there is much to recommend a short offer letter, accompanied by the main terms and conditions in reasonable, but not excessive, detail. The offer letter or the terms and conditions will in turn refer to a staff handbook relating to procedural matters. The handbook may form part of the employment contract and will be made available to the employee either just before or just after work commences. In this way, although the handbook is strictly introduced after the contract is signed, a sensible balance can be struck.

Contract terms

This section sets out some of the main terms which might be included in the contract of a senior company executive. It is not intended to be definitive. In any case the minimum terms and conditions as set out at the end of this chapter (often known as the 'section 1 terms') should be covered in all employment contracts. As employment law continues to change rapidly, no business should assume that the contract which was the state of the art a year or two (or even six months) ago will not now need revision.

Above all other terms in any employment contract, the law will imply a duty of trust and confidence between employer and employee. Higher standards are usually expected of employers, who should therefore act not only to the letter of the agreement but also within its spirit. The fact that an employer has a contractual right, for example, to relocate an employee, does not mean that the right can be exercised in any event, but only when it is fair and reasonable to do so in all the circumstances. To relocate a production worker from Birmingham to Leeds away from family and community, especially on a few days' notice, would be unreasonable whatever the contract says. It could also on its own be a breach of the duty of trust and confidence, which would entitle the employee to resign and claim constructive dismissal. The same principle may apply to material adverse changes in employment terms which an employer tries to enforce on its staff.

Term of the agreement

As with any other good contract, the employment agreement will have specific provisions as to how long it is intended to last. In some cases there will be a fixed-term contract which will automatically expire at the end of the stated period. This practice has been on the increase, especially in media-related and local authority or state-funded jobs, although it is less common in other businesses. Most employment contracts are for an indefinite period, subject to termination on notice. The notice period will tend to be anything from one week to three months, but may be longer in the case of more senior executive positions. The contract should state whether both parties have to give the same period of notice or, for example, whether the employee can give a shorter notice period than the employer.

Statute law lays down minimum notice periods which over-ride any conflicting term of the contract – one week's notice for each complete, continuous year of service up to 12 weeks. In a few exceptional cases, where the contract does not specify a particular period, common law might imply longer notice than the statutory minimum. Case law authority, for example, suggests that a reasonable period of notice for a managing director should not be less than six months. The contract should also include a start date and the date when any previous period of service commenced, where this is an extension to the total service of the employee. It is also wise to include a normal retirement age for the job in question, which must not discriminate between men and women.

Job description and duties

The description of the employee's duties, rather than the job title, is a key term of the contract. It can still be the most difficult piece of information to obtain! Job specifications are best agreed internally within the business before the job is advertised and then used as the basis for selection. The benefits are:

- being clear what the vacancy is (it is surprising how criteria can change during the recruitment process)
- communicating this clearly to applicants to avoid mis-understanding
- providing a reference point for applicants who subsequently find that the job was not quite what they thought
- providing a yardstick (and not merely a stick) for appraisal, and
- establishing a base for disciplinary action, if necessary.

At the same time it is sensible to include a 'flexibility clause' which allows the employer to direct employees to similar quality and status work in the future and a 'mobility clause' for reasonable relocation.

Remuneration and benefits

Remuneration is a package of pay and reward for work. In some jobs salary is everything and in others it may be less than half the total remuneration. Either way the contract will set out the salary or wages and whether they are calculated and paid by the hour, week, month or year. It will also normally include the dates for salary reviews and details of bonuses or commission. The contract should make it clear how those calculations will be made, by whom and when payment will be made.

As a precautionary measure it is recommended that the contract gives express power to the employer to deduct amounts due to it out of remuneration payable to the employee. If there is no such clause and the employer makes an unauthorized deduction, this will result not only in the amount being repayable to the employee but also in the employer being precluded from claiming it back later.

Benefits include:

- provision of and terms relating to a company car and fuel – or a car allowance in lieu
- pension arrangements
- medical expenses insurance, possibly also for the executive's family
- long-term sickness or permanent health insurance (PHI)
- share options (another fast-changing area where up-to-date advice is required)
- four, five or even six weeks' paid holiday.

Larger companies may present their employees with a choice, a 'menu' of possible benefits and scales – for example, some want a smaller car and less insurance but more holidays.

Confidentiality, copyright and non-competition

The common-law duty of fidelity which an employee owes to an employer during the course of an employment largely protects confidential information whilst the job continues, but not afterwards. The employment contract should therefore include an express confidentiality clause and a provision assigning to the employer all copyright material created during the employment period. (For more detail on these subjects and the suitability of restrictions against future competition by the employee see Chapters 6 and 15.)

Termination of employment

Employment is normally terminated on notice given by employer or employee, although even the expiry of a fixed-term contract may give rise to employee claims. The repercussions are now considered.

Wrongful dismissal

If the contract is broken because due notice is not given, damages for breach may be payable. Dismissal in breach of contract is known as 'wrongful dismissal'. Except for cases of gross misconduct justifying summary dismissal, the length of notice will be the starting point to determine how much compensation will be paid to the dismissed employee. The length of notice is also relevant if the employer seeks to enforce 'garden leave' (also called 'gardening leave') by requiring a departing executive to stay away from work (and not contact suppliers or customers) during all or part of the notice period. A longer notice period can therefore be a mixed blessing for each of the parties. For the employer it implies an obligation to continue paying and providing remuneration and benefits but the possibility of keeping a potentially competitive employee out of the market for the notice period; for the employee it means greater apparent security in the form of time to look for another job or compensation, but the risk of being kept out of the business for several months if he or she is seen as a potential threat.

The consolation for the employer is that dismissed executives normally have a duty to mitigate their loss by seeking suitable alternative employment. The earnings from the job they take, or should have taken, then have to be brought into account and only the difference is payable by the employer.

Where, however, there is a clause entitling the employee to pay in lieu of notice, the courts may regard this as a liquidated damages clause payable in any event without the employee seeking to mitigate loss.

Unfair dismissal

The dismissal may also be 'unfair' under the Employment Rights Act (ERA) if it is not carried out for an 'admissible reason', one which is accepted by the industrial tribunal as being in accordance with the ERA, and/or a dismissal not carried out fairly in accordance with proper procedures. Most contracts contain a disciplinary procedure requiring a series of disciplinary hearings and warnings, which should be properly carried out. Failure to do so, quite apart from being a breach of contract, potentially makes the dismissal unfair under the ERA. Incorrect procedure on its own can make a dismissal unfair and increase compensation to cover the additional period which would have been worked if the correct procedure had been followed. Again specialist knowledge or advice is recommended.

An employee who is alleging unfair dismissal can apply to the appropriate industrial tribunal within three months of the date on which his/her employment ceased (the 'effective date of termination'). The employee must have served a qualifying period of continuous employment, currently two years. This period is under review both by the courts and as part of government policy[1]. When a claim is substantiated, the tribunal will usually award compensation, but there are a number of other remedies available to it including the power to order the employee's reinstatement into the original job or other re-engagement by the employer. The maximum levels of compensation which the tribunals can award are regularly reviewed and up-to-date figures should be checked. Much higher awards may exceptionally be given if the employer does not comply with a reinstatement or re-engagement order or if the dismissal involves certain anti-union or health and

[1] A White Paper on 'Fairness at Work' introduced in Spring 1998 proposes to reduce the period of two years to one year.

safety issues. Where there is sex, race or disability discrimination, the compensation is unlimited[1].

Business transfers and employment rights (TUPE)

As long ago as 1977 the European Commission introduced a directive to protect the rights of employees (known in Eurospeak as 'workers') to retain their jobs and job entitlements when their business was transferred to new owners. Generally known as the Acquired Rights Directive, it was brought into English Law in 1981 by the Transfer of Business (Protection of Employment) Regulations 1981, also known as TUPE or 'the Transfer Regulations'. The new laws were not only late but also defective, from the days when the British Government thought that European directives worked on a 'pick and mix' basis. They have therefore been much amended and 'clarified' by subsequent legislation and court decisions, many of them from the European Court of Justice. An understanding of how these regulations affect employment rights is important for anyone working with business contracts.

TUPE – key points

- TUPE applies where a business passes from one owner (the 'old owner') to another (the 'new owner'), even if there is no direct transfer.
- Employees assigned to the business (or the identifiable part of it which is transferring) are taken over by the new owner on the same terms and conditions as their employment with the old owner.
- Dismissal of the employees (by redundancy or otherwise) by the old owner to facilitate the transfer will in most cases be automatically unfair dismissal.
- Dismissal of the employees by the new owner for reasons connected with the transfer will be automatically unfair,

[1] The 1998 White Paper also proposes that the limit on compensation claims for unfair dismissal be removed entirely.

unless the new owner can show a specific economic, technical or organizational (known as 'ETO') justification requiring a change in the workforce generally.

- Employees are not forced to transfer, but if they elect not to, they are treated as resigning without any claims against the old owner or the new owner.
- Prior consultation with the transferring workforce is required either through recognized unions or through employee representatives elected for the purpose.
- The usual two-year qualifying period is still required for any employee to claim unfair dismissal (subject to further case law or statutory change on the subject).
- Changes in terms and conditions before or after, but connected with, the transfer which are detrimental to the employee are liable to constitute constructive unfair dismissal or be entirely ineffective.

TUPE checklist

1   Is there a business or an economic operation retaining its identity which is being transferred? A takeover or merger by sale of shares is not a TUPE transfer. Alternatively, is there a business, or an identifiable part of a business, or operation which ceases (or reduces) in one ownership and reappears in substantially the same form elsewhere?
2   Who was employed by that business, and assigned to the relevant part of it, when the sale or cessation was first planned? How long have they been employed?
3   Are all the employees likely to be required after completion of the transfer? Do they include key people who are essential to the new owner to maintain the value of the business?
4   Will the new owner pay at least the same rates of pay, benefits and bonus as the old owner?
5   Will there be any problems for the new owner in having employees with two (or more) different sets of employment terms after completion of the deal?

If the answer to question 1 is 'yes' and to questions 3 and 4 is 'no' or to question 5 is 'yes', seek further advice from a specialist about the individuals covered by question 2.

Obligations under TUPE

Where TUPE applies, the contract of employment is treated as if it was originally made with the new owner of the business. As a result the new owner has all the obligations of the old owner under the contract, except for criminal liabilities and rights attaching to occupational pension schemes. The effect of TUPE is that the employees can claim from, and sue, the new owner for any arrears of pay, bonus or benefit, or any Equal Pay Act or discrimination claims, and can resign and claim constructive dismissal if the new owner breaks the contract. Where TUPE might apply, the new owner should seek a warranty of the accuracy of the information given as to the terms of employment of the employees and the absence of claims by or arrears due to them. The new owner is also advised to seek a specific indemnity for any claims which result from the transfer. Very clear contract provisions and indemnities are necessary to cover these points.

It is a key requirement of TUPE that proper information must be given and consultation take place with the employees affected and/or their representatives. These representatives may be elected by the staff themselves for the purpose or they may be union officials where one is recognised by the employer. The information given to employees must include the identity and plans of the new owner in relation to the business. The duty to consult then applies in respect of changes which are likely to result from the transfer. If the business transfer contract does not cover the issue, it follows that the new owner will acquire the liability for any breaches. The handling of the statutory requirement to provide this information against a background of confidential sale and purchase negotiations can create great problems in practice. The benefit to the new owner is that it can now usually sense the mood of the workforce before the transfer takes place – and vice versa.

Although not a TUPE obligation, restrictive covenants should be reviewed by the new owner immediately after the transfer. The transfer will not destroy the covenants, since the contract is treated as having been made between the employee and the new owner, but the covenants will be treated cautiously by the courts. The covenants may, for example, relate only to the customers of the old owner and therefore be of no benefit to the new owner unless they are changed. Those changes will, in turn, require careful negotiation and employee consent.

Cost implications

As mentioned in relation to agency and distribution contracts and agreements for services, TUPE liabilities may arise on the termination of those contracts, in addition to outright business sales. The following costs need to be considered:

- notice periods payable in any event for any employees dismissed
- redundancy payments
- unfair dismissal or constructive and unfair dismissal orders or reinstatement/re-engagement orders
- liability for holiday pay claims, equal pay claims, sex/racial discrimination, unlawful wages deduction claims and other past liabilities
- compensation of up to four weeks' pay for each employee affected where the TUPE consultation requirements have not been complied with.

The message for business is clear – look after your employee contracts and include TUPE considerations in your contract planning checklist from the outset. Failure to do so and to review carefully the cost and benefit implications of your actions could seriously damage both employee relations and your pocket.

Section 1 requirements

1 Names of the employer and the employee.
2 Date on which the employment began.
3 Date on which the employee's period of continuous employment began.
4 Rate of remuneration and intervals at which it is paid.
5 Terms and conditions relating to hours of work.
6 Terms and conditions relating to holiday entitlement, sick pay and pensions.

7   Amount of notice which the employee is obliged to give and entitled to receive in order to terminate the agreement.
8   Job title or description.
9   Length of the intended period of employment.
10   Place of work.
11   Any collective agreements which directly affect the terms and conditions of the employee's employment;
12   Confirmation of whether or not the employee is required to work outside the UK for a period of more than one month and, if so, details of the terms and conditions affecting that employment.

Where any of this information is not relevant, the ERA requires a statement to that effect. Failure to refer to any of the above matters entitles the employee to apply for clarification of the terms of employment to an industrial tribunal.

Summary

Section 1 of the Employment Rights Act 1996 requires certain minimum particulars to be given to employees within eight weeks of starting work (see above). These terms of the employment contract should be incorporated in the offer letter before the employee accepts the job and starts work. There may be conditions attaching to the offer. In any event the offer should clearly set out the term of employment or notice periods, job description and duties, remuneration and benefits together with relevant provisions as to confidentiality and non-competition. Employers must, during the employment period, take care to show due trust and confidence in their employees and to follow proper disciplinary procedures at all times, particularly where dismissal may result. Where an identifiable part of a business is sold or transferred, the contracts of employment of the employees of that business or the relevant section or division may pass automatically to the new owner of the business. Alternatively employers should plan for redundancy costs, which may be significant. (See also Chapters 1, 6, 8 and 9.)

■ 11

Intellectual property

The expression 'intellectual property rights' may sound intimidating. The term is, however, a useful description of rights, such as patents, trade marks and copyright, in non-physical property but which result from personal or corporate effort or skill and which deserve legal protection. The concept therefore represents a form of property which derives from the mind or intellect. Such rights frequently play an important part in commercial transactions. For example, the exclusive right to reproduce the design of a product may, in time, be more significant than the pure right to buy or sell the product.

Patents

● A patent gives the owner a monopoly right to the exclusive use of an invention which may be a product or a process. Like any form of property right a patent may be bought, sold or licensed.

- To obtain patent protection an invention must be novel, contain an inventive step (one which is not obvious to a person skilled in the particular art), be capable of industrial use and not be specifically excluded from patentability.
- The invention must not be something which is already generally known. Once it is published or made available publicly, the novelty is likely to be lost and the invention cannot be patented.
- Full confidentiality of the invention should therefore be maintained up to the time that the patent application is made. The greatest mistake is to show a potential patent to someone without first protecting confidentiality.
- Excluded from patent protection are matters such as literary works (protected by copyright), scientific theories, immoral or offensive discoveries and plant or biological processes.
- Patents last for 20 years subject to certain renewal fees being paid and the validity of the patent not being impugned in the meantime.
- Patents may be registered in the UK or through a general international application and now through the European Patent Office in Munich.

Patents are a specialized field and professional advice is recommended from the outset. The relevance of patents to contracts is most likely to arise in relation to exploitation rights for third parties. The owner of the patent, not necessarily being the first inventor, may exploit the patent or may assign or license it to another in return for a lump sum or royalty or a combination of the two.

There are many sad tales told by disappointed inventors. They need to remember that, once a patent has been sold, it is the buyer who decides what to do with it. The buyer may never succeed in selling the product and the high hopes of the inventor will be dashed. Worse still, despite vague statements about market potential, the buyer may never even try to develop and sell the patented products and may buy the patent simply to squash it, for example, if it competes with one of their existing products and has the potential to spoil an existing lucrative market. The inventor who is aware of these possibilities could seek to negotiate a substantial advance fee or minimum royalties, or even a buy-back option if the patent is not developed. In the absence of such provisions many valuable inventions have been lost for twenty years with minimal return for their original developers, despite enormous market potential. Others may be bought out for a modest sum (sufficient perhaps to repay the bank overdraft) only to make millions for their new owners.

On the other hand, if you are buying a patent from an inventor, especially if you are paying a large lump sum or setting up a production capability for the purpose, you will want to be satisfied that the invention was novel and the application valid and that there is no chance of the patent being revoked. Make sensible checks before the agreement is settled and also appropriate warranties (possibly backed by a suitable retention) against claims from the inventor or other patent owner.

Trade marks

A trade mark is a distinctive name, design or sign given to products or services which distinguishes them in the marketplace. The mark aims to build up brand recognition and reputation and will thus form part of the goodwill of a business. Brand names today frequently have a high market worth in their own right. By the same token, confusion can easily arise in the marketplace if there is duplication or overlapping between trade marks, especially relating to the same product or service area. To limit repetition, references in this chapter to trade marks will be only to goods or products, but the same principles apply equally to services.

The law has long recognized that reputation, whether of an individual or a business, is a valuable asset deserving protection in much the same way as a patent protects an invention. Accordingly both statute and case law have built up over the years to protect those rights.

Registered trade marks

Trade marks exist in registered and unregistered form. Factors common to both are an identifying name, symbol or style, or even the presentation of a particular product, which is distinctive and not merely descriptive and which is therefore clearly recognizable. Any thought of washing powder or hamburgers, for example, immediately brings to mind brand names which are protected by trade mark registration and a strong market reputation which affects our selection processes. Registration offers greater protection to the owner of the mark because breach arises by the very fact of conflicting use by a third party. The trade mark owner need only then show registration and ownership of the trade mark and conflicting use in relation to the same type of goods. The mark must generally be identical. Where it is merely similar to the registered mark, the claimant must show that the public has been confused. Where the goods are different, but the mark is identical or similar, the claimant needs evidence of unfair advantage being taken or that the infringement damages the distinctive character or repute of the mark.

A colourful example of the distinction arose in 1996 when the courts had to decide whether a soft porn TV series called 'Babewatch' infringed the registered trade mark of the well-known surf-pounding programme 'Baywatch'. Here the names were not identical and the style of the two programmes was different enough for the court to decide that there was insufficient confusion for an infringement. The law reports do not reveal how many viewings were required to establish this finding!

Two important practical points should be noted. First, it will not be possible to register a trade name which is purely descriptive of the products or services – a trade mark must be distinctive in order to be registrable. Second, trade mark searches should be done both at the outset when a new trade mark or name is first thought of to check that there are no existing registrations or similar marks which are likely to cause confusion, objection or even dispute, and again shortly before the new brand is about to be launched. Failure to follow this simple precaution could lead to the threat or reality of an injunction for infringement (or passing off – see below) and to the launch being cancelled and the whole brand design being aborted.

Registration of a trade mark is important for many businesses. The first step is to check that there is no similar mark registered already and that the proposed mark is indeed distinctive enough to be registered. This check will also disclose existing marks which might be infringed by the proposed use. To be registrable, a mark must be capable of being represented graphically and must distinguish the goods or services of one business from those of another. Since the Trade Marks Act 1994 came into force it has been possible to register a wide range of marks including those relating to words, designs, letters, numbers, the shape of goods, their packaging and even smells, provided they can be clearly described in writing. Trade mark registration applies for a ten-year term which can be extended on payment of a renewal fee. The marks are registered in relation to certain classes of goods or services (with separate fees for each class) and may straddle two or more of the 42 registration categories.

Registration in several countries is time-consuming and expensive. There are therefore various forms of international trade mark registration, most notably the European Community trade mark (often known as a CTM) which will cover all EU countries and the fuller-scale (but in practice rarely used) international registration via the World Intellectual Property Organization.

Unregistered trade marks

By contrast, if the mark or name is unregistered, the owner has to establish, first, an existing reputation in the goods and, second, that people have been confused into believing that the infringing items were associated with the owner's business, even if the infringement is by way of an identical name. Breach of an unregistered trade mark is known as 'passing-off' because the infringer passes off its products or services to look like those of the real owner. The courts treat this as a misrepresentation and will intervene to protect the rightful owner and to avoid confusion in the marketplace, and also to protect the owner's reputation which could otherwise be damaged by the imitation. It is normally also necessary to show that loss or damage has resulted or will result to the rightful owner.

Harrods, for example, objected to the name 'Harrodian School' as infringing their reputation in a name which they guard zealously. The school buildings had previously been used as the Harrodian Club for Harrods employees but the court held (in 1996) that there was no evidence of confusion in the circumstances because people dealing with the school would not believe that they were dealing with Harrods.

Domain names

Harrods was more successful in relation to the protection of its domain name on the Internet when it obtained an injunction against a company which had registered some 54 famous names, including Harrods. The decision is, however, unreported and the Harrods application was uncontested. Greater difficulty has been experienced by companies, including those in different countries, which already use similar names and which apply for registration of the same domain name. This area of law is now developing rapidly and there is enough evidence to suggest that businesses should register their domain names earlier rather than later. They also should beware of the law of passing off if they lead people to deal with them in the belief that they are another business with a similar name. Those considering a new trade or product name should also carry out domain name searches to alert themselves to possible conflicting uses.

Trade mark licences

Any assignments or licences which permit third parties to use a registered mark need to be registered. Typically licences cover particular countries and types of goods or services, such as franchise agreements (see Chapter 12) and many forms of manufacturing or distribution agreements. The effect of trade mark infringements can be substantial. If you buy in a large quantity of fashion merchandise, for example, which has been pre-sold at a healthy profit, and you then find that the labels or, worse still, part of the design, infringe third-party trade marks, it is possible that the stock will not only be unsaleable but will be impounded and that you will also have a claim from an irate buyer. You will want to be able to claim against your supplier. This clear case of material risk should be covered by an express warranty and indemnity in the sale agreement, if there is one. The advantage of an indemnity in such a case is that you may be able to involve your supplier from the outset, rather than having to wait for judgment against you and then claim under the warranty. In cases of fashion goods or publications, there may also be copyright issues to consider.

Copyright

Copyright is a negative property right which prevents other people from doing certain things to a copyright work. Like any other form of property, copyright can be licensed or assigned. It should be distinguished from trade marks on the one hand and design right and registered designs on the other. The law may grant protection to detailed plans or designs under these design rights, but as the rules relating to them are technical and the rights much less used than copyright they are not covered here.

Outlines

Copyright law is substantially contained in the Copyright Designs and Patents Act 1988, to which there have been some amendments, largely as part of European harmonization. The main points are set out below:

- Copyright can subsist in literary, dramatic, musical and artistic works, as well as sound recordings, broadcast and cable programmes and the typographical arrangement of published editions of work.

- No formalities are required to acquire copyright protection. Provided the work qualifies for protection in the first place, the right arises automatically as and when the work is generated. However, in the case of literary, dramatic and musical works copyright does not arise until the work is recorded in some permanent or semi-permanent form.
- To acquire copyright protection a work must be original. Obviously no one person has a monopoly on facts or ideas; it is the expression of the facts or ideas, involving skill and labour, which is a necessary component and which is awarded copyright protection.
- Compilations such as computer databases or TV programme listings will also obtain copyright protection as original works if labour and skill have been used to produce the work (even though there is not necessarily any artistic merit).
- Adaptations may acquire copyright if skill and effort are used to produce the work, but the consent of the owner of the original work will be required; otherwise copyright infringement will arise.
- There may be several copyrights in the same work. In a musical recording, the composer will have copyright together with the musicians and the artistes. Their rights will need to be contractually established between them.
- Some works are the result of input from various labour sources. Thus, if the individual person's work cannot be distinguished, all the contributors are entitled to a joint claim of authorship and hence authorship of the copyright in the whole work. On the other hand, if the contributions are easily distinguishable – for instance, authors who each write an individual chapter of a book – then the authors will not be joint authors of the whole literary work but rather of their particular chapters.
- In the case of literary, dramatic, musical and artistic work the author or director is the owner of the copyright. Special rules exist with regard to sound recordings, films, broadcasts and cable programmes.
- If a literary, dramatic, musical or artistic work is made by an employee *during the course of employment* the employer is the first owner of any copyright in the work subject to

any agreement to the contrary. It therefore follows that if the work is made by the employee in his or her spare time and not as part of their job, the employer is not the owner of any copyright in that work. The copyright may need to be specifically secured.

- Copyright in literary, dramatic, musical and artistic works now subsists for 70 years from the end of the year in which the author or director dies. With regard to sound recordings, film, broadcast and cable programmes, copyright subsists in the work for 70 years from the end of the calendar year when the sound recording, broadcast or cable programme was made.

- There is now a separate publication right for works which are out of copyright but which have never been published in the UK or another European Economic Area country. The duration of the right is 25 years.

- The copyright owner has the right to copy the work, to issue copies of the work to the public, to perform, show or play the work in public, to broadcast the work or include it in a cable programme service and to make an adaptation of the work or do any of the above in relation to an adaptation.

- There are four so-called 'moral rights': to be identified as author (the paternity right); to object to derogatory treatment of the work (e.g. parody and burlesque); not to be falsely attributed to a work, and to privacy of certain photographs and films. These moral rights last for as long as copyright subsists in a work, except with regard to false attribution which applies for 20 years after a person's death. Any of the moral rights can be waived in whole or in part in writing; otherwise they should be asserted by their owner.

Commercial exploitation

The person who creates the work in which copyright subsists can transfer ownership by assignment or licence to another in return for a lump sum and/or royalty payments. Such arrangements should be in writing and expressly state the terms and conditions between the parties. Future copyright works can be commissioned, assigned and sublicensed, for example a painting or a book where there is a contract to produce the work, so that the copyright becomes immediately subject to the assignment or licence as soon as the work is created. Nevertheless, the fact that a painter produces one painting on a commission basis and sells it to a buyer will not prevent the same painter from producing a substantially similar work for someone else (see also the *Cala Homes* case on p. 171).

Infringement

Copyright includes the right to prevent someone reproducing your work without your permission. Infringement of a literary, dramatic, artistic and musical work therefore occurs when all or a material part of a work is copied without the consent of the copyright owner. Issuing copies to the public of the work or performing the work in public are also infringements. Secondary infringement occurs when infringing copies of literary, dramatic or musical works are imported, for example, pirate video tapes for distribution in the UK.

There is likely to be a copyright aspect in anything from a pair of jeans or the design of a suitcase to a video or CD recording. Breach of copyright can be a criminal, as well as a civil, offence, and the infringer may be met by police as well as by lawyers' writs. In any event breaches of copyright, when they come to light, must be met with swift action. Publishers and other copyright owners cannot generally afford to wait and see what transpires and injunctions are issued very speedily if there is clear evidence of breach and unequivocal undertakings to cease and hand over offending material are not given. If you are involved with contracts in these areas you must be vigilant to avoid being severely out of pocket if there is serious infringement affecting your products. Be prepared to act fast.

Permitted acts

Not all copying is infringement. Some acts are permitted, such as fair dealing – for instance when a person wishes to carry out research or private study in relation to a work. If you wish to review, criticize or report a work then you should acknowledge the copyright owner. Commercial use of work will not, however, be fair dealing and is likely to amount to infringement. If in doubt, seek advice from a lawyer with experience in this area or from one of the copyright licensing organisations.[1]

International aspects

The UK is party to the Berne Convention, which states that, as between the signatories, no legal formalities are required to protect copyright, and the Universal Copyright Convention. Whilst it is not a requirement of protection under English law the Universal Copyright Convention recognizes the use of the symbol © and the name of the copyright owner and date of first publication of the work as ingredients for international recognition of the rights of the copyright owner. The use of the symbol is therefore advised if the work is likely to be used abroad.

Computer software

Software has not historically had its own form of legal protection but is dealt with under the law of copyright supplemented by European directives and UK regulations. The hardware side of a computer contract is largely covered by sale of goods law and the maintenance side will be subject to the legal principles applicable to the supply of services. Software, on the other hand, is an intellectual property right and copying will be breach of copyright unless especially permitted. Restrictions against copying are likely to be contained in all written licences, including the so-called 'shrink-wrap' licences

[1] For example, the British Copyright Licensing Agency Ltd, 90 Tottenham Court Road, London W1P 0LP, telephone 0171-436 5931.

contained inside, but visible from outside, the packaging around program disks. Licences will generally permit a back-up copy of the software for security purposes. Most consumer software sales will contain a licence for an indefinite period provided that the terms of the licence are adhered to. More substantial programs may be licensed on an annual basis, automatically renewed provided the relevant fee is paid.

Although the negotiation of computer and other IT contracts is a specialist field in its own right, here are some general points for guidance:

- The software clearly must be fully compatible with the hardware system and backed up by suitable training, new release and support mechanisms from those who really know the product. Troubleshooting response time periods may be critical.
- The contract may limit the use of the software to certain machines and/or users, which can become restrictive and expensive as a business expands and has to move – a clear variation path should be set out.
- If the software house becomes insolvent or otherwise unable to support the software, the effect can be dramatic for a business relying on that software. In larger contracts for bespoke software, some measure of security is provided by lodging the source code and/or object code, written by the programmers, with a stable independent third party called an escrow agent. Access to the code can then be obtained if the software house fails to provide the required support.
- Software agreements will normally be prepared by the supplier and will contain a range of exclusion and limitation clauses. These must be carefully checked and, if necessary, negotiated.
- Databases are the subject of specific regulation under the EC Databases Directive of 1996, effective from 1998. For this purpose a database is a collection of independent works, data or materials with literary, dramatic, musical or artistic content arranged in a systematic or methodical way. The directive operates to cover the database both by its own copyright and by a new, independent database

right which prohibits unauthorized extraction of material from the database and applies for 15 years. If the database is constantly changing, the 15 years may, in effect, be perpetually renewed.

These brief pointers should be borne in mind by businesses dealing with IT contracts. All too often the effort that goes into the system and software selection process relaxes at the point of negotiating the contract. That effort must be maintained throughout the contractual process to ensure the best prospect of the desired result or, if the worst occurs, financial recovery for the loss involved.

Know-how

Although without statutory protection, know-how has become a significant intellectual property right. It extends to all manner of discoveries, processes, designs, methods, drawings, formulae, reports and the manuals or computer programs in which they are held. Training procedures and marketing techniques may also be included, although transferors of know-how should take care not to leave open-ended commitments in relation to training. Being a non-statutory right, know-how requires protection by contract. Careful drafting is required to obtain a sensible balance of protection without creating an unreasonable, and potentially unenforceable, burden on the licensor or transferor of know-how.

Summary

Intellectual property rights are becoming increasingly important and valuable in business life and are liable to be relevant to a broad range of contracts. You must be familiar with these rights so that your business contracts are protected. Patents affect only a minority of companies, but where there may be patentable rights full confidentiality is essential from the outset. Registered and unregistered trade marks and trade names are, on the other hand, applicable to businesses of many kinds and at all levels, if only to protect trading names. Copyright is also relevant beyond its immediate apparent importance, in view of the ease (and prevalence) of unauthorized copying and the fact that innocent companies become caught up in disputes relating to product design as well as text. This principle extends to software where the rights to reproduce, or even to use, programs may be strictly limited and where large software companies take immediate and vigorous action to protect their products from infringing use. (The way in which these rights and the know-how in a method or system are typically dealt with by contract is considered in Chapter 12.) Points to consider here include:

- Is there a patentable element involved and, if so, is full confidentiality being maintained?
- Have you carried out a trade mark search for identical or similar marks to your own (or proposed) mark? This necessary safeguard should be updated regularly. Many trade mark agents will provide a 'watching' service to advise you of any similar applications in the future.
- Is your name or logo distinctive enough for registration and do the costs and procedures justify it?
- In how many countries would you need to be registered and is an international registration viable?
- Before you use a new name, have you checked in relevant trade journals and directories?
- Are you legally entitled to use and continue to use (and perhaps develop) your name, logo, original material and software?
- Is your know-how as protected as it might be?
- Have you checked any conflicting domain names and/or registered your own?

(See also Chapters 6, 8, 9, 10, 12 and 13.)

■ 12

Franchising and licensing

Commercial licensing agreements apply to a full range of products, services and situations where intellectual property rights are used by a business which does not own those rights. Such licences may cover manufacture, assembly, marketing, sales, service or any other facet of exploitation or support of a patent, trade mark, technology or know-how system, copyright or design. The main specification is that the licensor, who will either be the owner of the rights or a licensee of them for a particular geographical or market sector, will grant the licensee the right to deal with them in a specific way for a specific period.

Features of a commercial licence agreement

Most agreements contain some or all of the following features:

- the right to use a – clearly defined – product or service

name, design, methodology or technology – and subsequent improvements to those features
- limited to a stated purpose, territory and period and possible renewal rights
- with strong obligations of confidentiality
- subject to maintenance of quality standards and, where applicable, suitable sales methods
- with warranties by the licensor as to the validity and exclusivity of the IP rights and the absence of disputes relating to them
- obligations on the licensee to inform the licensor promptly of any known infringements and to co-operate in any infringement proceedings
- payment by the licensee of a flat annual fee and/or unit fee and/or a royalty based on sales, production or shipment levels with detailed provisions for accounting and payment
- limited rights to assign and sub-license
- termination provisions on default/insolvency/change of control;
- restrictions on competition during and, for a limited period, after termination of the licence.

A typical negotiation area is that of target production or sales, especially if the royalty rate decreases as sales increase. In some cases the licensee may be required to guarantee a minimum royalty, even if production or sales are negligible. Similar considerations apply here to minimum sales obligations of distributors. One effect of the licensee failing to meet minimum levels of production, sales or licence fee may be that the licensor will have the right to terminate the licence. Again the licensee should not let wild optimism cloud commercial judgement. Because of the range of commercial licence agreements, it is probably easiest to consider one specific type of arrangement, which is also one of the best known – the franchise. Many of the principles which apply to franchising illustrate the issues which will arise in other licence agreements.

Franchise agreements

Our view of a franchise is likely to be connected with health products, ties, underwear or fast food. We are probably more familiar with 'business format franchising' where, to the outside eye, there is little or no difference between the outlet which is directly owned by a business and the outlet that is franchised. So what goes on behind the scenes? A typical franchise relationship contains most, if not all, of the following features:

- The franchisor has a distinctive name, associated with a trade mark, experience and reputation in a particular area of business and an established procedure for conducting that business, all of which are suitable for 'packaging' and applying to strongly branded premises, and/or types of services.
- The franchisee is an independent business, which buys the right to use the trade name and the know-how for the period of the franchise.
- The detailed operation of the business is set out in one or more manuals – possibly supported by bespoke software systems. The manual contains highly confidential information with which all franchisees will be required to comply and which will change with improvements in the running of the business.
- The franchisee pays a capital sum at the start of the franchise term followed by regular payments, generally based on the turnover of the franchised business.
- These fee obligations are backed by the entitlement of the franchisor to review the accounts and, if it wishes, the books and records of the franchisee.
- In many franchises the franchisee is required, by the contract or by practicality, to buy raw materials or completed products through approved suppliers in order to maintain product and service quality for the benefit of all franchisees.
- The franchisee is obliged to keep the franchised business separate and distinct from any other business, to use the trade mark and trade names and know-how exactly as

prescribed by the franchisor and to maintain the confidentiality of all the know-how.

- The franchisor retains sufficient control over the business to ensure that the franchisee complies with its obligations and maximizes the potential of the franchise.
- To assist this the franchisor provides detailed guidance on the premises and the whole of the set-up arrangements together with training for the key employees of the franchisee.
- The franchisor provides national advertising and probably assists with, and retains close control over, local marketing.
- The franchise is limited to a given area or range of products or services and the franchisee has no right to establish a base outside the agreed territory or range of products or services.
- There are restrictions on the ability of the franchisee to assign or transfer the business since the franchisor would wish to maintain a strong degree of control over the choice of any incoming franchisee.
- The agreement typically lasts for between five and ten years, and perhaps longer, with the right to renew for a further term.
- There are rigorous provisions enabling the franchisor to terminate the agreement if the franchisee seriously breaches the agreement .

Business advantages of franchising

The growth of franchising owes much to the advantages which it offers to both parties. It gives the franchisor the chance to build up business and turnover at a faster rate than cash and personnel resources might otherwise permit and to tap into the extra energy of franchisees owning their own businesses. It gives franchisees the opportunity to run their own businesses and be self-employed without the need to be specialists or total innovators. On the financial side, there should be a reduced risk of failure in following a pattern with an established success record and correspondingly less difficulty in raising start-up finance. But franchisees must pay for the privilege and accept tight control by their franchisors. When the franchisee considers it could do everything on its own, it becomes the franchisor's potential competitor. Although there are restrictions on the franchisee, it may be difficult for a franchisor to stop, for example, another member of the franchisee's family setting up in competition and using many of the same techniques. The strength of the franchisor's brand and reputation and levels of cost and service will be critical here.

Franchisors need considerable resources. The cost of piloting successful viability trials, setting up the infrastructure, finding, equipping and training the franchisee and providing ongoing support are considerable. Provision must also be made for a fighting fund to defend the brand against imitators and, if need be, to take over the business of defaulting franchisees until replacements can be found. Trade mark registration is normally an important ingredient of franchising but much of our brand awareness arises from the visibility of high street names of shops or products. Products or services without a strong brand image, and which rely essentially on an idea or technique which others can learn, are extremely difficult to protect.

Franchisor's liability for information provided

Although there are, as yet, very limited statutory controls over business format franchising in the UK (unlike many of the US states where there is federal and local control regulating the position even before discussions commence with potential franchisees), the normal laws of misrepresentation and negligence apply. A franchisor will be liable for the accuracy of the information it supplies to prospective franchisees[1] and any attempted exclusion of liability will have to pass the unfair contract terms tests to afford protection. Optimism is not enough. Collateral contracts may easily be created if specific promises or warranties are given, even orally, and are shown to encourage the franchisee to enter into the agreement. Even encouraging franchisees to sign on the grounds that other

[1] See the comments on *Williams* v *Natural Life Health Food*, p. 94.

would-be franchisees are ready to do so may amount to action-able misrepresentation if it cannot be proved to be true.

Franchising and pyramid selling

The name franchising is sometimes given to schemes which are in fact pyramid selling or 'muli-level' marketing – a number of levels of distributors of products, or even money, where distributors are encouraged to recruit more distributors and are given financial incentives to do so. The incentives may be direct, by payment for the recruitment, or indirect, for example by charging the distributor next down the chain a higher price for the goods. The incentive for participants is to recruit more of their number rather than to sell more products. Such schemes tend therefore to abuse the rights of the lower levels of participators and do nothing to improve competition in the marketplace.

Pyramid selling schemes are now closely regulated by the Trading Schemes Act 1996 and subsequent regulations. Breach of the Act is a criminal offence and payments or obligations to pay may be unenforceable. The Act is widely drafted and may catch what would formerly have been regarded as legitimate franchises. To fall outside the regulations there must be either single-level agreements (meaning that all franchisees have broadly similar rights direct from the franchisor and only a nominal maximum charge by the franchisor – a requirement which immediately rules out most legitimate franchises) or that all parties involved in the network are VAT registered, including the franchisor. Non-resident franchisors must now be VAT registered in the UK to maintain exemption. It seems likely that the regulations will be further amended and the latest provisions should always be checked.

Master franchise and area development licences

Franchisors may wish to appoint a licensee for a larger region or separate country. For example, a US franchisor of a well-known brand may wish to seek one or more licensees for the

UK and permit them in turn to license or franchise individual units within their territory. If the licensee of the larger territory is to operate those outlets itself, the agreement is likely to be an area development licence, whereas if the licensee intends in turn to grant individual franchises to third parties, the arrangement will be a master franchise. Other options include setting up a subsidiary in the countries concerned, a distribution agreement or a joint venture. Whichever route is chosen there will be many factors to consider in reaching a decision. The requirements of the local law and the tax structure will require a thorough analysis before a decision is made. There may also be cultural and legal differences in operating in other countries, which are best investigated at an early stage to test the viability of the plans. Certain countries (including France and many US states) have registration requirements with varying degrees of formality before franchises or similar arrangements can be signed. Other countries may also require, by law or custom, a strong element of local ownership of the outlet, which will affect the structure and terms proposed.

Effect of competition law on intellectual property licences

Because exclusive territories are often given and controls imposed on licensees and franchisees, such agreements can be used in a way which would carve up markets and restrict competition. Competition law considerations, therefore, are always just round the corner when dealing with licences and franchises (see Chapter 6, p. 69). So far as the Restrictive Trade Practices Act is concerned, registration may be avoided by the licensor and franchisor granting a 'sole' right in the territory rather than an exclusive right, i.e. agreeing not to grant rights to others in the territory but not barring itself. A fail-safe application may nonetheless be recommended. The Fair Trading Act is more concerned with monopoly operations or practices and is unlikely to apply unless the licensor or franchisor supplies or receives more than a quarter of all the goods or services of a particular kind or there is a co-ordinated arrangement with other similar suppliers which could restrict or distort competition.

The Treaty of Rome may be relevant in the larger franchise operations for two main reasons. First, any arrangement whereby the same sort of agreement is entered into by a single licensor or franchisor with a large number of licensees or franchisees should be treated as a whole. By analogy, an agreement for the tied supply of beer to a small café in the corner of Holland or Belgium could infringe European competition law if agreements with the same restrictions were entered into with many other small cafés. The cumulative effect of all these agreements would have the perceptible effect that if, for example, you cycled round the Benelux countries seeking refreshment, your choice of beer would be limited and competition would be restricted as a result. Second, although an agreement may apparently operate only in one European state, it may potentially affect trade between member states if the licensee or franchisee is limited in practice from setting up in competition in another EU member state.

Technology transfer and research and development block exemptions

The technology transfer block exemption will probably apply to cases relating to patents and know-how where intellectual property rights (IPRs) are licensed in return for payment, typically of royalties. As with other block exemptions, the principles are most important where there may be a perceptible effect on trade between or affecting member states of the EEA and where the turnover of the parties (and their associated companies) and/or the market share of the products are outside the *de minimis* thresholds referred to in Chapter 6. In such situations there is an inherent conflict between the monopoly status of the IPRs by virtue of their originality – and registration where applicable – and the free trade principles of the Treaty of Rome. Articles 30 to 36 of the treaty prohibit the prevention of marketing of products in one state which have been previously marketed in another member state with the consent of the IPR owner.

The provisions of the block exemption are complex but recognize that most types of technology licensing will encourage rather than restrict competition. To fall within the exemption, a licence must broadly be either a pure patent licence, a pure know-how licence (provided the know-how remains secret) or a mixed patent and know-how licence. Other IPR licences will not be covered by the block exemption except to the extent that the rights are ancillary to the technology covered by the exemption. The exemptions are subject to details which require careful study, but one of the main provisions is to limit the permitted restrictions to the patent period or 10 years from the date of first marketing of know-how and so long only as this remains confidential. The object is to ensure that licensees cannot be restricted where others would be free to exploit technology which had become public knowledge.

There is a further block exemption relating to research and development. Again, these areas should be pro-competitive. The exemption, however, distinguishes between collaboration on the pure research and development stage, which it supports more readily, and the second stage of joint exploitation, which is regarded with caution as more likely to restrict competition. Again, the exemption is very specific and requires detailed consideration in appropriate cases.

The franchise block exemption

Given the uncertainty and experience with a number of applications relating to franchise agreements, the EC published in 1988 a block exemption relating to franchises. It is limited to franchises involving retail sales and master franchises, and does not cover area development licences. It specifically permits many of the main provisions which franchisors wish to include in their agreements. For the most part, therefore, the agreement will be unlikely to infringe European law unless it includes some of the 'black clauses', for example:

● forbidding the franchisee from *supplying* outside the allocated territory
● establishing maximum or *minimum resale prices*

- requiring that products for the franchise are *obtained* only from the franchisor or another nominated supplier.

The principles of the law relating to restraint of trade also need to be borne in mind in relation to franchising and licensing agreements. Consider the extent of confidential information which may have been made available to the franchisee and decide what level of protection is reasonably necessary for the franchisor to protect that information. It is unlikely that much more than a lengthy restriction will be justified; the block exemption specifically mentions one year as being a period which would not, of itself, infringe the exemption. The territorial impact of the restriction should also be carefully drafted to cover only the main catchment area for the outlet in question.

Summary

Intellectual property rights can be important to a business and so should be governed by contracts which set out the position clearly. The main provisions will establish the permitted extent and areas of use of the rights, protect the rights and reputation of the licensor and establish payment for those rights which reflects their value and can, if necessary, be independently checked and verified. Franchising is an example where there is now a general format with inevitable variations between different industries. Care must be taken with the new regulations under the Trading Schemes Act and international licences raise important questions on the conflict of laws of different countries and choices as to jurisdiction and similar matters. With restrictions, the terms of the relevant block exemptions may also be relevant. Points to consider include:

- extent of the rights being licensed and whether improvements and derivations are included
- area covered and whether the licence is exclusive or non-exclusive
- term of the agreement and provisions for notice or other termination

- amount and payment arrangements for the licence fee and any royalties
- any requirements for minimum sales or payments and effect of failure to achieve these
- obligations as to record-keeping, reporting and auditing the records
- provisions on quality control and observance of agreed procedures
- licensor warranties on ownership of the rights, registration, non-infringement and right to enter into the agreement with appropriate indemnities for breach
- provisions for dealing with third party claims
- limitations on liability and insurance requirements
- confidentiality and non-competition clauses
- rights of assignment, subcontracting and sublicensing
- boilerplate clauses
- buy-out provision or termination.

(See also Chapters 4, 6, 8, 11, 13 and 16.)

PART II

Contracts in practice

■ 13

Planning the contract

It is an easy leap from agreement on the outlines of a deal straight into detailed contract drafting. Once the framework of the written contract is set, it assumes a life and resilience independent of its original creators. In extreme cases, the contract draft becomes a Frankenstein's monster which threatens to disrupt harmony and destroy the original basis of agreement. This chapter proposes a general approach to planning contracts in business which will give the maximum chance of the contract serving its intended purpose and the minimum risk of becoming an agent of destruction. In that sense, clarification and anticipation are recommended as the main driving forces, with protection a secondary, although important, issue. Most areas of protection will be easier to identify after the main contract areas have been fully clarified.

Contracts are often prepared against tight time deadlines and there is a tendency for businesses, as well as lawyers, to rely on some familiar format or precedent and regard the exercise as no more than filling in some blanks and changing some clauses. Considering the following issues will help to establish whether indeed that format is right and, if not, how the issues and then the contract should best be structured.

Subject

The subject of a contract is normally straightforward to identify. What is the contract about? This could range from the purchase of ten filing cabinets or a maintenance contract for computer hardware through to the construction of a hydro-electric dam. The subject is the immediate focus of attention in most cases.

Object

Like the classic sentence the classic contract has a subject and an object. The object will be the broader objective or purpose. It may be immediate or longer term or belong to a larger plan, such as part of a large office reorganization in the case of the cabinets, a new form of accounting in the case of the computers or a new power generation project in the case of the dam. The object will affect the choice of contractor, the degree of supervision and the level of comfort relied on and each will affect the type of contract which is chosen.

If the objectives are lost sight of contract negotiations can involve hours of deliberation over small issues at the expense of the main issues which will make or break the relationship and be the real difference between success and failure. It is important to identify the objective of the contract and the point at which an effective result has been achieved. Will there be a clear, measurable outcome? If so, how can this be defined and what happens when it has been achieved? What will be necessary to consolidate and build on that measurable outcome? If not, how will the objective, and the attainment of adequate performance levels, be measured?

Effect

One test of the objective is to project the possible results of the contract being performed. It should not only clarify the objectives but also show up side effects – beneficial or otherwise. A common cause of contract disputes is an effect of actual performance which had not been anticipated. Assume, for example, that you run a house-building company, looking for appealing new house designs. Market research indicates that converted railway stations have great appeal as homes, so you engage designers to prepare plans on this basis. The houses are popular and your competitors are showing interest. What could be easier than for them to go to the same designers and ask for the same design? There will be no breach of copyright because the copyright belongs to the designers and not the client; the designers are free to reproduce the design, with or without amendments, for your competitors.

This is not a flight of fancy, but substantially what led to litigation in *Cala Homes* v *Alfred McAlpine* 1996. Here extra zest was added by the fact that the managing director of Cala left to join their competitor, McAlpines, and took the idea with him. Cala took McAlpines to court but found that, although the McAlpine design was effectively a copy of the Cala house design, the copyright in the design had not been assigned to Cala. Although the whole point of the design was to obtain business advantage for Cala, there was nothing in the contract with the designers to protect the design. In the event, the court took a pragmatic approach to the situation and held that Cala had effective editorial control over the drawings and such an input into the design through their employees that the copyright was owned jointly between them and the designers. Cala, as joint copyright owner, had not consented to the licence to McAlpines and could therefore prevent McAlpines from copying the plans. So Cala finally succeeded, but it took court action and – to some extent – new law to achieve the success. The moral is that the effect of success should be considered in advance, not merely the effect of failure.

Cost

The cost, or at least the apparent cost, is normally calculated at the outset. The true cost, however, may be very different. In an employment contract, for example, both parties have a clear view of what will be paid in terms of salary. For the employer costs will include obvious items such as national insurance and employee benefits and also less obvious items, such as secretarial and administrative support, additional equipment, office space, facilities management and training. Unless the employer takes these factors into account the budget may not balance. The employee, too, needs to consider other factors. Travel expenses, for example, and perhaps the cost of child-minding. Office hours may be a poor guide to the level of commitment expected and there may be unseen costs to social life and even to health.

In relation to the sale of goods, if the filing cabinets referred to earlier are for resale to a specific customer, the specification must be an exact match. If they are for speculative resale, on the other hand, their marketability may well depend on factors such as colour. If the colour is wrong and there is no redress, the buyer may be faced with the high costs of respray or a heavily discounted resale. The process of negotiating standard terms is, for this reason, mainly geared to identifying and allocating the relevant costs, as well as the risks, of the sale and purchase of the products or services. This is also the time to test the assumptions made in the initial negotiations in order to evaluate the true cost of the deal. The assumptions, once tested, should in turn be incorporated in the contract either as principal clauses or by way of warranty. A typical example would be the warranty in a licence to exploit trade marks and know-how, that the licensor of those rights did indeed own them without third-party claims, was entitled to license them and that there were no infringements of the rights of third parties in doing as proposed.

Benefit

Are you obtaining the benefit you expect from the contract? What is the legal position if you contract to buy a Porsche at the price of a Ford but receive only the Ford? On the face of it you could resell the Ford at the price you paid for it and seemingly suffer no loss. Whilst that is true, it is not the end of the story. The law says that you are entitled to the benefit you expected to receive if the contract had been properly performed. If you contract to buy a Porsche, you are entitled to damages for loss of bargain, being the difference in value between that and what you actually received.

It therefore makes sense for the parties to a contract to specify the precise benefits they expect from the deal. The contract should cover their requirements and provide for appropriate redress if the benefit is not received. But if the buyer is coy about the benefits and these could not reasonably be known to the seller, the courts will be reluctant to award the buyer any more in the way of damages than would have been contemplated by both parties at the outset. If you need something for a particular reason, it is worth saying so.

There is also the danger that, in the course of negotiations, the parties will lose sight of the original objectives and principal benefits of the deal. There is great advantage in writing them down clearly at the outset and checking them regularly against the point reached in negotiations. Allied with this is the concept of a 'rolling memorandum' setting out the points agreed in the negotiations as they progress. The memorandum will give an all-round view which can in turn be checked against the original statement of objectives and benefits to ensure that significant advantage has not been lost in some of the more material areas in order to achieve gains of less strategic or long-term importance. This process will also enable a faster and more reliable assessment to be made if there is, as so often, a renegotiation of the price.

Risk

Risk is, to some extent, the counterpart of both cost and benefit. If you do not receive what you ordered, what are you likely to lose? The filing cabinet issue is fairly straightforward, but what about the effects of failure of the computer contract or the hydro-electric dam? The failure of the computer company to make a visit or to mend a fault might be that the system crashes at a critical time, just as the failure of one vital component might cause a complete system to be useless for its intended purpose. Either case could cause a great loss and perhaps breach by the computer buyer of its obligations to a customer. The issue becomes even clearer when looking at the hydro-electric dam contract. The construction is as strong as its weakest link but there are massive power and property interests, and human life dependent on the dam working properly. In such cases, the risk factor may outweigh all others and will influence the entire process of selecting and agreeing terms with designers, engineers and contractors.

Contracts are not like a card game, and should not be a gamble. If you are planning a commitment that has a high potential downside, it pays to think at an early stage how that risk can be limited. Will the other parties agree to limit your liability to a certain figure (assuming that such a limitation does not fall foul of the law)? Could the risk be covered by insurance and, if so, on what terms? You may agree to lose some of the profit you might otherwise make in return for a sharing of the risk by the other contracting parties. Computer contracts are a classic breeding ground for problems of this kind. In the leading case of *St Albans City Council* v *ICL* (see p. 35) the early software was defective and a substantial loss was incurred by the council, which successfully sued ICL. Much has been written about this case. In contract planning terms the following issues are important:

- In computer contracts, as in many technical agreements, the specification is important. Unusually in the St Albans case the specification (in the invitation to tender issued by the council) was clear as to performance. ICL agreed to produce 'a system to cope with all statutory requirements for ... the community charge'. As such they undertook to supply not simply the goods but also the result. As seen in Chapter 3 this goes beyond the statutory requirements in relation to the use of reasonable skill and care in the supply of goods and services by undertaking to achieve a stated result. It directly increased risk for the seller and reduced it for the buyer.

- Beware, however, the 'kitchen sink' specification. The St Albans contract consisted of nine documents making up the specification. The possibility of inconsistency and confusion tends to increase in proportion to the degree of detail.
- In some respects the council won because it had issued the invitation to tender. If the sale had been negotiated on the seller's terms, it is likely that the specification would have related to functionality and description rather than result, which shows the advantage of being in the driving seat in the negotiations.
- The contract limited ICL's liability to £100,000 or the amount of the contract price, whichever was the less. The £100,000 bore no relation either to the contract price (c £1.3 million) or the possible loss. Following the principles referred to in Chapter 4 (exclusion clauses and unfair contract terms) the limitation was held unreasonable, thus exposing ICL to the full amount of the claim. Whilst it is unlikely that a blanket exclusion clause would have been regarded as enforceable any more than it would have been acceptable to St Albans, it might have been possible, following a careful risk analysis, to negotiate a clause limited to the type of liability, the cause of loss and the extent of loss. It is safer to define the obligation narrowly than to include a broad obligation with an exclusion or limitation clause.

Tolerance factor

Tall buildings are designed to move. If they did not, the tension in their construction would break them apart, either slowly or dramatically, when the stresses of their environment proved too strong for the rigidity of their framework. We can see expansion joints clearly on motorway bridges. In known earthquake zones buildings are now built to withstand minor tremors and to cause less destruction if they collapse. Yet businesses often seek to draft all-encompassing contracts with strict terms and time limits with little or no tolerance built in for the inevitable commercial strains. Both the circumstances and the people involved may also change. The person with whom you negotiated the deal and worked well with may suddenly leave and be replaced by someone else with no understanding of the background. Worse still, their agenda may be completely different.

The principle is illustrated by an actual case, although I will assume here that the business in question involved bakery products. Clients were selling their production business in order to concentrate on added-value distribution. They were at the same time entering into a distribution agreement with the buyer to distribute the same products into a particular market in which they were specialists. Quality, consistency, freshness and thus speed of delivery of the products were of the essence. In order to secure the sale of the production business the distributors had to agree not to compete in the production or purchase elsewhere of the same type of bakery products for an agreed period. The bakers insisted that the restrictions in the sale and distribution agreements were absolute in the restriction period, even if they themselves were unable to produce and deliver the right quality products on time.

The bakers no doubt started with good intentions but two things happened. First, those negotiating the deal had not clearly enrolled the bakery production manager into the agreement; second, the baker's own sales team succeeded in bringing in other business more quickly than was expected. The quality and reliability of the deliveries to the client started to suffer, but the baker refused to let the distributor go elsewhere for its supplies or, even temporarily, to produce the food itself. When customers started pulling out, something had to give. In the end both parties suffered through customer loss and legal costs because, however apparently justifiable, there was no tolerance allowed in the equation or subsequently against an outcome, even though that outcome had been predicted at the outset.

Making it work

Contracts rarely exist in isolation. Elementary economics tells us that the fulfilment of any demand may stimulate more demand. As shown earlier in this chapter, this effect should be anticipated from the outset. If we assume that the baker finds a new style of baking or a magic new ingredient which starts to sell superbly, the distributor will want exclusivity of that product, particularly if it has established the product in the first instance by effective marketing. For its part, the baker will want to protect the recipe and prevent the distributor from setting up its own bakery or obtaining equivalent, but cheaper, supplies from someone else who has not made the same investment. An ideal contract will accept that both principles are at work and set down clear objectives and time scales for achievement. Exclusivity should be avoided unless a clear business case can be made out which would not adequately be achieved in another way, for example by turnover or volume targets. Where exclusivity is appropriate, it can be regarded as a right which is contingent upon satisfactory ongoing performance of those benefiting from it.

At the same time there are limits as to what you can plan and provide for. You need to strike a balance between what is possible and what is practicable. It is not sensible to turn a Nelsonian blind eye to the future and ignore what lies ahead, but it is equally unrealistic to expect lawyers to cover all risk areas without a careful analysis of likely or possible outcomes and what should sensibly be covered in the agreement. The legal contract with automatic focus has not yet been invented.

Implementation

Implementation of a contract should start at the point where the outlines of a deal are agreed, and well before signing. Communication within an organization can make the difference between success and failure. Check implementation procedures so that each stage of the process is seen to be achievable in the way and in the time-scale anticipated. The following checklist is applicable:

● What are the delivery arrangements and is there available transport and storage capacity?

- What personnel follow-up is required?
- Are the information systems compatible?
- What else will be required in technology terms and what implications does this have?
- What other support will be necessary and will it be available?
- Are the financial formulae workable and can the accountants act on the basis of the information given in the agreement to produce any certificates which are required?

In larger transactions it may be helpful to pass on the principal procedures at an early stage to the managers who will be responsible for implementation and to request them to provide a schedule of action or requirements. These schedules can in turn be fed back into the ongoing negotiation process. Any procedural issues can be highlighted and action schedules adapted for consistency so that the documentation proceeds alongside and is compatible with the implementation planning. Whilst this means that time and attention must be given to matters of detail before the deal itself becomes certain, it ensures that practical issues are settled from the outset and that everything is ready to roll the moment the contract is signed.

Planning for the uncertain

Even the most clairvoyant of business people or suspicious lawyers are not able to predict certain issues in advance. An obvious example is the price of goods where there is a volatile commodity market. Long-term supply agreements are bedevilled by the problem of price. We have seen that, although an obligation might be implied on one party where it is necessary to make the contract effective, the courts will generally not imply a commercial term where the parties have simply left matters open, for example on price, quantity or delivery date. The exception is that the courts will enforce contracts where the parties have set up in advance a clear procedure or machinery to resolve the issue, maybe by means of reference to an agreed price index or third-party arbitrator or expert. A mere agreement to agree is likely to be unenforceable and may, as a result, make the whole contract ineffective.

Thus the temptation to omit the difficult clauses, or to provide for discussion and agreement later, should be stoutly resisted. These provisions often go to the root of the deal. The following questions may suggest a way to resolve the issue:

- Is there an acceptance test that could be devised to establish the position such as in the case of computers or technical equipment?
- With prices, is there an active market for the products in question?
- In a manufacturing agreement should the price increase in line with raw materials, labour and other overheads?
- Is there to be a maximum increase in any one year?
- Will increases be permitted at any time or only at certain times of the year?
- Are retrospective rebates appropriate, based on the volume of business conducted in the period?[1] (Retrospective price increases are unlikely to be viable for any buyer!)
- What about reductions in raw material costs, especially if these are at an historic high when the deal is negotiated? Is the rate of inflation relevant and, if so, which index might be used? How far is it safe to predict inflation in view of past volatility?

Summary

It is at this stage that the task of preparing the right contract may begin to look daunting. But the right contract is the right contract for the occasion, not the definitive draft for all occasions. The comprehensive document which is designed to cover all eventualities and fiercely protect its own corner is rarely agreed and more rarely signed. The definitive contract, despite the ingenuity of the best lawyers, does not exist because no two sets of circumstances are the same. It would be inappropriate to take the same precautions for a walk in the

---

[1] But beware anti-competitive discrimination (see Chapter 6).

park as a walk in space, and yet they are both excursions. What distinguishes them most is technical difficulty, importance and risk. Despite this, there is a tendency to prepare similar contracts to cover entirely dissimilar situations.

A sense of proportion and relevance is at the root of contract planning. If you asked a lawyer for an infallible contract for your spacecraft, you would never take off – no contract can cover everything that might go wrong. You must achieve a balance between action and protection and it is up to you, the person who knows the business, to decide what sort of document you want. More comprehensive documents are longer; longer in length, longer to prepare and longer to negotiate. Such documents may not be the most appropriate for the occasion, but you must decide at the outset as the mould is set by the first draft.

My own thesis goes one stage further. I suspect that in a typical legal document 90 per cent of the substance is in 10 per cent of the content. The extension to this is:

1   If you start with a relatively short document, each 1 per cent of protection that is built in above 90 per cent will double the length of the document.
2   You can never reach 100 per cent.

You should therefore emphasize what is important to make the contract reflect the obligations of the parties, what is needed to make it work and what should happen if it does not. When that foundation and load-bearing structure has been established, you can safely add the detail. The process of identifying subject, object, effect, costs, benefit, risk and the tolerance factor should all help to plan that foundation and structure for the relevant terrain. Points to consider include:

● What is the subject of the contract and is it clearly covered, e.g. by a detailed specification?
● What is the objective of the agreement, is it measurable and what are the conditions of achievement?
● What will be the effect of the contract and what new pressures might this produce?
● Have you worked out all the cost implications and covered them in the contract as far as possible?

- Have all assumptions been checked and recorded in the contract?
- What benefits do you hope to achieve and are they all covered by the contract?
- What are the risks and how are they dealt with? Are there exclusion or limitation clauses to be negotiated? Is suitable insurance cover in place?
- Has some tolerance been built in to the equation?
- Will the deal work in practice and have you done every-thing necessary to make it work as effectively as possible?
- What areas of uncertainty still exist and how far can they sensibly be covered?

This chapter relates to every other part of this book and should be regarded as overlaying the specific comments in all other chapters.

■ 14

Standard form contracts

Contracts come in all shapes and sizes but most businesses need a framework for day-to-day trading. Sales and orders must be processed with speed, accuracy and consistency. Standard contracts and standard conditions of business provide the answer in many cases and are now considered in more detail. Many aspects can make a serious difference to the advantage to be obtained. The emphasis in this chapter is on conditions of sale but, although the orientation will be different, the principles apply equally to conditions of purchase.

Preparing standard conditions of business

In preparing standard conditions, there is a tendency merely to plagiarize another company's terms. This may be an over-simplistic and inappropriate approach. An over-extensive process of drafting and redrafting should be avoided likewise. The best way forward in most cases is for the business to consider and record its policy and practice and then to instruct lawyers to incorporate those principles within a draft. Experience suggests that it is often quicker and more economical for your commercial lawyers to adapt their precedent documents to suit your needs than to spend time reviewing and amending your draft. The process should ensure that the terms and conditions, when implemented, match the philosophy of your organization. Otherwise there could be inconsistency between the theory of the standard terms and the practice followed in the business. This inconsistency in turn may spill over into the way that supplies are ordered and orders are processed with serious incompatibilities in the event of a dispute.

This principle extends to the question of risk. Each business should assess the likely areas of risk with the benefit of its own experience, resulting in better procedures and improved prospects of success if a dispute arises. The tolerance factor is also relevant. If the standard terms give no margin or impose unreasonable deadlines, there will be conflict because unreasonable terms will be rigorously enforced or inconsistency created because they are not followed up. To take an extreme view in written terms but apply leniency in practice may only confuse and alienate those customers who do take the trouble to read the small print, or cause uncertainty on the part of employees who have to operate the policy. The terms and conditions must reflect the practices of the business and those heading the purchasing or order-processing functions, including the directors, should be fully involved in the process.

Identifying the goods or services

In any contract for the sale and purchase of goods or services both supplier and buyer should know exactly what to expect. The order or sales confirmation documents should set out exactly what is ordered or supplied, which may range from the permitted bacteriological content of food products through to a clear analysis of what specific services are or are not covered in a contract for professional services. They may define precisely how particular products are to be packaged and labelled or even the precise type of pallet on which they are to be delivered, and the ownership of that pallet after delivery. Since the chances are that any dispute, other than one arising from the buyer's inability to pay, will arise from an unfulfilled expectation of the buyer, the clearer the buyer's requirements, the less likelihood there is of serious dispute.

Delivery and inspection

The delivery and inspection process will often require the buyer, within a reasonable time, to inspect what has been delivered and report back to the seller any apparent deficiencies. What is a reasonable time will depend on the circumstances, as will the ability of the buyer to detect whether the goods supplied differ from the earlier sample or from the quality identified in the order. With bulk goods a tolerance of plus or minus 10 per cent from the volume or weight originally ordered may be appropriate, which will affect not only the total price paid but also whether the buyer will have sufficient supplies to satisfy its requirements. It is also reasonable that the buyer should promptly notify the seller of any deficiency on inspection, but if the goods are intended for resale in their existing packaging, there is little likelihood that the buyer will discover that they are defective. That problem may arise when the goods are finally delivered to and used by the ultimate consumer. If they are defective, the business which sold to that consumer will doubtless have to repair or replace them and a claim for redress will be carried back up the supply chain. There is thus a fundamental difference between requiring inspection of products intended for immediate use and those intended for resale in their existing state and packaging. Different terms are applicable in each case.

Failure by the seller to supply on time may create even greater problems. The seller or supplier will want to state that delivery is not guaranteed by any particular date and that time is not of the essence of the contract, but the buyer must consider this carefully. With food products, for example, the time of delivery and the freshness of the product may be critical. If delivery of the product is delayed, even if it is safe to eat, it may be rejected by the retailer, ultimate supplier or consumer. Whilst some tolerance may be acceptable, a clear latest date for supply is likely to be essential. Other cases are not necessarily time-critical and it is for the buyer to let the seller know if timing is important. If, for example, a new computer system is required for a shop opening, the potential losses in delaying the shop opening could be substantial if the system is not installed and properly functioning in time. This relates to the level of risk allocated between the parties. If the buyer has insisted on a heavy discount, it may have to accept a greater risk. The seller should avoid giving way on both price and risk. The parties may also wish to negotiate a specific liquidated damages clause to quantify and limit the potential loss and both parties should consider corresponding terms in any contracts with their own suppliers and subpurchasers.

If the delivery date is of great importance, the buyer should stipulate that the time of delivery 'is of the essence'. This hallowed legal phrase means that a failure to deliver on time amounts to breach of a fundamental term such that the buyer could terminate the whole contract and/or claim damages if the delivery date is missed, even by a single day. A seller should agree such a clause only if certain of performing on time and should look out for it in a buyer's standard terms of purchase. Even a liquidated damages clause might be preferable.

Price and payment terms

Unilateral price increase clauses, which give no opportunity for the buyer to withdraw from the contract, are invalid in consumer sales and may be ineffective in business sales. However, certain circumstances justify a seller increasing the price. In that case a reasonable opportunity should be given to the buyer to terminate the contract, particularly if the increase exceeds a stated amount. Buyers should carefully monitor and act on any such notices where necessary. Delivery costs should be made clear at the time and customs duties and other taxes, packaging costs and insurance should also be considered. Buyers, on the other hand, will stipulate a fixed price in their purchase orders.

The date for payment is an important part of any well-drafted conditions of sale and should be brought clearly to the attention of the parties on the face of the contract document. Different industries tend to have different norms, ranging from 7 to 90 days or, in some cases, even longer. The terms should clearly state the date from which time periods run and where and how payment should be made. If payment is calculated as a number of days from invoice, sellers should deliver the invoice at the same time as the goods. The buyer, on the other hand, will want to check that the invoice is not dated prior to the date of delivery and, particularly in overseas cases, that a copy of the invoice is sent by fax. The terms should specify currency and may require payment direct to the seller's bank net of all bank charges. Take care with contracts that stipulate delivery of goods by instalments or where payments are required on account. The seller may wish to ensure that date for payment of the instalments or on account is of the essence of the contract. Buyers here should beware time-of-the-essence provisions for payment, unless they are completely certain of their ability to fulfil and there are foolproof reminder systems in place. (See the discussion on this point in relation to breach of contract, p. 232 *et seq.*)

Risk and insurance

Risk will pass at the same time as title to the goods unless the contract specifies otherwise. Most conditions of sale, however, specify that risk passes on delivery. The practical effect is that the buyer takes the risk of loss or damage to the goods after delivery and should insure them from the point of delivery. The contract should specify when delivery is deemed to occur as this is a classic area for dispute. Delivery may be deemed to be anything from the moment of departure from the seller's premises to the point of safe receipt in the buyer's premises. There is a range of options in between, especially in international sales, such as delivery to the port of lading in the seller's country, shipment from that port to the nearest port in the buyer's country and delivery from that port (possibly across further international boundaries) to the buyer's premises. These issues are inextricably tied to the provisions relating to price. Concepts such as FOB (free on board) and CIF (carriage, insurance and freight) have been commonly used over the years. To avoid misunderstanding the meaning of these similar phrases refer to the standard INCOTERMS – recognized international rules for the interpretation of trade terms published by the International Chamber of Commerce.[1] The seller should also check whether its insurance would still cover the position if the goods are destroyed and the buyer fails to pay.

Title and retention of title

The statutory provisions for deciding when title passes were considered in Chapter 3. The problem for sellers arises when the goods are delivered but not paid for, particularly if the buyer then becomes insolvent. Once it becomes clear that the buyer will not pay, the seller will want the goods back, if they are of any value. If title has passed, the seller has no right to the goods and stock is one of the first assets which an administrative receiver of an insolvent buyer will want to sell.

To counter these problems sellers will seek, in their conditions of sale, to retain title to the goods until payment has been made by the buyer. It is best that the clause not only retains title to the goods covered by the particular outstanding invoice but also until all payments due by the buyer to the seller have been made – the so-called 'all monies' or 'running account' clause. In both cases if the buyer resells the goods to an innocent third party the retention of title will cease to apply. In limited circumstances the clause could preserve the title to the original goods where they are mixed with other products, although this right would be lost if the goods lost their identity and could not be recovered in their original form.

A term retaining title to goods covered by specific invoices will generally be upheld by the courts, but its use does require

[1] Publication number 460 ISBN 92-842-0087-3, ICC PUBLISHING S.A., International Chamber of Commerce, The World Business Organisation, 38 Cours Albert 1er, 75008 Paris.

a seller to identify particular goods to particular invoices. For this reason a running account clause may be preferable and should be more far reaching, although in some cases it could be more difficult to enforce. To support the power of enforcement retention clauses should also include:

- an obligation on the buyer to keep the goods in their original packaging and clearly marked as the seller's until payment or resale, and
- permission for the seller or its agents to have access to the buyer's premises on demand to recover the goods at any time after payment becomes overdue or notice of insolvency is received.

A seller faced with the insolvency of a buyer who has not paid for goods should lose no time in notifying the administrative receiver or liquidator of the defaulting company and pressing home the retention of title clause. Such rights are not generally available against an administrator, who has greater statutory protection from creditors. Take care in regard to VAT. Customs and Excise may take the view that if the goods are recovered, there can be no VAT reclaim by the seller on the bad debt. They may use this argument even if the goods are not recovered but there is a right to do so. A retention of title clause should therefore be used only if recovery of the goods would be of some material value to the seller. It is unlikely, for example, to be of much use in the case of fresh food or other perishable products.

Exclusion or limitation clauses

Chapter 4 established that exclusion or limitation clauses must be drafted very carefully and tailored to the particular circumstances. Standard terms must also comply with the reasonableness test (except in the case of international sales) and may not exclude certain liabilities. In commercial agreements the parties should specifically negotiate and agree exclusion or limitation provisions to increase the prospects of their enforceability from the point of view of the unfair contract terms tests.

Buyers need to take special care with such clauses which are, for the same reason, unlikely to appear in any buyer's standard conditions of purchase.

Bringing the terms into the contract

Once a contract has been created any amendment will be ineffective unless agreed by all parties. Conditions of sale must be spelled out before the contract is finalized. In technical terms they must be 'incorporated' into the contract. Reverting to the example of the contract between Morris and Williams (Chapter 1, p. 13), if Morris had written to Williams (rather than the other way round), Morris may well have added the sentence: 'The cabinets will be supplied on our standard conditions of sale, a copy of which is enclosed for your reference.' Such standard conditions should be introduced at the earliest opportunity and referred to clearly in all relevant correspondence.

In the event of a buyer's insolvency, in order to consider a claim a receiver will wish to know how and when the relevant condition was incorporated in the contract for sale of the products. The seller will therefore need very clear records of what conditions were in force at any one time and how they were notified to the buyer. For this reason, when sellers first adopt or later change their conditions of sale, they would do well to submit copies to all customers and further copies with all estimates and quotations. With written quotations standard conditions may be printed on the reverse or sent in full at the same time as the estimate/quotation. If, however, orders are generally taken by telephone and are legally effective on order, the terms and conditions must be notified to potential buyers beforehand. Printing standard conditions on sales order confirmation notes or invoices will not suffice, since the contract will come into being before the invoice is submitted.

Course of dealings

There is one exception to this last general principle. Where there is a regular course of dealings between the same parties and the parties accept, expressly or by implication, that their dealings should be governed by terms and conditions used previously, those terms may be regarded as incorporated in the contract. Whilst it is unwise for sellers to rely on this fact, buyers should take note that if sellers do, for example, include conditions of sale on the reverse of their invoices and also refer to the existence of standard terms and conditions on paper-work circulated before the contract is made, those conditions may well form part of the contract.

The battle of the forms

What if the seller sends off a set of conditions of sale and the buyer responds with standard conditions of purchase? From the same example, what would be the position if Mary Morris had handed Walter Williams a set of the Morris terms and con-ditions when they met and Williams had responded with his letter and a set of the Williams standard terms? The terms will probably differ in several respects. The answer is to follow through the principles set out in Chapter 1 to find the point at which the contract is created. An acceptance on different terms destroys the original offer and creates a counter-offer. If Morris and Williams meet, Morris passes to Williams a copy of the Morris standard terms and they then agree products, price, delivery and payment dates, a contract will be created on those terms, including the Morris terms and conditions. If, however, Mary Morris states her terms and Walter Williams says that he will consider them, there will be no contract unless and until Williams accepts on the terms proposed. If his acceptance introduces new terms, it destroys the Morris offer and creates a counter-offer by Williams, which it is up to Morris to accept or reject. If there is no further correspondence and Morris de-livers the goods, there will be deemed to be an acceptance of the Williams counter-offer by Morris' conduct and the Williams terms will apply. If Morris replies, noting the Williams offer but sending a new quotation form for Williams to counter-sign incorporating the Morris terms, this will be a further counter-offer which Williams could accept by signature. The Morris terms then apply.

A clause stating that the conditions of one party will prevail over those of the other will be ineffective, since the dealings must be analysed to find out the precise point offer and acceptance occurs. What matters, in the battle of the forms, is 'who fired the last shot', so be vigilant and determined not to be outflanked!

Summary

Probably more business contracts are entered into on standard forms than any other basis, yet they are frequently regarded as the Cinderella of the business. If you take time to prepare – and regularly review – the terms and conditions and their relevance to the particular business and its methods it will be repaid many times over in avoiding disputes or being able to solve them rapidly and effectively. Consequently your sales and purchasing teams must understand the process and act consistently with your own terms of business, particularly so that your terms are brought into the contract rather than those of the other party. They must also be able to see where the two might differ and what issues would then arise. Consider the following points:

- The existence of the standard terms must be clearly indicated, incorporated into the contract and tie in with the sale or order details on the front of the form or contained in other documents.
- When drafting sale terms, check that the goods or services and the delivery and (if applicable) installation provisions are sufficiently identified to establish that the contract has been properly performed.
- If drafting purchase conditions, tie them in with a clear description of the specification of the goods and the performance criteria in terms which can be tested in practice. The payment obligations can then be linked, if necessary, to acceptance tests.
- There must be clear provisions for delivery, inspection, price, payment, risk and title to the goods.

- Do not override your carefully drafted standard terms of business by misrepresentations of your products or services.
- Whose terms apply may also depend on the custom and practice of the industry and on the buying or selling power of the businesses concerned.
- Unusual term should be drawn to the attention of the other party. Non-standard situations or high risk/high liability areas require specifically negotiated terms.
- Consider and provide for the buyer failing to collect or accept delivery.
- Consider the standard or boilerplate provisions (see Chapter 15).
- Clear your terms, conditions and procedures with your insurers to check that your cover is not jeopardized.
- Check those contracts which set out various options as to liability/insurance cover and their cost/risk implications. For example, certain car rental agreements charge a low basic hire but the hirer is fully responsible for all loss or damage. Cover for various risks may then be purchased on a 'menu' basis.
- Make sure that you fire the last shot in the battle of the forms.

(See also Chapters 1, 3, 4, 5, 11, 13 and 15.)

■ 15

Boilerplate clauses

There are some general clauses which are not covered elsewhere in this book which are typically included in business contracts. They are often collectively referred to as 'boilerplate' clauses. Although the word suggests something mundane, the function of a boilerplate is to hold the framework together, and they should be regarded as an integral part of the contract construction and given due care and consideration.

Preliminary clauses or recitals

Lawyers can bemuse their clients by referring to recitals in the middle of a discussion about contracts. The reference to a recital should be taken as an invitation not to a musical interlude but to consider the paragraphs at the start of a contract which explain or recite what has happened so far. They may also set out the broad intentions of the parties when entering into the agreement. Recitals are intended to be descriptive, not to set out express obligations or terms which are still to be fulfilled.

Courts look to recitals to give an indication of the background to the agreement and what the parties were hoping to resolve in the written terms. They therefore must be drafted with care so that they do not conflict with any of the later operative terms. In short form contracts, preliminary clauses (rather than pure recitals) may also be used to set out the main definitions. Consider the following example (which assumes supplier and distributor have already been defined):

> The Supplier has agreed to appoint the Distributor its exclusive distributor for multi-drawer upright filing cabinets ('Products') for resale to office furniture and supplies wholesalers and retailers ('Customers') in England and Wales ('Territory') on the terms set out in this agreement.

This clause is more than a recital. It sets out the main thrust of the agreement and introduces the main definitions which are to be used. It also suggests some of the clauses which will follow, for example restrictions against the distributor operating outside the agreed territory and customer market.

Term and notice to terminate

One of the central issues in any contract, other than for a single transaction, is how long should it remain in force and what factors might bring it to an end within that period. Consider the following general factors:

- If there is a specific project, how long will it take to reach a conclusion?
- If the arrangement is in progress, what would be the shortest and the longest period during which it should remain in force?
- Should there be separate time periods, such as a primary and secondary term and, if so, what notice or other step, if any, will be required to continue or terminate at the end of each of those periods?

- Should either or both parties have the right to renew the agreement and, if so, can the terms of renewal be decided now or is it practical to include reference to arbitration?
- Are there any conditions, such as target levels of turnover, which must be satisfied either for the arrangement to come fully into effect or for it to remain in force?
- What is the interaction between the period of the agreement and the restrictions, such as exclusivity, to be contained in it?
- What rights should any of the parties have to terminate the agreement, other than on default by another party, before the end of the term or any specific period within the term?
- Should any party in breach be given the opportunity to remedy the breach before a termination notice can be served upon them?
- If so, what about persistent defaults?
- Will a change of control entitle the other party to terminate?
- Will there be automatic termination on insolvency and how will insolvency be defined (see p. 244)?

Many commercial agreements will have a fixed initial term and will then run on indefinitely unless and until terminated by one of the parties by written notice to the other. The notice period will be anything from three to 12 months. Consider this period carefully as it may be necessary to wind down the whole relationship within the notice period, which may mean allowing time to complete current work in progress and sell off stock in hand. If there is insufficient notice, the party giving notice will be liable for the loss caused to the other for the missing period.

Some contracts require good faith negotiations to take place within a specific period before a fixed termination date. Such a provision may be advantageous in management terms, since it sets a timescale for discussion against a clear background. Whilst to date an obligation to negotiate in good faith would not be binding under English law, we are beginning to see a change in judicial approach and such clauses are likely to play an increasingly familiar role in the interpretation of business contracts in the future. They are already legally binding in some other jurisdictions.

Should there be a specific compensation or liquidated damages clause? The compensation or indemnity provision of the Commercial Agents (Council Directive) Regulations (see Chapter 8) is an example of a statutory provision. The regulations came into force because the European Commission recognized the one-sided nature of many agency relationships and the need to build in a common basis between different member states of the Union. Such provisions are rarely negotiated in business agreements because the parties are reluctant to contemplate breach or termination except as a remote 'what if' possibility. This is exactly why such possibilities should be anticipated and the question of compensation relates directly to the whole issue of risk. The lack of a clearly set out compensation mechanism may well increase the risk.

Interpretation clauses

There is little more disheartening, when dealing with a complex legal document, than being faced immediately with a mass of interpretation clauses. By the time you have read them all you find you are at page eight and have only just reached clause one. For this reason, consider whether to put detailed definition clauses in the first schedule at the back of the agreement, rather than at the front as some form of barrier to the main text.

Nevertheless interpretation clauses can be some of the most useful and important in the document. They define words or terms which are used in several places and set down some rules of interpretation. For example, it is useful to refer simply to 'person', and define this as including reference to a firm, unincorporated association or company, without repeating these alternatives at each stage. The same applies to singular and plural and male and female (or vice versa). Words or phrases defined in many contracts include confidential information, control (very relevant in company transactions), group (of companies), and term (i.e. period of the agreement). In agency, distribution and similar contracts the definition of 'products' may be one of the most important terms of the agreement. Provisions for accounts, turnover and profits will also need considerable scrutiny by both accountants and lawyers.

The advantage of definitions is to avoid repetition of the same words, which can have a brain-deadening effect. It may also be helpful to take out of the body of a clause a concept which would disturb the flow of the wording and which would be better considered on its own. The advantage of putting the definitions in a schedule is that you can find them easily. Do not include definitions for their own sake.

Confidentiality

The subject of confidentiality is considered in more detail in Chapter 6, but there are some basic questions which are applicable here. How relevant is confidentiality? How is the confidential material to be circulated? What announcements are to be made about the deal covered by the contract and by whom? If confidentiality is important, look again at the circumstances and see whether you are adequately covered or, if you are on the receiving end, over-protected. These questions might also trigger issues of copyright or patents or other intellectual property rights and the protection of employees who could be approached by the other contracting parties to join them.

Notices

Most contracts specify that notices must be in writing and how they should be served. It is standard practice to require first-class post or personal delivery with some evidence of posting or delivery in case due service is ever questioned. Fax is also commonly included as an acceptable means of serving notices, although some clauses require a confirmatory copy by post. Where there is reference to telex or fax, make sure that there is a working receiver and that messages are retrieved from it. Failing to pick up and deal with a message containing a formal notice under the terms of a contract can have serious consequences. It may be helpful if notices are addressed to a specific person (by name or function) with a copy to that party's solicitors as an additional safeguard and prompt to action. Remember to include details of the other parties to contracts in your lists of those to be notified if your business moves, otherwise you might lose valuable time in responding to an important notice.

Allow adequate time for service abroad. It is useful to specify and define delivery after a certain number of 'working' days in the country of receipt or service during 'business hours' in that country or place. Many countries require service by registered air mail with return receipt and do not recognize the first-class post concept. It may also be an advantage for the contract expressly to permit service of any legal proceedings on a representative in the home country, thus avoiding complex procedures and delays.

Force majeure

'Force majeure' is a phrase from the French Napoleonic code which has so far escaped an up-to-date English translation, other than 'act of God', and which has no specific definition under English law. The Concise Oxford Dictionary (9th edition) suggests: 'an unforeseeable course of events excusing a person from the fulfilment of a contract'. Force here is used to mean a power beyond the control of the parties, and the object of a force majeure clause is to prevent one (or more) of the parties from being in breach of contract simply because of events outside their control. English law gives relief only if the contract becomes impossible to perform. A simple force majeure clause might read:

> Neither party is liable to the other for failure to perform any obligation under this agreement if and so long as the failure is caused by any factor outside the reasonable control of that party.

Many clauses go into more detail and cover such disparate events as war, acts of terrorism, riot and civil disturbance, fire, explosion, flood, theft (of goods), malicious damage, strike and new acts or regulations of government. There are various optional extras such as fog or bad weather (to be used carefully since such excuses may easily be invoked and are difficult to define), inability to obtain fuel, power or even raw materials, malfunction or breakdown of machinery and denial of export or other essential licences. Reference to 'acts of God' is common, although the interpretation of this clause by terrestrial courts, of whatever country, could give rise to other problems.

These events should all have in common the facts that they are not expected to happen and are beyond the reasonable control of the party seeking the protection of the clause. A strike caused recklessly by an intransigent employer or an equipment breakdown resulting from poor maintenance should not give rise to protection. As part of the planning process it is sensible to consider what force majeure events should be contemplated by the parties, what the effect of those events would be and who should bear the risk. In appropriate cases, such as an order for products where time is critical, the contract should provide for termination if the force majeure continues beyond a suitable specified period.

Entire agreement and no variation clauses

An 'entire agreement' clause aims to establish that the parties may rely only on the written terms in the contract and that they waive or give up any claims to anything which preceded it and confirm that they are not relying on any pre-contract representations. Such clauses are common but will be closely scrutinized by the court. They may also be adjudged as another form of exclusion clause to be read subject to the unfair contract terms legislation, especially where the contract is in standard form. Take care with any existing agreement term which is not intended to be subsumed in the new contract.

Variations of a contract can also give rise to problems. If the contract says one thing but the parties habitually do something else, does this amount to a variation? The variation clause will normally set out that the agreement may only be varied in writing duly signed as an agreement or deed in the same way as the original agreement. In practice, many agreements are varied by letter, and it will generally suffice for the clause to permit the contract to be varied in writing signed by a duly authorized director or representative of each of the parties. These general variation clauses are very different in their nature from a provision in the contract which enables one of the parties to vary what is to be produced or delivered under the contract, for example:

> Our policy is one of continuous improvement and we reserve the right to change the detailed specification of our products at any time without prior notice.

A buyer faced with this sort of clause, quite apart from any statutory rights, would do well to add qualifying words to temper the extent of the seller's power. The wording will depend on the circumstances, but could be as follows:

> ... but so that no such change will affect the basic form, fit, function, [colour], performance or key features of the products or their suitability for the purpose for which the buyer is acquiring them as previously notified to the seller.

Counterparts

Where there are several parties to an agreement, the various parties can sign at separate locations and create a contract by having separate copies – or counterparts – signed by only one of the parties. This works perfectly well provided that each of the parties ultimately signs at least one counterpart. Obviously all copies must be identical apart from the signatures and it is sensible to include a clause such as:

> This agreement may be signed [or executed as a deed] in any number of counterparts, each of which is deemed to be an original, but all of which together constitute a single agreement.

Other typical boilerplate clauses

- *No agency, partnership or joint venture*   Clarification that the parties do not intend the agreement to be regarded as any of these particular legal relationships. It is no more than a statement of intention and will not prevent a true agency or partnership agreement from being construed as such by the courts if a dispute arises.

- *Further assurance*   There may be other documents to be signed or help to be given to enable the parties to perform their obligations or receive their full entitlements under the contract. A simple clause might read: 'Each party will if and when called upon by the other execute any further documents or take such action as may be reasonably required to give full effect to the provisions of this agreement'. Note that this is not a permission to renegotiate the contract and seek to add terms that might have been included but were not!

- *Illegality and severance*   Illegal contract provisions are liable to be held to 'taint' the whole contract so badly that the entire agreement will fail. Minor offending provisions, for example, relating to an over-zealous exclusion clause or restrictive covenant, may be settled by the so-called 'blue pencil' approach. Some clauses in international contracts go further and provide for the parties to negotiate in good faith the nearest alternative clause which would be valid. Such a provision has questionable effect in English law.

- *No waiver*   A no waiver clause can be a useful way (for both parties) of making the point that failure or delay by one party to enforce rights under the contract against another will not automatically release those rights. A basic example would be: 'No party will be prevented by reason of delay or forbearance from subsequently enforcing any provision of this agreement'.

- *Non-merger*   Obligations in the agreement will remain in force notwithstanding completion of the agreement.

Summary

Boilerplate clauses are relevant to all contracts and operate as a reminder of some of the principles covered in more detail elsewhere in this book. For that reason no cross-references are given here. Points to consider include:

- Is the term of the agreement expressed clearly together with the circumstances and manner in which it can be terminated? (See also Chapter 19.)
- Are the key words and phrases defined in a way that would be intelligible to a judge with no prior knowledge of the circumstances?
- Are there suitable confidentiality provisions? (See also Chapter 6.)
- Is there clear notice procedure?
- Is force majeure appropriately covered?
- Should there be entire agreement and no variation clauses?
- Do you want counterpart agreements?
- Is there anything which requires a further assurance clause?
- Is there an electronic contract or international dimension? (See Chapter 16.)

■ 16

New technology and the international dimension

Methods of communication have changed radically in recent years. As they continue to develop, the use of technology in business is likely to increase exponentially. While it is to be hoped that humans will not, as a result, lose the power of speech and the ability to communicate face to face, there is no doubt that the electronic age will revolutionize the way business is done as fundamentally as the telephone has in the past. Since electronic communication often takes place across international boundaries, questions soon arise as to which legal régime might apply. These cross-border issues are considered in a later part of the chapter.

Electronic contracts

Four main forms of electronic communication, plus video conferencing, currently apply in relation to forming business contracts. These can be summarized in turn.

Fax

Fax is now an indispensable business tool and is also in regular domestic use. It links two or more compatible systems via a communication interface. The information typed or processed into one system is transferred by telephone (or cable) to the other system. Although generally thought of as a document-based system, the fax message can, depending on its hardware, either be processed from paper to paper or direct from one screen to another, or a mixture of the two, but will be in human readable form (as opposed to machine readable form) on screen or paper.

E-mail

E-mail is normally typed out on one screen and then transferred electronically to another, where it can, if appropriate, be printed out. The main difference from fax is that, although e-mail can be very fast, it does not necessarily go directly from one sender to one receiver. Most e-mail is either within an internal system, where it is unlikely to form part of the contract creation mechanism (although this may change as more key relationships form within an intranet system), or via a third-party internet service provider (ISP), of which Compu-Serve and Demon are examples. In effect the ISP can be likened to the post office, taking over the process of delivery of the message from sender to receiver.

The worldwide web

The worldwide web is an extension of e-mail. It permits messages to be set up and available to all who have access to the web. The significant difference is that there is a specified sender but an unspecified receiver. Further, the sender may be known in terms of name but not necessarily in terms of location and pedigree. Thus there is considerable scope for confusion of identity issues and corresponding questions of creditworthiness (see Chapter 2 and elsewhere within this book).

Electronic data interchange (EDI)

EDI, in many respects a further extension of the process, provides a means of transferring data which is confidential and where accuracy is essential. Banks, for example, rely increasingly on EDI to effect their international transactions. EDI is really beyond the scope of this book, although the principles mentioned here apply equally well, subject to additional protection being built into EDI systems against fraud, hacking and viruses. Because of the significance of the issues, we can expect greater regulation in this area. In the meantime the European Union has published a model EDI agreement and there is also, as from 1996, a UN Commission on International Trade Law (Uncitral) model law available on EDI and related means of communication.

Video conferencing

Video conferencing is another technological revolution which is starting to impact on business. By adding vision to sound, the quality of communication, listening and decision making is enhanced. There is, in effect, direct contact in the same way as if the parties were all present in the same room – with face-to-face discussion and, where necessary, the parties can see one another sign. The contract is made there and then by the parties agreeing that the documents, as signed, are released to one another in much the same way as now happens with most conveyancing exchanges of contract. The signed documents are then entrusted to the lawyers for delivery to one another.

Implications for businesses

The new technology affects the way in which business contracts are created. Consider the following questions:

- What constitutes an electronic offer?
- When and how is an electronic offer accepted?
- Can an electronic contract be made in writing?

- Is it possible to sign an electronic contract?
- Which law governs an electronic contract made across national borders?

The electronic offer

Since an offer, except for certain consumer contracts, can be made orally or in writing, it can also be made electronically. Always check that the offer has been made and received in complete form. It could refer to conditions available on another document or file which may be accessed, or even to conditions set out on a website.

Electronic acceptance

Acceptance of an electronic offer is more complex, partly because of different national rules. Whilst in England it is sufficient to post a letter of acceptance in a letterbox or to hand it in at the post office, many other jurisdictions require the acceptance to be delivered to the person making the offer. This is an important factor when deciding whose terms and conditions apply to the transaction and also whether a withdrawal of the offer was received by the person accepting it before or after that person properly communicated acceptance. Communication by fax is like the telephone. The connection is direct and the message is usually received at the same time as it is delivered, subject to delay for transmission and printing time on longer messages.

Most of the issues surrounding electronic communication have yet to be considered by the courts and our conclusions are based on the limited cases that have been reported, the experience of other countries and professional opinion on the subject. Acceptance of a fax does not appear to depend on anyone picking up the fax sheet from the fax basket or going to the screen to check for faxes. The message would seem to be received as surely as if the letter had landed on the mat, even if the intended recipient had gone on holiday or the letter had been dismembered by the dog. It is important that the sender keeps the transmission slip as a record of sending the fax.

E-mail via an ISP, on the other hand, is more like posting a letter – the first stage is to entrust the message to the service provider who will then deliver it. We do not yet know whether the English courts will regard transmission to the ISP as equivalent to posting in a letterbox. If they do, how will that square with the principle adopted elsewhere, and indeed the general principle under English law to which the postal rule is a specific exception, that acceptance is not communicated until it has been received by the other party? The question of which law applies may then become all important.

Electronic contracts as written contracts

The Interpretation Act 1978 defines 'writing' with reference to 'representing or reproducing words in a visible form' and current opinion seems to be that digital information is not a visible form, only a means to produce a visible form. Although there are exceptions in relation to copyright – the Copyright, Designs and Patents Act 1988 permits courts to interpret 'writing' as including 'any form of notation or code' regardless of how it was recorded – it seems unlikely that communication in electronic form can be classified as writing.

The following considerations apply:

- Is writing necessary for the contract you wish to enter into?
- If so, must the contract be made in writing?
- Or does the contract merely need to be evidenced in writing?

The second and third questions need further analysis. In the case of a contract which must be *made* in writing, it is not sufficient for the information to be displayed on screen, whereas it would be sufficient if the contract need only be *evidenced* in writing since, at the moment that the words appear, the requirement for a visible form of words will be satisfied. The difference may seem academic, but the same method of communication may make a guarantee (which needs only to be *evidenced* in writing) effective and an agreement for the sale of land (which must be *made* in writing) ineffective.

Electronic signatures

The main function of a signature is to authenticate the identity of the person and their commitment to a document in a particular form. Again there is a distinction here between those documents which must be 'signed' and those where signature is used as authentication but there is no statutory requirement for it. In the former case, an actual signature may be necessary, even if it is reproduced electronically, for example by fax, where it is scanned into the system beforehand and reproduced for specific purposes or by some form of electronic pen.

In *Standard Bank London Ltd* v *Bank of Tokyo Ltd* 1995, the courts accepted that where there is an established system of reliance on electronic signatures, in this case in the form of a secret electronic code, it would be accepted as sufficient authentication of the transaction where there was no technical requirement for signature. The chosen code can vary according to the extent of security and confidentiality required. The codes may be personal to individuals or personal to the particular computer from which they are sent. Because the authentication of a communication will be on behalf of an organization, and the use of the code will generally be restricted to persons having the authority to authenticate, the system has an element of built-in security for those receiving authenticated messages. It seems that the greatest challenges in relation to electronic communication lie with those originating them. Good internal practices will therefore become of paramount importance.

Internet *sans frontières*

The Internet was established as an open system and transmissions may go through a variety of routes with different levels of security. Nevertheless, in communicating by the Internet or the web you will be entering legal territory just as surely as in any other form of business exchange. Moreover, you may be doing so across national borders and, as with GSM mobile phones, you may not even know where the other party will be receiving the message. It may not be obvious at the time to consider such matters as choice of law and jurisdiction clauses, but remember that, where the contract does not make the choice, the relevant law will probably be that of the country where the contract is to be performed which raises issues of where any dispute will be heard. These subjects are dealt with in more detail later in this chapter. Suffice it to say here that, especially with e-mail and the web, it is much easier to become involved in a binding legal commitment with one or more businesses in different jurisdictions. Complex conflicts of law issues may arise and the extent of your benefits, obligations and risks may become much more difficult to establish. It is better to address these issues in the contract itself.

Practical pointers

Here are some suggestions on how to use electronic business contracts to your advantage:

- Treat e-mail with the same respect as any other form of written communication – get the message right in the first place and consider who may read it and who may rely on it. (Remember too that the defamation laws apply!)
- Remember that, if there is a dispute, electronic messages are required to be produced as evidence in much the same way as any other communication – don't use e-mail where you don't want to keep it; keep all messages either electronically or in printed version as they may have to be 'discovered' in litigation. (Reconstituting e-mails can be an expensive task.)
- Keep fax transmission slips with copies of the faxes.
- Keep tight control of internal authentication mechanisms.
- Coded authentication (through encryption techniques) can improve security in the right situations, but if you are using EDI ensure that the electronic systems are compatible.
- Draft the contract so as to clarify the régime that is suitable for the circumstances and to reduce or avoid doubt on what would be due notice of acceptance, authentication or signature – this may be as simple as saying that acceptance

may be given by any of certain methods, which are then specified, and when the acceptance is deemed effective.

- If you believe in reducing paperwork, see where and how that can be achieved whilst retaining sufficient separate electronic records to ensure that legal requirements or practical levels of protection will be met.
- Remember that what is legal in the country where the web message originates may be illegal in the country where it is received (almost anywhere). If appropriate, add a clear statement that the communication is intended only for those in stated countries where you know that the product or service and the method of marketing are legal.
- Outside the UK documents are sometimes required to be authenticated by a notary. This traditional figure in cyberspace terms is called a trusted third party (TTP) whose role is to verify identity, authority and encryption powers and to give the equivalent of the Hague Convention apostille or seal of approval.
- Use technology as another business tool rather than as something remote and mysterious to which different laws apply. There may be specific laws on these subjects in future, but in the meantime look out for further developments and their practical implications.

Choice of law and jurisdiction clauses

International issues are of growing importance and the law and practice in this area is set to change rapidly. This section covers some general propositions. The first is to be aware of the potentially international nature of your agreement. The effect of your goods being sold on abroad or your buyer having a head office in another country may be enough for international law to apply. Where the other party is based outside England and Wales, even the issue of how and when the contract is formed may be affected (as seen in the previous section).

The main considerations, all of which interact with one another, are:

- Which law should apply to the contract?
- Which country's courts should have jurisdiction over disputes?
- How should disputes be dealt with?

Choice of law

The choice of law is closely interrelated with the choice of jurisdiction:

- The English courts will generally give effect to the parties' express choice of law under the contract.
- Under the Rome Convention, to which the UK is a party, the courts of the EU states will, subject to certain exceptions mentioned below, apply the parties' own choice of law, even if there is no other link with the country in question.
- The parties' own choice of law may be overridden to the extent that there are rights under local law which give greater protection to a resident of that country.
- Other questions, such as the way in which the contract is to be carried out in a country and the capacity of the parties resident in that country to enter into it, may also fall to be decided in accordance with local law.
- The courts of one country may decline to accept the choice of law of another country where the contract is wholly connected with another legal system so that proper interpretation of the contract under other laws would be entirely inappropriate.
- A suitable clause will state that the contract is to be governed or interpreted under the stated law or that the stated law is to apply to the agreement. You could consider matching the language of the contract with the applicable law, but if there are to be versions in different languages, the contract should state which language is to prevail.
- English law is the law of England and Wales. Scotland and Northern Ireland have their own laws which, whilst similar in many respects, may in others be significantly different from English law. These differences should

reduce over time as the harmonization of the European legal process continues.

The contract will generally be drawn up in the country of the party selling the goods, establishing the network or granting the rights, where those concerned will be more familiar with their own law. Where there is an international context, some issues may nevertheless fall to be considered under one law and some under another.

It is always advisable to take early opinion from commercial lawyers of the other country on the relevant implications of local law. If the parties do not make their own choice of law in the contract, the Rome Convention states that it will be the law of the country with which the contract has the closest connection. This in turn will often be the country where the contract is to be performed, which could mean that different countries' laws would apply where the obligations of the parties are to be performed in several member states.

Consider at the outset the relevant factors, including:

● What is the extent of the international aspect and which countries might be involved?
● Is the contract one of a series where consistency is important?
● What parts of the contract have to be performed where?
● Are the other parties likely to accept your choice of law?
● Where do you want to enforce the contract and how easy will it be to do so?
● Should you seek local legal advice and, if so, when?
● Where will you be better protected?

Jurisdiction clauses

Jurisdiction clauses set out which courts should deal with enforcement of the contract and any disputes that arise. In England, the relevant court will normally be the High Court of England and Wales. Many other countries have federal constitutions and it is best, for the sake of certainty, to specify the state or city of the court as well as the country. Where there is exclusive jurisdiction, only the courts of the named country may deal with any disputes. If jurisdiction is non-exclusive the courts of a named country may deal with a dispute but other courts are not precluded from doing so.

If, therefore, an English supplier appoints a French distributor, the contract may provide for English law to apply and for the courts of England to have non-exclusive jurisdiction. The French distributor could not then object to the supplier going to the English courts for redress, but the supplier could, if it wished, go direct to the French courts for an order directing the French distributor to pay or to cease selling competing goods. Some courts nevertheless take the view, especially in EU or EEA states, that reference to non-exclusive jurisdiction simply puts the question back to the default rules. What if the French distributor goes to the French courts before the English supplier takes action in the English courts? Where jurisdiction is non-exclusive, the courts of a country 'first seised' (that is, first dealing with the case) will generally have the right to continue with the case and any other country's courts should decline involvement.

If the contract does not stipulate the forum, complex rules of private international law may apply. In the European Union the principles are:

- A defendant is generally to be sued in the courts of the country in which that person is domiciled – for the most part, the country where they normally live.
- In disputes relating to land and the validity of trade marks, patents and other registrable IP rights, the courts of the country in which those rights are held must have jurisdiction. In relation to the supply of goods and services and consumer loans, the consumer has the option to be sued in their own country or that of the other party (as their rights might be greater there). In most other cases the parties can agree on the jurisdiction or forum in which the case is to be heard.
- A judgment in one EU member state is to be recognized in all others provided that it is not against the public policy or inconsistent with the existing law of that country. Judgment is then enforced in the same way as any other judgment in the country where enforcement is required.

When deciding which court or forum to choose, consider the speed, predictability and cost of the alternatives available. If you find that jurisdiction clauses result in sudden bouts of xenophobia, consider another approach. This reflects the fact that each party wants to make it as difficult as possible for the other party to sue them. Accordingly each accepts that any proceedings it brings must be in the courts of the other party. The costs and logistical difficulties of bringing such a case are increased but the home player is comforted by knowing that the issue is going to be serious if the away team is prepared to travel to take action. It also means that neither of the parties can be forced to use foreign courts except to enforce its own rights. This 'stand-off' approach is not ideal but may avoid a dispute before the contract is even signed. Where you would need to enforce the contract in the other country, it may be best to accept that the courts of that country, and possibly also its laws, will have jurisdiction in order to avoid lengthy delays in legal proceedings.

Arbitration and alternative dispute resolution

Arbitration can be viewed as an alternative to litigation or as an addition to it. Some cases are particularly suitable for arbitration, such as the decision of a specialist in a matter of valuation of products or a business or shares in a company. The parties must decide what they want – someone who will listen to and weigh up all the arguments on all sides in a judicial way before arriving at a conclusion based on the evidence supplied, or someone who is an expert in the field in question who can weigh up the evidence in the light of their own knowledge and experience and arrive at their own professional decision? In the former case they should choose an arbitrator who should act as such, but in the latter they should choose an expert.

Arbitrator or expert?

Arbitrators must act in a balanced way and follow established principles before reaching judgment. It is difficult to appeal against their decisions except where they have worked on an incorrect understanding of the law. Experts, on the other hand, can decide what evidence to receive and how far to listen to arguments from the parties before making a decision. Their decisions can normally only be challenged if there is a 'manifest error' (which must be something very wide of the mark) or the expert is found to be acting fraudulently. There is no appeal if the decision is just plain wrong. The parties are open to this risk in deciding to appoint an expert.

Arbitration or litigation?

As a decision by an arbitrator is generally faster than court proceedings and is more difficult to appeal against, arbitration may be preferred to litigation, where the agony of proceedings and appeals can be prolonged for years. Costs are also a factor. The costs of a complex arbitration are not necessarily less than a full court hearing, but again there is much less risk of costs running out of control on an appeal. Strangely, it can be easier to enforce an arbitration award than a court judgment in some countries. The New York Convention on the enforcement of arbitration in awards, for example, has already been ratified by over 100 countries.

Drafting arbitration clauses

Where the parties to an international contract opt for arbitration, they will probably adopt one of the international arbitration procedures. Notable in Europe are the International Court of Arbitration of the International Chamber of Commerce (the ICC based in Paris), the London Court of International Arbitration (LCIA), and the American Arbitration Association (AAA) in the US, each of which have their own rules and procedures. In many cases the arbitration rules of the United Nations Commission on International Trade Law (Uncitral) are adopted. The parties can also choose a neutral forum and in Europe there are strong candidates in Holland, Switzerland and Sweden, for example. These bodies all have their own recommended wording for suitable clauses.

Even then there are decisions to be made. Are there to be three arbitrators or just one? Where will the arbitration be? What language will it be conducted in? Each decision has potential cost and time implications. The procedure in England has recently been overhauled and set out clearly in plain English in the Arbitration Act 1996. This Act adapts many of the Uncitral rules but tries to streamline the procedures where possible and defines the duties and powers of the arbitrator and the relationship between the arbitration and the role and powers of the courts (see also p. 254).

Checklist for the international element

Faced with this range of possibilities, how can a business make the best decisions? Here are a few suggestions:

- Is there any international element? If not, consider providing for English law and the exclusive jurisdiction of the English courts.
- Is there any likely technical or factual element that would be better decided by arbitration, such as a future price? If so, consider whether it would be best decided by an arbitrator acting in a judicial way or by an expert seeking evidence and coming to a professional opinion. Specify the issue clearly and which body should nominate the person concerned if you cannot agree on a choice beforehand or at the time. Don't leave it open 'to be agreed' without specifying the consequences.
- If there is an international element, consider whether there are aspects on which local law will prevail. Check or ask your lawyer to check with lawyers in that jurisdiction how you will be affected and get their view at an early stage on arbitration in that country and what is best left to the courts.
- If the other law is to play a leading role in the contract, consider how much work would need to be done to amend the contract so that it is consistent with that other law. Try to avoid a main 'cultural' redraft unless it is really necessary.

- Will there be trading in several countries and will the other parties have assets in several jurisdictions? If not, exclusive jurisdiction may be appropriate.
- If choice of law or jurisdiction is becoming a bone of contention, step back and look at the issues and how critical they are in terms of your objectives, the rewards of the contract and the risks of non-performance. Then review the law and jurisdiction aspect again.

(See also Chapters 1, 6, 8, 12, 13 and 19.)

■ 17

Transferring contracts

Despite the importance of knowing who you are dealing with, the question of whether and how contracts can be transferred or delegated is often treated as one of minor concern. In fact the issue may be of considerable significance. This chapter deals with transfers and subcontracting of rights and responsibilities and looks at contractual issues which arise when a company is taken over.

General principles of transfer and assignment

The word 'transfer' is technically used to refer to something which is physical, such as goods or products. 'Assignment', on the other hand, is the transfer, whether by sale or gift or simply as part of a commercial bargain, not of a piece of property but of legal rights possibly coupled with legal obligations, such as a contract to sell those goods. Goods themselves may normally be transferred freely, but the basic rule of contracts is that, whilst you can assign or pass on your rights, you cannot assign your obligations. If you sell on the benefit of the contract to a subpurchaser, therefore, you can as a matter of contract between yourself and the subpurchaser, require the sub-purchaser to pay the seller for the goods, but this does not relieve you of your own obligations to pay the seller if the subpurchaser does not.

Delegation is an alternative approach, which is typically done by subcontracting or sublicensing. The former, most notable in property law and the construction industry but common and perfectly viable in many other situations, in-volves the original parties remaining the parties to the (head) contract and one of them entering into one or more sub-contracts under which other parties perform part or all of the functions of the head contractor (see below). Subcontracting may be overt, known to the other party to the head contract, or covert and not known.

Some contracts expressly permit subcontracting, but only on the basis that the subcontractor gives an express undertaking to the parties to the head contract to perform the relevant obligations. In a construction contract the head contractor may bring in a specialist subcontractor to carry out part of the work. The advantage to the client of a direct undertaking from the subcontractor is to establish a direct contractual relationship, which the client could enforce against the subcontractor if necessary whilst retaining its rights against the head contrac-tor if the subcontractor fails to perform. This would also con-centrate the mind of the head contractor who would remain liable for any failures by the subcontractor. The subcontractor, not being party to the original negotiations and only brought in later, is often faced with a fait accompli and the risk of being without remedy against the client if the head contractor fails. Unless the subcontractor has obtained a cross-undertaking from the client as to payment, he could be left with an un-secured claim in the insolvent liquidation of the head contractor.

Similar considerations apply to sublicensing. This is a form of specialist subcontracting under which the sublicensee is given the power to exploit certain rights, such as copyrights, trade marks or technology. Here it is of considerable advan-tage for the owner of the right to have direct recourse against the sublicensee in order to take rapid action on any breach of the express contract terms. For example, the owner of a trade mark (licensor) may grant a licence to a company which is strong in production and marketing (licensee) to produce and sell goods which carry the trade mark. The licence will set out the terms of the arrangements, clear guidance on what the licensee can do and the relevant quality standards. When, however, the licensee grants a sublicence to a third party to manufacture and sell the same products in another territory, the licensor will have no direct control over the actions of the sublicensee. The licensor might therefore either bar any sublicences without consent, and negotiate specific terms when requested, or require in the main licence that any sublicence is in equivalent terms to the main contract with a direct covenant by the sublicensee in favour of and directly enforceable by the licensor.

Exceptions to the general principles

There are some important exceptions to the rule that you can assign or delegate the benefit but not the burden of a contract. For example, certain contracts are 'personal' by nature. In these cases the law recognizes that the parties were chosen specifically for who they are and that only the named individuals are to provide the services in question. An obvious example of this is the employment contract. The employer would not be prepared to accept someone else chosen by the employee to take the place of the employee, and the employee would not accept being passed to another employer without consent. Even with a transfer under the Transfer Regulations, the employee has the right to decline to transfer. A personal consultancy is similar, whereas a larger scale consultancy may involve permitting the consultant to nominate the team to be used. A less obvious example is a publishing contract where the law has long recognized that the relationship is personal. It seems clear in the case of an author, since the publisher wants the named person to write the book, but the principle also applies to the publisher. Over a century ago the courts established that an author will select a publisher with care on the basis of an expectation of personal dealings with that publisher. It is not open to the publisher simply to pass on that relationship to someone else without the consent of the author. This principle makes the transfer of publishing contracts an uncertain exercise.

Where contracts are of a personal nature, subcontracting or delegation of functions may itself be a fundamental breach of the contract for the same reasons which prohibit assignment. Publishing again is a good example. One can distinguish between the main publishing activities – liaising with the author, overseeing the editing, instructing the typesetters and granting third-party rights – which cannot be delegated and other functions – printing, sales and marketing – which are frequently delegated in practice without undermining the personal nature of the publishing relationship. If the whole of the publishing function is delegated, either by way of sub-contract or agency or any equivalent arrangement, the author may claim that the publisher has permitted the contract to be 'vicariously performed' and treat this as a fundamental breach or repudiation of the contract. (The effect of repudiation is considered further in Chapter 19.)

The contract may also expressly prohibit assignment. In some cases this is an express prohibition and in others there may be reference to the contract not being assigned without the consent of one or both parties. Unlike the position with leasehold property, there is no implication that any such consent may not be unreasonably withheld unless the contract expressly says so. References to consent not being unreasonably withheld can make an enormous difference to the respective bargaining power of the parties. They impose an objective standard of reasonableness on any party refusing to agree. Without the reference, the party refusing can be as difficult as they like without fear of legal sanction.

There may be an overriding law which has the effect of transferring entitlements and/or responsibilities, for example the Transfer Regulations. The employment contract automatically passes to whoever acquires the business of the old employer *unless* the employee objects. This can be thought of as an assignment by operation of law, acting outside the contract itself.

Change of control

Assignment can also take place in practice when there is a takeover of one of the parties to the contract. Although the contracting parties remain the same, the control of one of them passes to another. There may be a drastic change in policy and approach as a result. Worse still, the new owners of the company may be competitors of the other party to the contract. The fact that the contract is personal or that it contains a non-assignment clause will not prevent the change of control from taking place nor invalidate the contract. A specific change of control clause is required in the contract. The effect of the clause is that, if there is a great change (normally more than 50 per cent, but sometimes lower) in the shareholding of one party to the contract, the other party may terminate the contract immediately or on a short period of notice. In some instances the power is limited to cases where the controlling shareholders are competitors, but such a clause can be difficult to draft with sufficient certainty and pure competition may not be the only issue.

Novation

Novation is similar to assignment except that the incoming party takes over all rights and duties of the party they replace and the party replaced is fully released from the contract. In effect a new contract (novation) has been created under which the new party takes over completely from the old party. This is the ideal position for a business to achieve if it is passing on a contract to another party, but it will only be possible if the other original party agrees or, quite exceptionally, the contract provides for novation.

Summary

Transfer provisions are easily overlooked but they play a significant role in planning and dealing with contracts. The issues should be thought through at the outset. Points to consider include:

- Assignments should always be in writing and formally notified by the person taking the assignment (the assignee) to the other party to the original contract, even if consent to assignment has been given. Only when it receives that notice can the other party safely deal directly with the assignee. Consider the case of a loan. The contract is not generally of a personal nature and the lender can assign to you the right to repayment from the borrower. You need to notify the borrower of the assignment, otherwise the borrower will repay the original lender and you could lose the money. You should give written notice of assignment to the borrower and ask for it to be acknowledged.
- There is, of course, a trap for the borrower here. If the loan is assigned and the borrower mistakenly pays the original lender *after* receiving notice of the assignment, the debt is not discharged. If the original lender decamps, the borrower will have to pay the money again to the assignee of the debt, the new lender.
- Even if there is no formal written agreement it is possible that consent to assignment or a novation may be inferred from circumstances. Again it is convenient to refer to publishing. If the publisher sells its business and another publisher takes over, the author must decide whether to deal with the new publisher or not. If the author starts to deal with the new publisher as his/her publisher, for example by submitting a manuscript, it will be difficult for the author to claim that the assignment is unauthorized. Either the author will be deemed to have acquiesced in, and therefore accepted, the breach of contract or the evidence may be that the contract has in fact been novated and the new publisher accepted by the author in place of the old publisher. If you are the author you must make it clear as quickly as possible if the change is not acceptable and not compromise the position by action (or even inaction) in the meantime.
- You must make provision for any outstanding breaches by one party to the contract, possibly by taking an indemnity from the party concerned.
- Does the identity of the other party matter to you provided the work is done? If it is important, make the contract

personal and prohibit assignment and subcontracting. You can always consent to specific cases when they arise.

- Is it important that you can assign or subcontract your part of the agreement? If so, ensure that you have the power in the contract to do so.

- If you agree to assignment and subcontracting, consider adding a clause which requires the assignee or subcontractor to enter into a deed undertaking to you personally to be bound by the terms of the contract. This will be a deed of adherence in the case of an assignment or deed of covenant in the case of a subcontract. You should also follow up that obligation in practice.

- If the financial strength or identity of the other party is likely to remain important to you, and you agree an assignment clause, do not agree an automatic release of the other party. Conversely, if you might want to assign your interest, try to negotiate an automatic release on completion of the assignment.

- Would you be affected by a change in the control or ownership of the other party? If so, include a change of control clause, but leave yourself the option of terminating rather than making termination automatic, which may be used against you. When dealing with a group of companies, you also need to consider how far up the group the change of control might occur.

- Pay particular attention to the whole question of assignment and delegation where material payment obligations will arise in relation to future work, or where you wish to have clear rights against any party undertaking work on your behalf. Client, head contractor and subcontractor all have different interests here.

When dealing internationally, remember that other countries may have different conventions and laws which apply even where issues are not expressly dealt with in the contract. There may also be different expectations on the part of those with whom you are dealing as to what is and what is not possible.

(See also Chapters 2, 6, 7, 8, 9 and 13.)

■ 18

Dealing with problems

When a contract is signed, it is not the end of the affair. At best it is a mid-point in a process that started with a concept and will ideally end with a completed transaction or project. Projects do not always reach completion and not all have an end date. Even when they do, there may be ongoing obligations under the contract. This chapter looks at some of the issues which may arise after signing.

The contract review

At the end of lengthy contract negotiations, the non-lawyers involved often remark that they hope to 'put the contract in a drawer and never look at it again'. Certainly the process of negotiation should have identified and pre-solved a number of issues which might have become problems, but to regard the contract as finished with at that stage, as a form of legal insurance policy, is to miss much of its value. Any medium- or long-term contract should be reviewed regularly. It is, for example, accepted wisdom that employees' performance should be appraised at least once each year and that any business plan should be regularly reviewed against the attainment of agreed milestones or broad objectives. In the same way, revisiting the contract will be a good yardstick by which to judge whether the objectives are indeed being achieved, what could be done better, how far performance has slipped from the original intention and what revisions now need to be made. Even the contract itself may need to be revised. The process can be as beneficial as personnel appraisals, carried out in time and fairly, in improving performance and reducing the risk of failed expectations and disputes.

There are good legal reasons for this approach. If there is a dispute later, the parties involved will review the contract, but there will be much less risk of resolving any areas of uncertainty once the battle lines of dispute have been drawn. The contract might, for example, contain a mistake. Although you have taken great care, there are sometimes errors in the final version, ranging from the obvious to a misunderstanding of the meaning of a particular clause. If you discover these errors early, the chances of resolving them and amending the contract are far higher than when disagreement has already arisen.

Rectification, waiver and estoppel

Rectification, the legal process of amending a contract to reflect the real intentions of the parties, is an uncertain remedy at the best of times. You must generally prove either a mistake by both parties in the contract not reflecting their joint intentions, or a clear mistake by one party on which the other relied in circumstances where it would be unconscionable for that other party to rely on the mistake. Lawyers frequently find that what the contract says and what the parties are actually doing are very different. The question then is whether the parties have mutually agreed to vary the contract (despite what the contract may say) or whether one party has, by its conduct or inaction, waived a breach by the other party ('waiver') or has acted in some other way so as to be precluded from claiming for that breach in the future ('estoppel'). In all these cases prevention is better than cure.

No contract

There may be another, less expected, result of a contract review. You may find that there is no clear contract in the first place, but simply a mass of conflicting correspondence and telephone attendance notes (at best!), which is remarkably common when strict procedures are not put in place. The construction industry, which should know better in view of its annual expenditure on legal fees, is a main offender. There is often pressure to carry on with the job in a belief that 'the paperwork will catch up'. Work starts on the basis of an initial specification of works which has not been finalized and either an indication of likely price or a detailed schedule with many unspecified sums. An example arose in the 1997 decision in *VHE Construction Ltd* v *Alfred McAlpine Construction Ltd*, where the judge said:

> On projects involving thousands and sometimes millions of pounds, when a dispute arises about payment, the first issue very often is to decide whether there was a contract and if so what were the terms of that contract, if any.

After a careful analysis of the facts the judge concluded that a contract had indeed been entered into and he identified the precise time that agreement was reached, which was during a telephone conversation between managers on each side reaching consensus on the last outstanding item. The terms of the contract were those which applied as common ground between the parties at that time. The judge stated that it was only relevant to look at the surrounding circumstances to find out if and when a contract had been formed, but that what happened after the contract had been formed was irrelevant to understanding and implementing the terms of that contract (for analysis, see Chapter 1). The relevance to the subcontractor was that, if a contract had been created, it would have fixed the price for the work. Because of the soil conditions, a report on which was available to but not studied by the subcontractor before the contract was made but of which it was deemed to have knowledge, the work was more costly to carry out than had been anticipated and the subcontractor wanted to be paid on a *quantum meruit* basis – a fair rate for the work carried out, available where there is no agreed price in the contract. In this case, as a contract had been created at an agreed price, the contract price applied.

Troublesome contracts

A contract is normally first reviewed when a problem comes to light. There is no finite list of what can go wrong and the law reports continue to show examples from the most banal to the most esoteric. Here are some suggested guiding principles.

Payment delays

Failure to pay on time is one of the most common problems, but its roots will lie elsewhere. The difficulty for the creditor is finding the truth of the matter. Who has not heard a debtor complain of cash flow difficulties? They may be anything from a temporary receipts blip to an irreversible slide into insolvency. The indulgent creditor may be increasingly sucked into the mire by continuing or even extending credit (for example, by providing further supplies) in response to personal appeals from the managing director of the debtor. Occasionally those pleas and the story given are grounded in reality and, if so, it is not unreasonable to ask for up-to-date management accounts; evidence of large orders just received – or, all too often, about to be received; a list of other creditors – how many others are in the queue? – and other evidence to support the claims. It may be the right time to request further supplies on the basis of cash on delivery or against directors' personal guarantees (see Chapter 1). There are sensible precautions that you can take at the same time – a renewed credit check and a visit by the creditor's representative to the debtor's place of business. Check the degree of activity and stock levels and even the possible change of name on the door which might indicate that you are being told less than the whole truth.

Many conditions of sale will include a term requiring complaints to be notified within a stated period after delivery. Whilst this may not always be possible, it does give some protection to a supplier against the persistent late payer. Services are more difficult because the issue is more likely to be about the quality of the service, a matter of individual judgement. The best protection is to be as explicit as possible on what will be provided, by whom, in what way and when (see Chapters 13 and 14). The intention is to avoid surprises and to avoid disappointments.

Customer follow-up and an efficient credit control system will also often detect non-payment as the first sign of a bigger problem. The business must react to prevent the sales team from continuing to sell and the transport people from delivering more products to a defaulting customer. There are many times when a deferred payment arrangement has been agreed and has started off well, but then rapidly fallen away, leaving a bigger exposure than ever. The following options are open to a supplier in this situation:

- Give written notice of breach to the customer – sensible if the contract is for a long term, but of little value if it is simply a series of one-off transactions.
- Serve notice making time for payment of the essence of the contract (see Chapter 14), if it is not already specified – again useful if there are further obligations on the supplier.
- Exercise any right of set-off under the contract or at common law – worth considering where there are payments due both ways.
- Claim interest under the contract where the terms permit you to do so (provided that the interest rate is not extortionate nor regarded as a penalty).
- Issue a winding-up petition against a company which has failed to meet a clearly defined payment obligation, possibly (but not necessarily) preceded by the service of a 'statutory demand' for payment – a notice in specified form under the Insolvency Act requiring payment within 21 days, although the procedure is only available in debts above £750 where there is no reasonably arguable defence to the claim.

- Issue court proceedings for non-payment (see below).

Commercial issues

The business world changes at an ever faster pace. Contractual commitments which are intended for the longer term will always risk being in conflict with pragmatic reactions to the turns of the commercial wheel. New opportunities and new threats for the parties to the contract will arise. There may be new management with different views. There may be a take-over which will result in a complete change of ownership and direction of the business. These changes will bring a new focus to the contracts involved. There may also be forgetfulness, a frequent cause of dispute where the mistake is not acknowl-edged and/or an opportunity not given to put it right. Ideally these aspects will have been considered when planning the contract (see Chapter 13) and, where anticipated, will be expressed in the contract in clauses relating to such matters as change of control and breach remedy.

It is often remarked that the contract will only need to be re-considered if its progress is going badly. Experience suggests that it is almost as likely that the review will occur if it is seen to be going too well. It is remarkable how the sight of one party doing better than expected can induce discontent in the mind of the other, even if that other party is itself doing better!

Emotional context

Behavioural analysts refer to three likely responses of the rep-tile (or even dinosaur) brain that directs many of our reactions – fight, fright or flight. The principle can be seen at work in the legal process. The fighter will immediately threaten to sue and may issue a writ first and explain afterwards. The fighter will regard the whole exercise as a trial of strength and will-power and may be reluctant to discuss or compromise even when the odds are overwhelming. Nothing less than total surrender may be acceptable and sometimes litigation is inevitable because the fighter will be surrounded and advised by those who respond to and encourage that style. Those who take fright, on the other hand, will freeze and do nothing. There will be no response to letters before action or the writ. The first action may come after default judgment when the bailiffs are sent in. Some claimants have indeed given up by then, but it is clear that taking fright and doing nothing is unlikely to deter a determined claimant. Taking flight is a variant of this based on the premise that to run away is to reduce the risk of being caught. The 'flighter' will have limited assets (at least in any local jurisdiction) and a history of starting again. All three styles tend to become a way of life and the signs may be there at the outset. It pays the other party also to recognize and plan for them at the outset.

Reacting quickly

The fighter will need no encouragement and will act quickly from the start. It would still be advisable for that action to be legally reviewed against the contract first. An over-hasty action can lock a party into expensive legal proceedings and the cure becomes more serious than the disease. Those who take fright will be graduates from the Ostrich School of Management. They will bury their heads in the sand for lengthy periods in the hope that what they cannot see, no one else can either. The flighter will already be on the run and unlikely to have time to take protective action. Whilst these are obviously stylized versions, there is probably an element of one (or more) of these reactions in the way most individuals respond to contract problems. The answer is to react quickly, even if you decide then to do nothing until a certain point. If, however, urgent action is required, do it quickly. Don't wait to see what happens.

At one extreme may be the need to seek an immediate injunction to prevent irreparable loss or the wish to get to your own national courts first in international disputes, in order to prevent the other party from applying to their courts (see p. 215). At the other extreme there are time limits to catch the tardy. The time limits within which legal proceedings must be issued, running from the date of the cause of action, which is generally the date of breach of the contract or when a loss is first sustained in the case of negligence, are as follows:

- three years for personal injury claims
- six years for contract and negligence
- twelve years for claims relating to land or documents executed as a deed.

These limits may be extended for up to three years from the date of discovery in negligence and other tort cases where the defect or breach could not reasonably have been discovered earlier, with a final backstop date of 15 years. There are also a number of remedies which are equitable and are thus at the discretion of the courts. That discretion will normally not be exercised where the party seeking it has delayed unreasonably.

Inducement to breach contracts

It is a civil offence to induce someone to break their contract with a third party. This principle was seen at work in the field of football management where one premier division football club was held to have enticed the manager of another to leave his existing club before the end of his contract. The important point in such cases is to assess whether there is an encouragement to break the existing contract or merely a request to join another team or company once the first contract has been properly brought to an end. If, for example, an employee on 12 months' notice was encouraged by a competitor to leave his or her employment and join the competitor immediately, this would entitle the employer to sue the competitor for damages for the loss of the employee's services (net of remuneration) for the notice period.

The better course for the competitor is to make the offer with a start date arising when the employee is legally free to join, expressly recognizing the validity of the notice but letting commercial logic dictate the result. If, for example, Richards the retailer went direct to Morris the manufacturer (see Chapter 1) and asked Morris to supply Richards direct and not through Williams the wholesaler, that would not be an inducement on the part of Richards for Morris to break the contract, unless Richards knew or should have known that there was a contract in place, such as a long-term exclusive distributorship, between Morris and Williams which Richards, by going direct, was inducing Morris to breach. If that were the case, Williams would still have a right against Morris to enforce the contract or claim for loss and would also have a claim against Richards for interference with the contract. To make matters more serious, if two or more parties jointly plan to induce a breach of contract, the interference then becomes a criminal conspiracy with potentially custodial results.

Anticipating defence

An innocent party to a broken contract should not assume that their claim will be straightforward. Illegality, unfair contract terms or some of the issues considered in Chapter 2, for example, might bar or limit the claim. The checklist at the end of that chapter (p. 31) indicates what possible problems lie ahead or, if you are a defendant, what defences are available. There may also be counterclaims by the defendant for breach by the party threatening proceedings (known as the plaintiff), not uncommon when relationships deteriorate.

You should specifically consider at this stage the issues of unfair terms, illegality and unfair competition. Is there a risk that the claim, or the defence, might fail because the terms relied on are unfair under the legislation or regulations referred to in Chapter 4? Are any of the terms potentially illegal? If so, it might be better to settle on reasonably advantageous terms at the outset, rather than to risk all against a determined defendant. Are there provisions restricting competition and, if so, how important are they to you? Is the other party prepared to agree a modified and more restricted form of non-competitive undertaking that will serve your commercial needs, rather than your seeking to enforce an all-round covenant drafted some time previously which may no longer be fully appropriate to your needs?

Default notice procedure

Many business agreements contain a provision that a default

notice must be served and give a stated time for remedying the breach (where it is capable of remedy). In that case the innocent party will be able to terminate if payment is not made, or the breach is not otherwise remedied, within the permitted time after a default notice. It can be useful to seek to limit the notice procedure to material breaches, since it is by nature a prelude to possible termination of the contract. There is no single test to decide what is a material breach, but the emphasis is on the party alleging the breach to show that it is material, or will have a significant effect, in relation to the contract as a whole.

There is less flexibility with a clause making time of the essence. Such a clause should be resisted in negotiations where its effect could be to give the innocent party the power to terminate a long-term contract if a single payment is one day late. On the other hand, persistent delays in payment can be a significant irritant, even if payment is made after a default notice, and some contracts provide for persistent breaches to justify termination. In other cases, time can be made of the essence in a written notice stating the default, giving a reasonable time for it to be rectified and making performance by that extended date of the essence of the contract.

Summary

Problems will probably arise at some stage in the implementation of a contract, especially a longer term agreement. The best approach is to take notice of all the signs, enquire and pursue the cause of the problem in order to find its source and then pursue your case firmly and consistently, but be realistic about the options, the risks and the best practical outcomes. Be as objective as possible and take advice to reinforce that objectivity and the options open to you. Other points to consider are:

- When preparing the contract clarify the level of performance required in each case, avoiding, for example, references to 'acceptable standards' and similar general expressions.
- Review current contracts regularly and check that you are still achieving the level of performance you expected.

- Check exactly what the contract says and that you are on firm ground. If not, adapt your strategy accordingly and try to strengthen the weaker areas.
- Where you consider the other party is falling short, tell them about it as quickly as possible, letting them know what you expect. Follow up immediately in writing so that there is a clear 'paper trail' if matters ever come to court – whether people settle litigation, or the terms on which they settle, is often determined by the strength of the incidental paperwork.
- Don't delay in seeking redress if your rights might be prejudiced as a result.
- If you negotiate on any of these issues, do so on a 'without prejudice' basis (see Chapter 1).
- If you agree settlement terms, they should be clearly set out in writing and signed, and there must be adequate consideration to make the agreement or release binding.
- Recognize the fact that if another party changes the rules, and you accept the situation, you are not only tacitly accepting their breach (or waiving your rights in legal terminology) but you may also be effectively agreeing to a variation of the contract.
- Check that you are continuing to deal with the same party that you contracted with, watching out for changes in company or business name, or in the directors or management which might indicate something more fundamental. Remember that the company number remains the same and perhaps carry out an occasional company search.
- Consider exercising any retention or reservation of your title rights to recover stock sold to the defaulter but not yet resold by them (see Chapter 14).
- Beware giving the other party cause to make counter-claims against you.

(See also Chapters 2, 4, 6, 7 and 19.)

■ 19

Endings and breakdowns

It may happen that the situation occurs where one or more of the parties to a contract comes to the conclusion that the relationship has broken down or that the contract must come to an end. This chapter outlines the remedies available for those affected by a breach of contract and their claims for legal redress.

Rescission

In certain circumstances an innocent party to a contract may bring the contract to an end by rescission, rather than termination as a result of breach or any other factor. The basis of rescission is that the parties should be restored to the same position in which they would have been if the contract had not existed in the first place. Rescission therefore may well be accompanied by a damages claim for the loss caused to the innocent rescinding party by the other party to the contract.

Examples of circumstances where rescission may be appropriate include:

● misrepresentation – where the party would not have entered into the deal if the true facts had not been misstated
● failure of a condition precedent – where the performance of the rest of the contract was dependent on some earlier condition which was not fulfilled
● total failure of consideration – where the other party completely fails to perform their part of the bargain.

In these cases the courts go back to the beginning and seek to restore the parties to their original position, so far as it is possible to do so, rather than merely compensating the affected party for the loss of the benefits it would have obtained if the contract had been duly performed. Rescission damages may also be awarded. Note that breach of a warranty alone will not justify rescission, whereas breach of a representation may do so. When negotiating contracts, therefore, it is worth changing references to representations, if you are being asked to give them, to warranties.

Restitution

Restitution has been called a remedy in 'quasi-contract', because it gives a right based on an assumed understanding of fairness between the parties to an arrangement even in the absence of, or outside, a formal contract. Where, for example, one person receives a windfall benefit at the expense of another, the principles of equity may consider the first person has enjoyed 'unjust enrichment' and order restitution to the second person of what they have lost and the first has unfairly gained. The same result can occur where the first person has received money or goods which were intended for the second, even though there has been no breach of any existing contract. In some cases, entitlement to restitution of goods can be traced to their proceeds of sale. As with other equitable remedies, there is a delicate balance of procedures and fairness to be established and the complex legal issues in this area require careful analysis.

Repudiation

Some breaches are so fundamental that they indicate the party concerned is no longer prepared to be bound by the terms of the contract, which may amount in law to repudiation. The effect is that the innocent party has a choice either to accept the breach and keep the contract in existence, or to treat the contract as at an end. In either case the innocent party can preserve the right to claim damages for any loss caused by the breach and/or the ending of the contract as a result. The choice, or election, must be communicated in some clear and effective way, even by conduct, provided the action shows that the party accepting the repudiation is indeed treating the contract as over. It is a significant step because, if the circumstances do amount to repudiation, the innocent party terminating the contract can avoid any further obligations under it and will be automatically discharged from any restrictive covenants. If the action is not justified, the apparently innocent party will have repudiated the contract and the converse proposition applies.

By way of example, consider a distribution contract between Morris the manufacturer and Williams the distributor. The agreement is for a three-year term for exclusive distribution rights in Northern Ireland and Williams has covenanted not to sell competing products in that territory for one year after the agreement terminates. There are no sales target figures in the agreement but, after some discussion about the need to improve sales, Morris starts selling and distributing in Northern Ireland through another company. Williams has three choices:

- to remonstrate with Morris and try to persuade Morris to restore Williams as its exclusive distributor
- to seek a court injunction preventing Morris from selling through anyone else
- to treat the Morris move as repudiation of the contract and find another supplier for the market. If repudiation could

be proved, the restrictive covenant on Williams would be ineffective and Morris would not be able to prevent Williams from dealing with a competitor.

Walter Williams will have to make up his mind fairly quickly. He can protest and threaten action, but if he carries on ordering from Morris as before, he may be deemed to have accepted the breach and affirmed the contract. There is no certainty that the action of Morris would amount to repudiation, but if Williams keeps the contract alive his chance to treat it as repudiated will be lost and he will be left at best with a claim in damages for the loss of exclusivity.

Another example of potentially repudiatory conduct would be the assignment or transfer of a contract by one party, or the subcontracting of all obligations, in circumstances where either the contract is personal or there is a bar against assignment or subcontracting.

Insolvency

It is usual and sensible to provide for immediate and automatic termination in the event of the insolvency of one of the parties. An innocent party will hardly want to continue to perform under a contract where there is little or no chance of being paid. The definition of insolvency will vary but will include liquidation (except a solvent liquidation as part of a corporate reconstruction exercise) and receivership. Administration is more difficult because the power to terminate may well be suspended to give the ailing company the chance to recover. If termination is not automatic, the innocent party should still consider termination by notice, where permitted by the contract on insolvency of the other party, or submission of a breach and/or time of the essence notice to force the receiver or liquidator to decide a course of action.

Death

The death of one of the parties will not necessarily terminate a contract unless it makes the contract impossible to perform, in which case the contract will end by frustration. Even then, although the performance may not be possible, any pre-existing liabilities will be passed to the estate. When planning contracts, it is worth considering what effect the death of a party would have and whether, and how, it should be covered in the agreement.

Frustration

Frustration of a contract applies where, through no fault of the parties, it becomes impossible for the parties to complete their bargain. The situation is, in fact, remarkably uncommon and is not to be confused with those where one of the parties has agreed to bear a particular risk or type of risk. For example, in relation to the sale of goods, either seller or buyer will generally accept the risk of loss of the goods from a particular point, depending upon the terms for carriage of goods incorporated in the contract. So if Morris the manufacturer agreed to sell and deliver cabinets direct to Richards the retailer, and the cabinets were stolen and lost, there would be no frustration of the contract. The parties would need to review the terms of the contract to see whether risk had passed and, most likely, which of them should then claim on their insurance policy. Morris may still be able to manufacture new cabinets to fulfil the order. A force majeure clause might be relevant for Morris if she retained the delivery risk. By way of contrast, the destruction of Morris' factory would make the contract impossible for her to perform, within any reasonable future time for the type of order in question, if there were no other means and if equivalent products could not be bought elsewhere. In that event there may be legal frustration of the contract.

Termination by notice

Many contracts are short term by their nature. Most sales of goods are, for example, single transactions which produce a rapid sale and purchase. Termination will probably only be an issue if the goods are not delivered on time. Even a trading relationship based on a history of transactions is unlikely to lead to termination, although it might result in problems about future refusal to supply. The position is different with longer term contracts, such as exclusive purchasing, agency, distribution, licensing, franchising and facilities agreements.

If the contract does not provide for termination, the courts will be very reluctant to presume that it was intended to carry on indefinitely and will treat the agreement as terminable at any time by either party on reasonable notice. Reasonable notice is always difficult to establish and the courts look at each case on its own merits. Regard will be had to the period that the arrangement has been in force, the capital and other investment put into the relationship and a reasonable period which the parties would need to bring their relationship to an end. Reasonableness of the notice period in this case is considered at the time the contract is terminated rather than when it was first made. Decisions involving long-running commercial licences have affirmed reasonable notice periods of six and twelve months, but in other situations between one and three months may be more appropriate. The exception is an agency agreement which is terminable summarily at common law, although where the Commercial Agents Regulations now apply between one and three months' notice will be necessary. Except with agency agreements under those regulations there is no statutory right against 'unfair' termination of a commercial contract, as there is with employment.

Most written contracts will specify the length of notice to be given, often after a stated initial term. The following is an example:

> This agreement will continue in force for a period of two years from the Commencement Date and thereafter unless and until either party serves not less than three months' written notice of termination on the other, such notice to expire on or at any time after the initial two year term.

There may be a number of variants on this format. The length of the primary term and the notice period will obviously vary; for example, six months' notice will be more common for distributorships. The contract may state that the notice may only be served on expiry of an anniversary of the commencement date which will be especially relevant for businesses with a clear annual cycle. The important point is that the party serving notice and the party receiving notice should examine the terms of the contract to ensure that they have been complied with, and that any provisions for the method of serving notices have also been complied with, since failure to serve a notice strictly in accordance with the terms will invalidate the notice and the server will have to start the process again. If the contract entitles you to terminate by notice because of a breach by the other party, follow the contract requirements carefully to make sure your notice is valid. Even then, only terminate as a last resort and bear in mind that, unless you can establish repudiation (see p. 243), your damages claim may be limited to past and not future loss.

Remedies

There are a range of remedies available to a party which considers it is or may be the victim of wrongdoing by another party.

Where a deposit has been paid, the contract may permit it to be forfeited. Where payment or performance is still due, it may be withheld – a fairly certain means to bring matters to a head. Repossession of goods sold under a valid retention of title has already been mentioned and, where the contract or circumstances permit, goods may be stopped in transit. These steps should always be considered before legal proceedings are taken.

Injunctions and similar orders

An injunction is a court order prohibiting a named person or business from doing something. A mandatory injunction, which is less common, is an order requiring someone to do something. An alternative remedy is specific performance which requires a party specifically to perform their obligations under the contract. These are all equitable remedies and will only be granted if the party seeking them has substantially complied with their own obligations under the contract and has not acted improperly – known graphically as 'coming to the court with clean hands'. Of these remedies, the prohibitory injunction is the most common. In the right circumstances an injunction can be obtained the same day, even over the weekend. The following conditions are usually required:

- a clear legal cause of action by the claimant (plaintiff) against the other party or parties (defendants)
- a summons or writ setting out the claim and commencing the legal action
- a strong initial (prima facie) case of material breach of contract by the defendants or the imminent risk of material breach in the case of what is known as a *quia timet* injunction
- the plaintiff has acted quickly
- the need to maintain the status quo until all the facts are ascertained and the case is fully heard
- an undertaking by the plaintif to pay the defendant damages for the loss and disruption caused to the defendant by virtue of the order if an undertaking is granted against the defendant and subsequently discharged on further hearing
- the court is satisfied that damages would not be an adequate remedy for the plaintiff, or that the defendant might not be able to honour a damages award so that the plaintiff would be uncompensated.

Injunctions are particularly important in protecting intellectual property rights such as patents, trade marks and the confidentiality of information, including employee competition. There is normally a two-stage procedure. The first stage is an interim injunction hearing, often on short notice, to decide whether an injunction should be granted to preserve the status quo pending the second stage, which is a fuller hearing as to whether an injunction should be granted or should remain in force. In the most urgent cases, interim injunction applications may be *ex parte*, that is without the defendant being present or represented. The plaintiff must be careful not to mislead the court in those circumstances as the court relies on the information supplied under oath on the plaintiff's side alone. If the *ex parte* injunction is granted there will be an *inter partes* hearing shortly afterwards, at which both or all parties can produce evidence. Again the case is normally resolved on the basis of affidavit, rather than oral, statements. In interim applications the court requires clear evidence that the plaintiff will suffer serious damage if the order is not made and that there will be more harm to the plaintiff if the injunction is not granted than there will be to the defendant if the injunction is granted (sometimes known as 'the balance of convenience' test).

Because injunctions are equitable remedies, the court has a wide-ranging discretion on whether to grant them or not and, if so, on what terms. It is unwise for potential plaintiffs to rush into injunction proceedings without careful consideration of the circumstances and possible outcomes. Substantial costs may be involved with the risk of paying damages and the defendant's costs (as in most litigation) if the application is unsuccessful. The case commences with the obligation to file detailed statements of claim and deal with the defence and all the issues that subsequently arise in a litigation claim. On the other hand, a potential plaintiff should act quickly otherwise the courts will refuse to grant an order if there has been unreasonable delay.

The injunction is, in theory, the first stage of the full proceedings which will conclude at trial (or even at final appeal three or four courts later). In practice, the outcome of an injunction application may determine the whole case. If the injunction is granted, the defendant will rarely continue to contest the action since the first objective will have been lost. If the injunction is refused, there may be little point in the plaintiff pursuing a damages claim, or the defendant may be prepared to settle for damages rather than an injunction.

Damages

The prime measure of damages in a claim for breach of contract is the cost of putting the plaintiff/innocent party in the position in which that party would have been if the defen-dant/defaulting party had properly performed the contract. As seen in Chapter 1 in relation to the Ford and the Porsche, the plaintiff is entitled to recover damages for loss of bargain in addition to recovery of any costs incurred because the plaintiff would have been entitled to the Porsche if the defendant had stuck to the bargain. The extent of the loss is that which can be seen to result from the breach (rather than any other cause). The test is whether, if the parties to the contract had contem-plated the situation at the outset, they could have foreseen that this type and extent of loss would be likely to result from a breach of the contract.

In some cases claims will exist both for breach of contract and in negligence for breach of the duty of care. The duty of one of the parties to the others may be greater in negligence than in contract and the possibility of an alternative claim should always be considered by both potential plaintiffs and defendants. The implications may extend to whether any exemption clauses in the contract cover liability in tort as well as contract, whether the measure of damages would be the same and whether the limitation period for bringing proceed-ings would be the same. When considering damages for loss of profit in breach of contract cases the general rule is that there may be recovery for loss of any contracts which were in force at the time, but not for 'economic loss' – loss of goodwill or potential future contracts, even with the same customer.

Chapters 5 amd 14 looked at the advantages of liquidated damages clauses, and the importance of ensuring that such provisions are not construed as unenforceable penalty clauses. Such clauses will avoid quantifying the loss actually caused, but they may also limit a claim. For the most part, although damages may be awarded for mental distress which has reached clinical levels, they will not be ordered for loss of enjoyment or disappointment where there is no other actual loss. There are two main exceptions to this general rule. The first relates to employment contracts where emotional distress may be a direct factor in compensation claims. The second is a contract, such as the package holiday, where pleasure and relaxation are the main purpose of the agreement. If you are in your twenties or thirties and book your Alpine holiday on the basis of the brochure emphasizing the convivial company and lively evenings around a frothing fondue, but find you are the only youthful person with a party of octogenarians, then you may, as did Mr Jarvis, have the basis of a successful claim against the tour company both for the value of the holiday and the lost opportunity of enjoyment (see *Jarvis* v *Swan Tours Ltd* in 1972).

A different disappointment arose for Mr Forsyth when he engaged builders to construct his new swimming pool. Mr Forsyth was keen on diving and stipulated that the pool be a minimum depth of seven feet six inches. The contractors excavated to a lesser depth. It was established that even a six-feet depth was safe for diving and that the value of the property as a whole was no different because of the lesser depth. Was the measure of damages the £22,000 required to rebuild the pool to the required depth, or a much smaller sum for the loss of amenity? The case went to the House of Lords (*Ruxley Electronics & Construction Limited* v *Forsyth*) who decided in 1995 that rebuilding would be unreasonable but that Mr Forsyth should receive some compensation for not getting what he was entitled to receive, even though he could not prove any direct financial loss. The Lords therefore restored the original decision of the first-instance judge to award him £2,500 damages for loss of amenity, ultimately a somewhat Pyrrhic victory for Mr Forsyth.

Where a party is affected by a breach of contract by another, the innocent party may not expect to stand idly by and let the potential damages escalate. They have a duty to mitigate their loss, which is perhaps best demonstrated in employment cases where a person dismissed without notice must nevertheless take prompt action to look for another comparable job. It is also relevant in cases of six months' notice or longer where it is quite possible that the plaintiff will obtain another suitable position. The ex-employee must then bring the earnings into account (or what they would have earned if they had followed up the prospect properly) by way of reduction in their overall claim. The same point applies in commercial contracts where the measure of damages is related to the plaintiff's loss and not to the defendant's gain. The position is different in many intellectual property matters where the aggrieved party may be entitled to choose between a claim for damages and a claim for an account of profits. In the latter case the claim will relate to the benefit to the wrongdoer, who may be required to account for the whole of the profit derived from the unlawful act, even if that profit appears excessive in relation to the loss caused to the plaintiff. Beware, however, threatening legal action for breach of an intellectual property right unless you are sure of your ground. If your threat is unjustified, you – and your lawyer writing the letter – can be in turn be sued!

Interest and costs

It is unlawful to claim interest in a debt where there is no contractual or other legal right to do so. However, a new government bill proposes a statutory interest charge on late payment which seems likely to be phased in over several years from 1999. In the meantime, once a writ or summons is issued the plaintiff may also claim interest on the amount due, at the rate of interest specified from time to time as applicable to judgment debts, together with the legal costs involved in the proceedings. The costs will be calculated on a fixed-scale basis in relation to undefended proceedings and will then be assessed according to the further work done in the case. A losing plaintiff will generally have to pay the defendant's legal costs. The amount recoverable is normally in the region of 60 per cent of the costs incurred between the solicitor and client, so that even in a case of supposed full recovery, the plaintiff may still be out of pocket for the irrecoverable balance of costs. These are all factors to be taken into account when planning litigation. The costs in terms of management time should also be considered, both directly involved in dealings with the potentially complex documentation and evidential requirements of a case and the disruptive and even emotional aspects of court proceedings. None of these are to be underrated.

Recovering damages

Winning the case may only be part of the battle. In many situations, the problem lies in recovering the damages. Whilst there are many weapons available to the successful plaintiff, including bailiff action and charging orders on property, the risk of the defendant becoming insolvent often looms large. Even the apparently well-off defendant can prove he is without assets by the time the case comes to trial. The issue then arises of whether the business concerned has quietly disposed of its assets so as to be able to go into insolvent liquidation if it loses the case. In extreme situations, especially where a defendant has most of its assets outside the UK, there may be concern that the UK-based assets will be removed from the jurisdiction and will be unavailable if the plaintiff wins the case. The courts have developed what is known as the *Mareva injunction* to deal with this situation; the defendant will be ordered not to dispose of or remove any assets until the case is finally settled or until further order. Another specialized form of injunction is the *Anton Piller* order which permits plaintiffs and their advisers, supported if necessary by the police, to enter premises of potential defendants without prior warning and to seize and retain incriminating evidence or counterfeit property. The courts may also make orders against either impecunious or non-resident plaintiffs ordering them to provide security for the costs which the defendant will incur and might be unable to reclaim if the plaintiff effectively disappears.

Despite all this, the successful claimant may finish up with a mere claim as an unsecured creditor in the bankruptcy of an individual defendant or the liquidation of the defendant company. Insult may be added to injury when the remainder of the defendant's liabilities are called up and any share that the plaintiff may have obtained in any surplus after costs of bankruptcy/liquidation is reduced by the amount of all the other creditors' claims. For example, the proceeds of a successful wrongful trading claim made by a liquidator are available for all creditors in priority order and in proportion to their debts, even if one creditor has effectively suffered more than others. All the more reason, therefore, for would-be plaintiffs to evaluate other ways of resolving disputes more cleanly and quickly.

Arbitration and alternative dispute resolution

As demonstrated, litigation may be lengthy, costly and uncertain. In some cases the main issues are sufficiently clear to be suitable for arbitration. The choices between litigation and arbitration and some of the international contract issues involved were reviewed in outline in Chapter 16. When the contract breaks down reconsider the choices made at the outset and the options now available before plunging down any particular path. The Arbitration Act 1996 has introduced a new, more customer-conscious arbitration system whose declared aims are to provide for the fair, speedy and cost-effective resolution of disputes by an impartial tribunal. Arbitrators are now expressly given certain powers to make interim orders previously only available to judges.

With the costs, delays and uncertainties of both litigation and formal arbitration, there has been a strong move to find an alternative method of resolving differences of commercial opinion. Alternative dispute resolution (ADR) brings in a neutral third party to mediate. A mediator tries to find and build on common ground and to seek consensus, whereas an arbitrator is asked to make a judgement and an expert to make a decision. ADR is not mutually exclusive with litigation or arbitration and can run alongside formal proceedings. The leading ADR contact in England in this area is the Centre for Dispute Resolution (CEDR) in London. Many industries also have their own mechanisms for resolving contractual disputes.

Summary

Contracts need to be drafted with a view to what might go wrong and what should happen if it does. Like a good set of board minutes, a contract should be a record of what has been agreed and how it is to be achieved and a reminder of the action required to fulfil those promises. When problems arise, the facts should be separated from the fiction and the emotion, and a sensible, but flexible, strategy worked out. Like the contract itself, that strategy should be regularly reviewed in the light of events. Practical solutions should be considered alongside legal redress and the longer-term objectives and risks analysed. Care must be taken not to interfere with the contracts of other businesses and, equally, not to fall into any traps laid by the other party. The party who was your partner may now be your opponent, but they may be in no greater rush to start litigation than you. Remember that communication is worth preserving and informal or even formal mediation might avoid the worst aspects of a dispute. Points to consider include:

- If you decide to take action, observe breach notice procedures set out in the contract so that any remedies are justified.
- Some breaches may be so great that they show an intention no longer to be bound by the contract, leaving the other party free to terminate and claim damages.
- If you feel that litigation is inevitable, evaluate with your lawyer the potential costs, risks and rewards before taking action. Once committed, prepare to put your efforts behind the action to maximum advantage whilst recognizing that enormous patience (and a deep pocket) may be required!
- Above all, when action is required, don't bury your head in the sand and pretend that all is fine with the world, or that it is not fine but you can't do anything about it. It is better to make an informed choice, even an informed choice to wait for a change, than to do nothing out of fear of doing something.

(See also Chapters 2, 4, 6, 7 and 19.)

■ 20

Working with contract law

Some people go through life without taking responsibility for anything that happens to them or anyone around them. Others seem to carry the cares of the world on their shoulders. You should approach both of them with care in relation to business contracts because the essence of a successful business contract is responsibility.

Responsibility

You must take responsibility for sensible planning and fore-thought, for agreeing the right terms, for making sure your part of the deal is performed, for supporting the other parties in achieving what they have undertaken, for reviewing performance and progress and for solving any problems that may arise.

People may say 'Well, we trust each other, so there's no need to worry', but what is that trust based on? It may be friendship at school, meetings at the tennis or golf club (often a testing ground on their own) or a business acquaintanceship strengthened by a convivial dinner. Is the trust based on shared values or simply shared experiences? Has it stood, and how would it stand, the test of a commercial relationship?

Trust, as we generally understand it, is an important ingredient in business, but by no means the complete recipe. It can add flavour and consistency to the mix, but it will not by itself make a series of incompatible ingredients into an edible product. All parties to a contract must understand fully what is required of them, accept responsibility for making the deal work and demonstrate, and continue to demonstrate, that commitment to the others involved. Trust is to be earned, not taken as given. The point where the negotiating process moves beyond practicability and beyond all fairness is the point where something will probably go wrong. When it does, there may be losers quite outside the contract itself. When businesses fail to meet their commitments, the effect on others may go further than would ever have been expected.

Responsibility means, among other things, using the money and people to do what you have undertaken, taking the time to follow through, being realistic as well as optimistic and not promising more of any of these than you are confident of being able to achieve. Having thought about it from your own perspective, think about the other party. Can you live up to their expectations of your performance? Are you confident that they can live up to yours? What evidence or assurances do you need? What is their financial strength and have you seen up-to-date audited accounts? Do they have the necessary financial backing for the essential new equipment or sales force, or are they still hoping to secure it? Are you prepared to support them in their objectives?

Always check your assumptions and be prepared to ask potentially embarrassing questions to satisfy your expectations. What is understood by those terms which are in common usage between the parties but which are not actually defined? In one case, a client and a contractor, aware of the problems of fixed price contracts, agreed to undertake a project on the basis of a 'partnering agreement'. The emphasis was on the allocation of costs but the question of allocation of risk had been overlooked. The contract concerned a power plant and the plant broke down. The contract was found to be only a collection of reports and correspondence with no clear statement of what work was to be done and who accepted responsibility for it.[1]

A good contract will be good for all those who are parties to it, although it will probably be better for some than others. If you think you are getting a particularly good deal, consider what the effect will be on the other parties. What are their expectations? Will they remain committed to perform when they find out the reality? If they just stop at that point, where will it put you? Will you be able to enforce your legal rights or in practice will you be more at risk by their failure than they are themselves? In these circumstances are you being responsible in signing the deal?

Negotiation

Many fine volumes have been written about negotiating and it is not the purpose of this book to do more than comment on the area in passing. The negotiating process is a fundamental part of the relationship between the parties to the contract because the effects of the negotiation will be long term. Winning the war but losing the peace can easily occur in commercial negotiations, and the approach to negotiation as a form of arm-wrestling contest may not serve the interests of any of the parties in the long run. The issue does not ultimately depend on who forces the other's arm down on the table first.

Here is my suggested ten-point negotiation checklist:

1 Negotiations need preparation and planning. Before you start you must have a clear idea of your authority in the negotiating process, what you want out of the deal and what you think the other party may be wanting.
2 Be genuine and do what works for you and the way you are, but be cautious about imposing opinions or conditions on others. Attempts at domination will sooner or later lead to reaction.

[1] See also the VHE Construction case, p. 231.

3 There will be doubt, concern and preconception. Listening carefully and not interrupting will not only give you a good insight into what the other parties are seeking but will also foster a spirit of mutual commitment. Creating and exploring areas of doubt may be the key to moving the negotiation forward, since only then may you be able to unlock some of the preconceptions with which the other party has come to the table.

4 To avoid the question of trust becoming personal remember that the people with whom you are negotiating now may not be the same as those who will later work with the contract. Check whether the other parties are honouring their commitments in the negotiating process itself, for example by turning up for meetings on time and by doing what they said they would do and, indeed, whether you and your team are doing the same! If they, or you, fail there, what will happen later?

5 Use the discussion process to question assumptions, even in the guise of procedural issues. Be prepared to go back to basics and check the supposedly obvious points. Check, for example, that you are dealing with the right people in the right company and that they have the authority to agree and sign the contract or, if not, who has that authority, and the will to make it work.

6 Regularly repeat and write down the points as they are agreed and identify areas to return to. This 'rolling memorandum' is particularly helpful in building up the contract terms by agreement and avoiding the shocks that can arise when the first detailed formal contract appears.

7 If an issue needs to be re-examined, brave any possible reaction ('... but we've already agreed that ...!') so that the parties finally enter into an agreement which they are committed to. In any good relationship it should be possible to disagree without falling out. On the other hand, friendship before the contract is signed does not guarantee friendship afterwards if the terms do not work.

8 During each of the discussion, proposal and bargaining stages check that the arrangements and the overall terms are workable and beneficial for all parties and where the strains are likely to come. Ask others in your company for

their views on what is proposed and so enrol them in the success of the project. It is all too easy to be swept along in negotiations with the tide of exciting visions unmatched by commercial reality, or to be so desperate to finish what has become a tedium that the nagging voice of doubt has been silenced by the wish to move on to something new. This applies particularly when you are negotiating under pressure or late at night. Keep your ongoing checklists available throughout to ensure that you are not varying one of the key factors of the deal and that the objectives are still in place.

9   Remember your desired outcome, the areas where you might be able to compromise and your minimum acceptable outcome. Can you see the same for the other parties? If you are at your optimum and you feel another party is at their minimum, ease up where you can.

10   The negotiating process may take some time (and is all too often rushed), but in the long run the exploratory build-up to consensus is more successful than any attempt to bulldoze the other party into agreeing something which they do not want and are not committed to. If this happens, they will never feel responsible for the result. A good deal is a good deal for all those making it and can be nurtured and strengthened by the process. A win for you and a win for them should be the ultimate goal and the best chance of ensuring a working relationship after the deal is done.

Writing it down

My experience in advising business people over the years is that over 95 per cent start with the best of intentions and a desire to act honourably, but memory becomes – at best – selective when personal interest is involved. Many times I have made file notes of discussions with clients who, when the pressure came later, could not recall what they had agreed at the time. Nevertheless, once they had reviewed those notes and the contract, they were ready to accept and adhere to what they had previously said.

A well-known car manufacturer once used an advertisement by-line – 'Quality is remembered long after price is forgotten'. I have observed a variant – 'A promise is remembered by those receiving it long after it is forgotten by those giving it'. A promise is also imagined more often than it is given. A clear written report will therefore avoid the fertile ground of dispute over situations when a listener interprets as a promise a statement that was intended to be a hope or expectation. Without a written contract, the lawyer called upon to advise can only speculate on what was done or said. You will need to recall conversations and the status of those conversations. The advice process will become longer and accordingly more expensive and the best course of action less certain.

It is sometimes thought that putting terms in writing might create a strain on a good business relationship and the trust between the parties. If the relationship is to fall apart simply by recording what is supposed to have been agreed, it is probably better that it does so at the outset before any real damage is done! Indeed, this does happen. The person negotiating may be full of enthusiasm, but his or her business partners or colleagues must also be committed to the deal and not threatened by it. Unseen problems may only come to light after several drafts of the contract have been produced and several meetings held. This perhaps is where the investigation and listening process referred to earlier can be put to good use.

Business people often fear writing down anything that might be a legal commitment. Various reasons are given but I suspect that those who are without professional legal training are simply too concerned about making a mistake and do not consider the issue is important enough to involve legal help. This book should demonstrate that the legal process is not as arcane as it might at first appear and that there is much that can be done to help put business dealings on the right legal footing.

Into the future

This book is based on my practical experience as a business

lawyer and the numerous technical articles which form part of the professional diet to keep abreast of specific issues and new cases. Some leading legal publications are now updated monthly to cope with the speed of change. So what can we expect in the future? Here are some of the main factors which I believe will shape the development of the law in the next decade:

- continued European development and harmonization of laws throughout the Union, which is itself due to expand
- the proposed monetary union and single European currency which, whether (and whenever) the UK joins, will inevitably affect the way business is transacted both inside and outside the Union – no doubt the European Court will need to be careful to support the rights of those states outside monetary union to ensure that there is no trade discrimination against them!
- increased access to and use of international law reports, from the USA, Canada and Australia in particular, and the greater development of international trading customs and protocols and their influence in shaping our commercial law
- digital developments and the electronic age, which already require but lack a consistent set of rules, are growing at speed and in a relatively unregulated environment – control of this development will call for a degree of international co-operation which historically has been hard to achieve and which, even if achieved, may be out of date by the time it occurs
- a greater choice between standard contracts, perhaps with optional extras, for speed, certainty and low cost, and carefully negotiated individual contracts where the circumstances require a proper and individual analysis and careful preparation
- An ever more sophisticated insurance market which will provide cover for a wider range of risks but subject to terms and conditions which themselves will need careful negotiation.

Summary

When a legal contract is created, so are expectations. There may be pleasant surprises when a first draft arrives which is well laid out, concise, readable and a fair reflection of the deal. All too often the expectation is unfulfilled and, sometimes, shattered by a document that is inappropriate in style and irrelevant in content. Whose responsibility is this? Where there are lawyers, they frequently take the blame, sometimes justly and sometimes not, but those involved in the project should consider the quality of their information and instructions and whether the paper product matches the old computer adage of 'garbage in, garbage out'. The aim of this book has been to show the framework and outlines of our law, the important distinctions which need to be drawn and some of the choices you must make when deciding the best way to reflect the commercial bargain between the parties. In that respect, the deal which disregards legalities is liable to result in frustration and unnecessary expense.

Contract negotiators or lawyers, be they your in-house colleagues or your chosen external practice, perform better in all respects when they are properly briefed and regarded as part of the team. Briefing takes time but it can yield great rewards in terms of better preparation and a more focused contract which will play its part as a positive management tool in the entire planning, implementation and completion of the project. I hope that the principles, examples and checklists in this book will likewise play their part in that process.

Contract guidelines

Some general principles to sum up:

- Both business people and the lawyers they consult have a responsibility to ensure that contracts work in practice as well as in theory.
- Many contracts can be administered without lawyers, but those negotiating should understand the legal principles which they are operating and the need for periodic review

of both those principles and their current practice. Business people who draw up their own contracts must see the process through with the same thoroughness that they would expect from outside professionals; the job should not be half done.

- Business people should believe that lawyers can help them to achieve more effective contracts but that they need sound information and a clear brief to do so.
- Previous documents or precedents may be appropriate but should not be used without a proper planning process.
- Planning should establish a specified outcome or result which is linked to the contract terms.
- Assumptions should be investigated, recorded and, if appropriate, warranted in the contract.
- Consider the possible tax implications in good time.
- Weigh up the costs and benefits at the outset and throughout negotiations and check them again before signature.
- The form, length and style of the contract should be suitable for the occasion and the degree of benefit and risk involved.
- The documentation should be appropriate for its intended audience and purpose, especially in international transactions.
- The documentation should be carefully scrutinized before signing and reviewed periodically afterwards.

A contract checklist

The goods/services (Chapters 3 and 14)

- Are the goods/services to be supplied clearly identified?
- What limitations should apply to the type or performance of those goods or services?
- What performance or quality criteria should be specified and how and when is conformance to these criteria to be measured?
- What transport and storage stipulations should apply (e.g. in relation to fragility or temperature control)?
- Are there special arrangements for packaging, labelling or pallet/container return?

The parties (Chapters 2 and 7)

- Are all relevant parties included?
- Are all names and addresses (and company numbers) correct?

- Have you checked the parties' company details and/or identities?

Time and delivery (Chapters 13 and 14)

- When must the supply delivery be made?
- Is time to be of the essence or merely estimated?
- How is the supply to be made and what is necessary to achieve this?
- Are there to be acceptance tests?
- Should proof of delivery or inspection on receipt be required?

Price and payment (Chapter 14)

- Is the price clearly set out or are there adequate provisions to fix it?
- When and how (place and currency) is the price to be paid?
- Has the impact of currency variations been taken into account?
- What credit checks have been undertaken?
- Has an irrevocable letter of credit been established?
- Are guarantees required (e.g. from banks, holding companies, directors or proprietors)?
- Is there a risk of set-off applying and should this be covered by the contract?

Risk and insurance (Chapter 14)

- When is delivery/collection due?
- When does risk pass?
- Has insurance been obtained and does it cover the circumstances and the risks?
- Is there a valid retention of title clause suitable for the circumstances?
- What sanctions apply for default in delivery, collection, payment or performance?

- Does a liquidated damages clause need to be negotiated?
- Have the customs requirements been taken into account (including any bonded warehouse requirements)?

Term and termination (Chapters 15 and 19)

- Are there clear provisions for how long the contract is to continue and how and when it can be terminated?
- Should performance targets be included in the contract?
- If so, does failure to achieve them give the right for the other party to terminate?

Commercial issues (Chapters 4 and 8)

- Are all the obligations of each of the parties to the contract set out in sufficient detail to be clear and, if necessary, measurable both to the parties and any third party called upon to adjudicate on whether those obligations had, indeed, been fulfilled.
- Are there any agency considerations?
- What warranties are required (e.g. as to fitness for specific purpose or trade mark rights)?
- Should there be any indemnity provisions on specific aspects?
- What limitations or exclusions of liability should apply?

Boilerplate and transfer (Chapters 15 and 17)

- Is there a breach notice procedure?
- Can one party terminate on notice of insolvency of the other?
- Is assignment or subcontracting permitted?
- Is there to be a change of control clause?

Confidentiality/competition (Chapter 6)

- What express confidentiality clauses should be included?
- Are there restrictions against competition and, if so, what? Are they reasonable?
- Are either of the parties to the contract dominant in their market?
- Are competition laws likely to be infringed?
- Are competition registrations necessary?

Law and jurisdiction (Chapter 16)

- Which law applies and which country's courts should have jurisdiction?
- Should there be arbitration provisions and, if so, should they be specific to certain matters or apply generally to any dispute?

Glossary

Note: the following are general descriptions – not legal definitions!

ADR Alternative dispute resolution – a form of non-binding mediation

Arbitration An alternative to litigation in which the dispute is heard by, typically, one or three arbitrators who will make a decision based on the evidence heard

Articles 85 and 86 The main anti-competition rules of the Treaty of Rome (now renumbered articles 81 and 82)

Articles of association A formal statement made by a company on incorporation (which can be subsequently amended) setting out its internal constitution

Assignment The transfer of a contract or legal rights/obligations

Bailment Lodging of goods by one party with another with an express or implied obligation to look after the goods

Black list A list of terms, particularly under European legislation, which will be invalid and unenforceable

Block exemptions   Specific exemptions from articles 85 and 86 in relation to specific subjects

Blue-pencil test   A test operated by the courts for deleting offending parts of a restrictive covenant or similar term

Collateral contract   An agreement running alongside the main terms of the contract

Comfort letter   A letter issued by the European Commission stating that it intends to take no further action under article 85

Common law   Judge-made law consisting of decisions from individual cases

Connected   A specific degree of association between two or more parties, particularly where the term is governed by the Companies Act 1985

Consequential loss   Loss arising from breach of contract, negligence or tort other than the immediate physical or financial damage or injury.

Consideration   Money or some other obligation which has real value

Constructive dismissal   Resignation of an employee as a result of breach of contract by the employer

Consultancy   Appointment of a person (other than an employee) to assist or advise in relation to a project or business

Consumer   Person buying products or services in a personal and non-business capacity

Contra proferentem   The principle that an onerous clause will be interpreted by the courts, in case of doubt, against the party seeking to impose it

Contract   (For the purposes of this book) an agreement which is legally enforceable

Copyright   The right to prevent another person from producing infringing copies of, or extracts from, an original work

Corporate veil   The protection of incorporation given by company law

Counter-offer   A revised offer made instead of an acceptance or rejection

Counterpart   One of several signature parts of a contract or deed

Course of dealing   One or more previous transactions between the same parties relating to a similar subject matter

Damages Compensation awarded by the courts for breach of contract, negligence and in other cases

Deed A document which is expressed to be executed as a deed, being duly signed and witnessed

Defendant A party defending court proceedings

Del credere **agent** An agency where the agent guarantees to the principal that the third-party customer will perform the contract

De minimis A low-level threshold, often used in relation to competition law but also sometimes used in relation to matters such as warranty claims

Directives Laws passed by the European Commission which are required to be implemented by the governments of member states, normally by regulations

Distributorship Relationship whereby a supplier appoints a distributor

Domain name The name used, particularly by an organization or business, to identify itself on the internet or worldwide web

EDI Electronic data interchange

EEA European Economic Area, comprising the European Union together with the additional states who were previously members of the European Free Trade Association (Iceland, Liechtenstein and Norway)

Equity Decisions of the courts of equity initially based on correcting the unfairnesses of common law, subsequently developing into even stricter rules, now giving the basis for 'equitable remedies'

Estoppel The rule that someone is prevented from denying that which they have previously stated as correct

European Union (EU) The economic and political union currently of 15 states, previously the Common Market or the European Economic Community, comprising Austria, Belgium, Denmark, Finland, France, Germany, Greece, Ireland, Italy, Luxembourg, the Netherlands, Portugal, Spain, Sweden and the UK. It is expected to be enlarged in the future to include Cyprus, the Czech Republic, Estonia, Hungary, Poland and Slovenia

Exclusivity A term denoting that one or more parties agree not to operate or compete in a specific area

Expert   A person qualified and experienced in a particular discipline who will make a decision from personal knowledge of the subject in question

Fiduciary duty   A duty to act honestly and in good faith in relation to another party

Force majeure   An event beyond the control of one or more of the parties to a contract

Franchising   The grant of certain intellectual property rights in relation to an established business format

Frustration   The point when a contract becomes impossible to perform through no fault of the parties

Further assurance   The obligation to take any further action necessary to perfect a contract or deed

Garden leave   The power of an employer to suspend an employee during a notice period

Goods   Items which have a physical character (other than money) but which may be specifically defined by individual statutes or regulations

Grey list   A list of terms, particularly under European legislation, which may or may not be invalid depending upon the circumstances (cf **White list** and **Black list**)

Horizontal agreements   Agreements governing the relationship between two or more parties operating in parallel to one another, such as two or more manufacturers of the same or similar products (cf **Vertical agreements**)

ICC   International Chamber of Commerce

Incorporation   The point at which a limited company is legally established

Incoterms   Recognized international rules for the interpretation of trade terms published by the ICC

Indemnity   Requirement in a contract or deed to repay another party for a claim made against them or loss incurred by them

Independent contractor   An individual who is not an employee of the other party

Injunction   A court order requiring a person to do something or preventing a person from doing something

Intellectual property rights   Patents, trade marks, copyright and other non-physical rights given legal protection

ISP   Internet service provider connecting two or more parties via e-mail

Jurisdiction The right of a particular court or the courts of a particular country or a tribunal to hear and adjudicate on a particular dispute

Legislation Statutes, regulations and directives

Limitation period The period within which legal action must be commenced

Liquidated damages Compensation which may be agreed in a contract as a pre-estimate of loss

Liquidation The point at which a company finally ceases to exist and is wound up

Litigation A dispute pursued in court

Memorandum of association A formal statement made on incorporation by a company (which can be subsequently amended) as to the business it is authorized to undertake

MMC The Monopolies and Mergers Commission – a UK government body

Negligence Breach of a duty of care owed to another causing loss or damage

Nemo dat The rule of law that you cannot give what you do not have

Non est factum This is not the type of transaction that I agreed to enter into

Novation The replacement by one party to a contract of another party

Null and void An agreement or deed which is deemed never to have come into existence in the first place

OFT Office of Fair Trading – a UK government body

Outsourcing A contract whereby a third party is instructed to carry out work previously carried out in-house

Part performance A situation where a person or company partly performs an agreement which another person leads them to believe exists

Personal contracts Contracts which by their nature are personal to the original parties and cannot be assigned without the consent of the other party

Plaintiff The party making the first claim in court proceedings

Public domain The accepted level of general public knowledge or information

Quantum meruit Payment of a fair rate for the work actually done (as opposed to a pre-agreed amount)

Rectification The legal process of amending a contract to reflect the actual intentions of the parties

Regulations Statutory instruments and other delegated legislation brought into force by the government as authorized by statutes; also laws passed by the European Commission having direct application in member states

Representation A statement of fact

Repudiation A fundamental breach of contract by one party which entitles the other or others to treat the contract as at an end

Rescission Cancellation of a contract as if it had never been in force

Restitution An order to restore another party to their original position, for example by returning goods or money to them

Restrictive covenants Provisions in a contract preventing one or more of the parties from undertaking certain specified activities

Restrictive Trade Practices Act (RTPA) Act requiring the registration of agreements which restrict the activities of businesses within the UK

Retention of title Reservation by the owner of goods to title in them until an event (such as payment for those or other goods) has occurred

Revocation Withdrawal or revoking an offer

Satisfactory quality An obligation as to the condition of goods implied by the SGA

Severance Deleting words from contract

SGA Sale of Goods Act 1979

SGSA Supply of Goods and Services Act 1982

Statutes Laws formally passed by Parliament

Statutory duty A duty set out in a statute

Subject to contract Words used to indicate that there is no intention to enter into a legally binding agreement

Time of the essence Stipulation in the contract that an obligation be performed strictly on time, failing which a material breach of contract will arise

Title   Right of legal ownership

Tort   A civil wrong, such as negligence

Transfer regulations   Transfer of Undertakings (Protection of Employment) Regulations 1981 (as amended)

Treaty of Rome   The founding statute of the EU, now significantly amended by the Treaty of Amsterdam of 2 October 1997

UCTA   Unfair Contract Terms Act 1977

Uncitral   UN Commission on International Trade Law (which publishes various model codes and laws)

Undue influence   Exercise by one person of influence over someone else relying on them

Unenforceable   An agreement or deed which is accepted as having come into force but which the law, for a particular reason, will not be prepared to enforce

Unfair dismissal   Dismissal of an employee in breach of statute

UTCCR   Unfair Terms in Consumer Contract Regulations 1994

Vertical agreements   Agreements governing the relationship of parties in a vertical relationship, such as supplier and distributor (cf **Horizontal agreements**)

Voidable   An agreement or deed which is subject to a defect that can destroy it

Waiver   The acceptance by one party to a contract of a breach of that contract by another party

White list   A list of terms, particularly under European legislation, which will be valid if strictly complied with

Without prejudice   Words used to protect a genuine attempt at negotiation from being produced in court as evidence of weakness

Writing   Representing or reproducing words in a visible form

Wrongful dismissal   Dismissal of an employee in breach of contract

Wrongful trading   Continuation of trading by the director of a company after the point when insolvent liquidation has become inevitable

Index

NOTE: Words in **bold** are described in the glossary. In some cases the index gives only the principal references.

acceptance *see* offer
Acquired Rights Directive *see*
    Transfer Regulations
act of God *see force majeure*
adherence (deed of) 227
advertisements 65–7
affect on trade *see* competition
agency / agent 29, 76, 80, 99–113
    commission 99, 102–8
    compensation on termination
        104–6, 112, 198
    del credere 101
agreement to agree 12
**alternative dispute resolution
    (ADR)** 216, 254
Anton Piller order *see also*
    injunctions 253
arbitration 12, 216–8, 254
articles 85 and 86 70, 77–82, 109–11

assignment 121, 149–50, 221–7
assumptions (when negotiating
    contracts) 172, 258–60
authentication 210
author contracts *see* publishing
    contracts
authority – actual and ostensible 22,
    88, 92–3, 102

bailment 40
bankruptcy – effect of *see* insolvency
battle of the forms 191–2
Baywatch 144
benefit (and burden) of contract
    221–4
Berne Convention 151
black clauses 81
block exemptions 79, 81–6, 109–11,
    162–4

blue-pencil test 48
boilerplate clauses 195–204
breach (of contract) 60–63, 76–7, 104, 197, 233
building contracts 41–4, 61–3, 231–32

Cala Homes v Alfred McAlpine 150, 171
carriage insurance and freight (CIF) 188
catalogues 65–7
change of control 197, 225
cheques 7
choice of law 212–14
collateral contract 24, 60
comfort letter 82
Commercial Agents (Council Directive) Regulations 103–6
commercial code 3, 43
common law 19, 48, 61, 67, 102, 132, 133, 246
Company Directors Disqualification Act 103–6
company law 21, 88–9, 91–5
company name/number 26–7, 93, 96–7
company search 96
compensation *see* damages
competition 69, 75–86, 133–4
    agreements of minor importance 80–82 *see also de minimis*
    Competition Bill/Act 77–8
    effect on trade 80–82, 161–2
computer contracts 151–3, 186
condition precedent 242
conditions of business 183–93
confidentiality 69–76, 120, 133–4, 142, 199
confidentiality undertakings 71–2
consideration 6–9, 24
construction contracts *see* building contracts
consultancy 115–25
consumer contracts 51–6
consumer credit 16, 67
Consumer Credit Act/Regulations 67

Consumer Protection Act (CPA) 53, 63–6, 95
consumers 15–16, 47–56
contra proferentem 49
control *see* change of control
Control of Misleading Advertisements Regulations 66
copyright 35, 133–4, 147–53, 171
Copyright Designs and Patents Act (CDPA) 147
corporate veil 94–5
cost 172
counterpart 202
course of dealing 10, 190–91
creditworthiness 101, 111, 232
criminal law 21, 58, 64–5, 67–95, 129

damages 61–3, 65, 71, 249–53
databases 152–3
death 49, 55, 58–63, 244–5
deed 9, 14
default *see* breach 237–8
defective contracts 4–5, 9–10, 12, 19–32
de minimis 77, 80–82, 162
del credere **agent** *see* agent
Director General of Fair Trading (DGFT) 77
directors 87–98, 117
Disability Discrimination Act 129
disk – goods or services 35–6, 132
Distributor/distribution/ **distributorship** 76–80, 99–113, 176, 215
domain name 146
domestic arrangements 7
dominant position 82–3 *see also* competition
Donoghue v Stevenson 59
drafting contracts 167–94, 257–65
duress 25
duty of care 59–63

economic loss 63, 121
EDI 207
electronic contracts 205–12, 263
electronic signatures 210
e-mail 206

employment 115–17, 127–40
  benefits 133
  constructive dismissal 131
  contracts 16, 127–40, 223–4
  disciplinary code 132
  discrimination in employment
    129, 135, 138
  dismissal 90
  duty to consult 138
  employment protection 72–5
    see also transfer regulations
  fidelity – duty of 72
  flexibility clause 132
  garden leave 75
  handbook 130
  mobility clause 131–2
  notice periods 131–2, 134
  unfair dismissal 135
  wrongful dismissal 134–5
entire agreement clause 201–2
equity 19
estoppel 230–31
European Commission 4, 55, 78,
  80–82
European Community Trade Mark
  (CTM) 145
European Economic Area (EEA) 79
European law 4, 34–5, 49, 70, 263
European Patent Office 142
European Product Liability
  Directive 63
exchange rates 108
exclusion clauses 44, 47–56, 61–2,
  175, 189–90
exclusivity 106, 161–2, 177
expert *see* arbitrator

Fair Trading Act 77–8, 161
fax 199, 206
fiduciary duty 88–91
fitness for purpose *see* goods
food supply contracts 176, 185
force majeure 200–201, 245
Form A/B 81
forum *see* jurisdiction
franchise block exemption 163–4
franchising 81, 94, 109, 155–65
Fraser v Evans 71

fraud 22, 95
frustration 245
further assurance 203–4

General Agreement on Tariffs and
  Trade (GATT) 83
General Product Safety Regulations
  64–5
gentleman's agreement 7, 10–11
gift 20–21
good faith 30, 53–4, 73, 88–92, 102–3,
  197–8
goods 35–45, 64, 99–101, 103, 184–5,
  198–9
  appropriated 37–9
  defective 52–3, 63–5, 185
  delivery of 36, 38–9, 108, 185–7
  description of 40, 49, 52
  fitness for purpose 36, 40–41, 44,
    49, 52
  misleading pricing 65–7
  price of/payment for 12, 36, 42,
    81–2, 92, 96, 108, 179, 186–7, 232
  property/title in 37–9, 49, 108,
    188–9
  safety 64–5
  sample 41, 49, 52
  satisfactory quality 35, 40–41, 44,
    52
  specific and ascertained 37–9
gratuitous permission 9
grey clauses 80
grey list 54–6
guarantee 13–5, 52
Guinness 93

Harrods 146
Hillsborough 58
horizontal agreements 80

ideas, protection of *see*
  confidentiality
identity 226–7
illegality 21, 203
implied terms 10, 44
incapacity 21
incomplete contracts 9–10
Incoterms 188

indemnity 25–7, 50, 62–3, 65, 124, 147, 227
inducement 236–7
infringement 150–51
injunction 76–7, 82, 150, 235, 247–9
insolvency 89, 95–6, 152, 189–90, 197, 222, 233, 244, 253
insurance 50, 54, 65, 68, 108, 187–8, 263
intellectual property rights 141–54, 162–3
intention (to create a contract) 7
interest 122, 232, 252
interference with contract *see* inducement
International Chamber of Commerce (ICC) 188
international element 34, 105–6, 205–19
Internet 210–11
Internet Service Provider (ISP) 210–11
interpretation clauses 198–9
invention 70

Jarvis v Swan Tours 251
joint venture 75
jurisdiction 212–6

know-how 153, 157–8

land contracts 54
licensing contracts 155–65
limitation clauses *see* exclusion clauses
limitation period 64
liquidated damages 61, 186, 198, 250
liquidation/liquidator 28–30
literary works *see* publishing contracts
litigation 247–53
logo – protection of *see* Trade Marks and copyright
loss of profit claims 63

Mareva injunctions 253
market share 80–82

market value 8
mediation *see* alternative dispute resolution
memorandum of association *see* company law
merger 77–8
minimum resale price *see* resale prices
minimum sales targets 107, 156
minors 21
misrepresentation 8, 23–4, 159–60
mistake 8, 27–30
mitigation of loss 134–5, 251–2
Monopolies and Mergers Commission (MMC) 77
moral rights 149

necessaries 21
negligence 49, 57–63, 93–4, 159, 250
negotiating 259–61
nemo dat 20–29
nervous shock 58
non est factum 27
notice / notices 199–200
  see also terminating contracts
notice period 103–4, 197
novation 225
null and void 9

object code *see* source code
offer (and acceptance) 4–8, 128–30, 190–2, 207–12, 231–2
  counter-offer 8, 191–2
  withdrawal 6
Office of Fair Trading (OFT) 55–6, 66
outsourcing 123–4

parallel imports 111
parole evidence rule 24
part performance 20, 29
partnership agreement 75
passing off 145–6
patents 141–3
pay in lieu of notice 135
penalty *see* liquidated damages
personal contracts 223–4
personal guarantee *see* guarantee

personal injury 55, 58–63
Photoproduction Ltd v Securicor 50
planning contracts 169–81
posting 6
price rises *see* goods – prices
product liability 64–5
products *see* goods
promises 262
public domain 72
public policy 21
publication right 149
publishing contracts 223–4
pure economic loss 63, 121
pyramid selling 160

quantum meruit 232

reasonableness 48–9, 52–3
receivership *see* insolvency
recitals 195–6
rectification 230
relevant market *see* market share
remedies 247–53
remuneration 133
repudiation 243–4
resale prices 100–101, 111, 163
rescission 24, 241–2
responsibility 257–9
restitution 242–3
restrictive covenants 72–82, 104,
    106–7, 110–11, 121–3, 133–4,
    138–9, 158–9, 197
Restrictive Trade Practices Act 77,
    161
retention of title 39, 188–9
review – of contract 229–30
revocation 6, 208
risk 51, 100–101, 112, 173–5, 184,
    187–8
Rome Convention 213–4

Sale of Goods Act (SGA) 33–45, 151
secret profits 88–91
Securicor 50
self-employed person *see*
    consultancy
service contract 90
services 123–4, 184–5

set off 233
severance 76
shareholders' approval 88–93
small print 54, 74
snail 59
software 35–6, 151, 174–5
source code 152
St Albans City Council v ICL 35–6,
    174–5
Standard Bank London Ltd v Bank
    of Tokyo 210
standard contracts 183–93, 263
standard terms of business 17, 48–9,
    53–6, 122
statutory duty 60
sub-contract/sub-license 117, 122,
    149–50, 211–7
subject to contract 11–12
supply contracts 12
**Supply of Goods and Services Act
    (SGSA)** 33–45

tax 116–7, 120, 123
technology transfer block
    exemption 80, 162–3
terminating contracts 107–8, 120,
    130–32, 196–8, 241–55 *see also*
    notices
thin skull rule 62–3
time of the essence 119, 122, 185–7,
    238
tolerance 175–6
tort 58–63
Trade Descriptions Act 66–7, 95
trade marks 143–7, 223
Trade Marks Act 145
Trading Schemes Act 160
trading standards officers 65
**Transfer of Business (Protection of
    Employment) Regulations
    (Transfer Regulations/TUPE)**
    109, 136–9
transferring contracts 221–7
Treaty of Rome 34, 53, 70, 77–83, 162
trust and confidence 131
TUPE *see* Transfer of Business

Uncitral 207

undue influence 25
unenforceable 10, 23–4, 82
Unfair Contract Terms Act (UCTA)
    47–56, 61
Unfair Terms in Consumer
    Contracts Regulations
    (UTCCR) 47–56
Universal Copyright Convention
    151

variations 15, 55, 201–2
vertical agreements 80
VHE Construction Ltd v Alfred
    McAlpine 231–2
video conferencing 207
void 9, 48
voidable 10

waiver 203, 230
white list 80
Williams v Natural Life Health
    Foods 94, 159
without prejudice 11–12
witness – need for 9
work permit 129
World Intellectual Property
    Organisation (WIPO) 145
world trade 83
World Trade Organisation (WTO)
    83
world wide web 206
writing – need for 12–17, 128,
    209–10, 226, 261–2
wrongful trading 96

Contract Negotiation Handbook

Second Edition

P D V Marsh

This new edition represents a thoroughly revised version of what is now a standard text. The structure of the Handbook follows the logic of the negotiating procedure.

Part One describes the background to planning. Three negotiating situations are identified - bidding, procurement and contract dispute - and the factors relevant to the planning for each are set out. Part Two identifies the problems involved in the selection of the negotiating team and the duties which they are expected to perform. Parts Three and Four move to the negotiating table to review the stages through which the negotiations will pass, how the expectations of the parties will be adjusted and the tactics appropriate to each negotiating situation.

Gower

Contracting for Engineering and Construction Projects

Fourth Edition

P D V Marsh

Peter Marsh's book has long been recognized as a standard work. With its emphasis on the commercial aspects of contracting, it represents an eminently practical guide to this complex subject for purchaser and contractor alike. It covers contract planning and contract administration, deals with both the preparation and the appraisal of tenders and explains in detail how to draft the key clauses in a contract to ensure the maximum advantage.

For this new edition the text has been thoroughly revised to take account of recent changes in law and practice, including the impact of the relevant EU Directives, the introduction of the new engineering contract, the issue of the Latham Report and the sixth edition of the ICE conditions.

In its revised version the book will continue to serve the needs of purchasing and contracts staff, engineers, quantity surveyors, project managers and legal advisers seeking a reliable source of guidance.

Gower

Comparative Contract Law

England, France, Germany

P D V Marsh

Despite the media emphasis on the 'Single European Market', people who do business across the EU are faced with radical differences between legal systems and philosophies. It is dangerous to make assumptions about another country's law.

Peter Marsh's book reviews and compares the main elements of English, French and German law as they relate to business contracts; especially those relating to the sale of goods and to construction work. He covers:

- drawing up contracts
- their validity
- the obligations of the parties
- the position of third parties
- the control of unfair terms
- remedies for non-performance.

As the only single-volume detailed comparative treatment of both French and German contract law in the English language this book will be invaluable to British businesses trading with France and Germany, to lawyers who may be called upon to advise such businesses, and to professionals in the construction industry who may be carrying out work in France or Germany.

Gower

Gower Handbook of Management Skills

Third Edition

Edited by Dorothy M Stewart

'This is the book I wish I'd had in my desk drawer when I was first a manager. When you need the information, you'll find a chapter to help; no fancy models or useless theories. This is a practical book for real managers, aimed at helping you manage more effectively in the real world of business today. You'll find enough background information, but no overwhelming detail. This is material you can trust. It is tried and tested.'

So writes Dorothy Stewart, describing in the Preface the unifying theme behind the Third Edition of this bestselling Handbook. This puts at your disposal the expertise of 25 specialists, each a recognized authority in their particular field. Together, this adds up to an impressive 'one stop library' for the manager determined to make a mark.

Chapters are organized within three parts: Managing Yourself, Managing Other People, and Managing the Business. Part I deals with personal skills and includes chapters on self-development and information technology. Part II covers people skills such as listening, influencing and communication. Part III looks at finance, project management, decision-making, negotiating and creativity. A total of 12 chapters are completely new, and the rest have been rigorously updated to fully reflect the rapidly changing world in which we work.

Each chapter focuses on detailed practical guidance, and ends with a checklist of key points and suggestions for further reading.

Gower

Making Major Sales

Neil Rackham

This work is based on the most extensive research project ever
undertaken in the area of selling skills. It determines the best ways of
selling high value products or services. The author and his team
observed and studied more than 35,000 sales calls made by 10,000 sales
people in twenty-three different countries over a period of twelve years.
Their analysis revealed that many of the methods developed for selling
low value goods just don't work in the environment of today's major sale.

The findings, published for the first time in this revolutionary book, will
overturn a whole collection of accepted sales truths. *Making Major Sales*
provides a set of simple and practical techniques which have now been
tried in many leading companies with dramatic improvements in sales
performance. The ideas described by Neil Rackham have already helped
thousands of people to become more successful with large sales.

Gower